The

HARVEST HANDBOOK™ OF KEY BIBLE WORDS

NEW TESTAMENT

HARVEST HOUSE PUBLISHERS
EUGENE, OREGON

Cover by Darren Welch Design, Mount Juliet, TN

Cover image © Heritage Image Partnership Ltd / Alamy

The Harvest Handbook™ of Key Bible Words New Testament
Copyright © 2018
Published by Harvest House Publishers
Eugene, Oregon 97408
www.harvesthousepublishers.com

ISBN 978-0-7369-7303-8 (pbk.)
ISBN 978-0-7369-7304-5 (eBook)

Library of Congress Cataloging-in-Publication Data is on file at the Library of Congress, Washington, DC.

Printed in the United States of America

18 19 20 21 22 23 24 25 26 / LB-JC / 10 9 8 7 6 5 4 3 2 1

Introduction

The New Testament was not originally written in English, but in Greek—specifically, *koinē* Greek ("street" or "common" Greek). The New Testament authors used this form of Greek because it was what most people in their time and place spoke. The best way to read the New Testament is to learn *koinē* Greek and read it in its original language, but not everyone has the time, desire, or calling for that. Actually, Christians today need not understand Greek to grasp the message of the New Testament. Modern translations are everywhere. But to have some knowledge of certain Greek words definitely helps clarify the meaning of the text.

William Edwy Vine (1873–1949) recognized this, which is why he used his expertise in New Testament Greek to develop a dictionary of New Testament words for the average layperson of his time. *The Harvest Handbook of Key Bible Words* is a condensed and modernized version of *An Expository Dictionary of New Testament Words*, by W.E. Vine, which was originally published in 1940. The entries in this handbook are keyed to what are known as "Strong's numbers," named after James Strong, who compiled *The Exhaustive Concordance of the Bible*, first published in 1890. You can use these numbers to look up words in the Greek dictionary in the back of Strong's *Concordance*, particularly if you want more concise definitions. There are 5624 Greek root words used in the New Testament, so there are 5624 Strong's numbers. This handbook covers 250-plus of the most important New Testament words. Because they are keyed to various numbers between 1 and 5624, you will often see Strong's numbers greater than 250. For example, *lēstēs*, "bandit," is keyed to Strong's #3027. A small glossary also appears in the back of this book for readers who may stumble across potentially unfamiliar terms such as "Septuagint" or "transliteration."

If you already know New Testament Greek, you can use an exhaustive lexicon (*lexicon* is a fancy word for "dictionary"), such as *A Greek-English Lexicon of the New Testament and Other Early Christian Literature*.[1] This handbook is primarily for the layperson. It is not exhaustive—that is, it doesn't cover everything. It is a resource for those who don't know Greek but still want to understand New Testament words in a deeper and more accurate way. If you use this handbook for a while and then want to step up to the next level and learn New Testament Greek, you will find these helpful:

- *Greek for the Rest of Us*, by William D. Mounce, gives the bare essentials of biblical Greek if you don't want to spend a lot of money on a full course, or if you don't have a lot of time to work through a first-year grammar.

- *Basics of Biblical Greek Grammar*, also by William D. Mounce, is sometimes a required text in seminary or Bible college courses, but it's very understandable and easy to use if you have the time and the desire to teach yourself.

The entries below often list the ways in which a word is used in the New Testament in addition to giving a brief definition. Many of the entries are accompanied by one or more quotes by popular Christian leaders or authors, either for an extra informational tidbit or for encouragement or inspiration. Some entries also include an additional insight related to the word.

We hope you find this handbook useful, as a Bible study tool, as a resource for Bible teaching, or simply for personal edification. A better understanding of key New Testament words can help Christians understand better and explain more clearly the message contained within all Scripture, which, as Paul tells Timothy, "is God-breathed and is useful for teaching, rebuking, correcting and training in righteousness, so that the servant [*anthrōpos*, literally meaning "man" or "person"] of God may be thoroughly equipped for every good work" (2 Timothy 3:16-17).

Abba

The word *abba* is an intimate Aramaic word for addressing one's father. A small child would use this word to talk to his or her father. Jesus used this word to relate to God the Father, as did Paul (possibly echoing Jesus).

Definition

abba (noun, Strong's #5)

Abba is an Aramaic word, found in Mark 14:36, Romans 8:15, and Galatians 4:6. In the Gemara (a rabbinical commentary on the Mishna, the traditional teaching of the Jews) it is stated that slaves were forbidden to address the head of the family by this title. It is like a personal name, in contrast to the proper name "Father," with which it is always joined in the NT ("*Abba,* Father"). This is probably due to the fact that *abba* had practically become a proper name, and as a result, Greek-speaking Jews added the Greek word *patēr,* "father." *Abba* is the sound articulated from the lips of infants, and suggests unreasoning trust. "Father" (*patēr*) expresses an intelligent understanding of the relationship. The two together express the love and confidence of a child.

Insight

Aramaic is the language Jesus and the early Christians spoke. It is a language similar to Hebrew in that it uses the same alphabet and shares many of the same features.

Quotes

"When I relapsed [into alcoholism], I had two options: yield once again to fear, guilt, and depression—or rush into the arms of my heavenly Father; choose to live as a victim of my disease—or choose to trust in Abba's immutable love."

> —Brennan Manning, *Abba's Child: The Cry of the Heart for Intimate Belonging* (Colorado Springs, CO: NavPress, 2015), 4.

"Probably the word 'Abba' [in Galatians 4:6], the Aramaic term for 'Father,' derives from the term that Jesus himself used in addressing God (cf. Mark 14:36), signifying that God is the loving and dear Father of those who believe in Jesus the Christ."

> —Thomas R. Schreiner, *Galatians: Zondervan Exegetical Commentary on the New Testament* (Grand Rapids, MI: Zondervan, 2010), 272.

Abyss

In Revelation, "abyss" refers to a bottomless pit where demonic hoardes are imprisoned, a holding place from which they cannot escape without God's consent.

Definition

abussos (feminine noun, Strong's #12)

Abussos is used as a noun denoting the abyss (NRSV: "bottomless pit"). It describes an immeasurable depth, the underworld, the lower regions, the abyss of *Sheol* (see below). It refers to these lower regions as the abode of demons, out of which they can be let loose (Revelation 11:7; 17:8). It occurs seven times in Revelation (9:1,2,11; 11:7; 17:8; 20:1,3).

Insight

This word primarily corresponds to the Hebrew Old Testament concept of *Sheol*, a shadowy underworld.

Admonition, Admonish

An "admonition" in the Bible has to do with warning, correction, and instruction. In the case of the most common examples, *noutheteō* (verb) and *nouthesia* (noun), it has to do with "putting a correction in mind." None of these words are necessarily meant to have frightening or unloving connotations. Paul uses the verb *noutheteō* in 1 Corinthians 4:14 in the context of warning the Corinthians as a parent would a child, from love.

Definitions

1: *nouthesia* (feminine noun, Strong's #3559)

Literally, a *nouthesia* is a "putting in mind" (*nous*, "mind," *tithēmi*, "put"). It's used in 1 Corinthians 10:11 about the purpose of the Scriptures (that they were written for our *nouthesia*). In Ephesians 6:4, it is paired with *paideia*, another "instruction" word that more specifically refers to the sort of teaching or discipline one would give to a child. *Nouthesia* occurs in Titus 3:10 regarding the "warning" to be directed at a person who causes trouble in the church. A difference between the words *nouthesia* and *paideia* is that *nouthesia* is generally training by word (whether through encouragement or reproof), whereas *paideia* generally stresses training by act, even though both words are used in each respect.

2: *noutheteō* (verb, Strong's #3560)

Compare with the noun above. *Noutheteō* means "to put in mind, admonish, warn" (see Acts 20:31; Romans 15:14; 1 Corinthians 4:14; Colossians 1:28; 3:16; 1 Thessalonians 5:12,14; 2 Thessalonians 3:15).

It is used of instruction and warning. In this way, it is different from the related verb *paideuō*, "to correct by discipline, to train by act" (Hebrews 12:6; compare Ephesians 6:4).

3: *paraineō* (verb, Strong's #3867)

Paraineō means "to admonish by way of exhorting or advising" and is found in Acts 27:9 describing an act of Paul (see also Acts 27:22).

4: *chrēmatizō* (verb, Strong's #5537)

Primarily, this word means "to transact business," or "to give advice to those making inquiries" (especially of official pronouncements of magistrates), or "a response to those consulting an oracle." It came to signify the giving of a divine "admonition" (instruction or warning, in a general way). See Hebrews 8:5, where it is translated as "warned" in the phrase "Moses was warned."

The word is derived from *chrēma*, "an affair, business." Names were given to people from the nature of their business (see the same word in Acts 11:26; Romans 7:3); hence the idea of dealing with a person and receiving instruction.

Quotes

"The verb translated 'to warn' [in 1 Corinthians 4:14] is a Pauline word in the NT. 'Admonish' probably catches the present nuance better. It has the primary connotation of trying to have a corrective influence on someone."

—Gordon D. Fee, *The New International Commentary on the New Testament: The First Epistle to the Corinthians, Revised Edition* (Grand Rapids, MI: Eerdmans, 2014), 200.

"We can choose to forget Him, forsake His commandments, and allow our prosperity and pagan influences to woo us away from dependence upon the Lord, but we do so at our own peril."

> —Chuck Swindoll, *Parenting: From Surviving to Thriving* (Nashville, TN: Thomas Nelson, 2006), 252.

Adulterer, Adulteress, Adulterous, Adultery

In the Bible, an adulterer or adulteress is one who has had sex with the spouse of another, which is in violation of God's law. God also accused Israel in the Old Testament of "adultery" in the sense that they pursued the affections of other gods in violation of their relationship with God, where God is pictured as Israel's spouse. God expresses displeasure with adultery committed among humans, as well as adultery committed by humans against God, even in the New Testament (for example, Revelation 2:22).

Definitions

1: *moichos* (masculine noun, Strong's #3432)

This word denotes one "who has unlawful intercourse with the spouse of another" (Luke 18:11; 1 Corinthians 6:9; Hebrews 13:4).

2: *moichalis* (feminine noun, Strong's #3428)

This word refers to an "adulteress" or a woman who commits adultery, and it is used

a. in the natural sense (Romans 7:3; 2 Peter 2:14), and

b. in the spiritual sense. In James 4:4, the author addressed hearers as "adulteresses" because of their wrong motives in asking God for something—from their love of the world. This is similar to Israel's breach of their relationship with God through idolatry, which was also described as "adultery" or "harlotry" (for example, Ezekiel 16:15-22; 23:43). Similarly, believers who cultivate friendship with the world (and who therefore break their spiritual union with Christ) are spiritual "adulteresses," since they have been spiritually united to Christ as a wife is to her husband (see Romans 7:4). It is also used as an adjective to describe the Jewish people when they transferred their affections from God, and can be translated in these instances as something like "adulterous" or "unfaithful" (Matthew 12:39; 16:4; Mark 8:38). In 2 Peter 2:14, the literal translation is "full of an adulteress."

Quote

"Adulterous relationships are based on deception. There is no truth involved."

—Cindy Beall, *Healing Your Marriage When Trust Is Broken: Finding Forgiveness and Restoration* (Eugene, OR: Harvest House Publishers, 2011), 199.

Angel

An "angel" in both Old and New Testaments is a "messenger," either a supernatural messenger from God (which is one sense of the term) or a human messenger sent by another person. The verb *angellō* means to "send a message," which is what the Greek term *angelos* ("angel") is based on.

Definition

angelos (masculine noun, Strong's #32)

An *angelos* is a "messenger," from the verb *angellō*, to "send a message." The message might be sent by God, by a human, or by Satan. *Angelos* is also used of a guardian or representative in Revelation 1:20 (compare Matthew 18:10; Acts 12:15).

Angels

a. are superior to humans (Hebrews 2:7; Psalm 8:5),

b. belong in heaven (Matthew 24:36; Mark 12:25), and

c. to God (Luke 12:8); they

d. are engaged in his service (Psalm 103:20),

e. exist as spirits without material bodies as humans do (Hebrews 1:14),

f. are either human in form or can assume the human form when necessary (Luke 24:4,23; Acts 10:3,30),

g. are called "holy" in Mark 8:38,

h. are referred to as "elect" in 1 Timothy 5:21,

i. are contrasted with some of their original number who sinned and left their proper home (Matthew 25:41; 2 Peter 2:4; Jude 1:6), and

j. are always spoken of in the masculine gender; a feminine form of the word does not occur.

Quotes

"Believers, look up—take courage. The angels are nearer than you think."

—Billy Graham, *Angels: God's Secret Agents* (Nashville, TN: Thomas Nelson, 1995), 39.

"Some angels render service directly to God and Christ. Other angels bring judgment against nonbelievers."

—Ron Rhodes, *The Secret Life of Angels: Who They Are and How They Help Us* (Eugene, OR: Harvest House Publishers, 2008), 24.

Anger

In the New Testament, "anger" (or "wrath") is a strong emotion of intense displeasure or hostility felt by both God and humans. God's anger often takes the form of judgment against sinful humans; we are saved from it through Jesus. Humans can be angry too, and our anger can be expressed in justifiable ways or destructive ways (for instance, see Ephesians 4:26).

Definitions

1: *orgē* (feminine noun, Strong's #3709)

Originally any "natural impulse, or desire, or disposition," *orgē* came to signify "anger," the strongest of all passions.

It is used of

   a. the wrath of humans (Ephesians 4:31; Colossians 3:8; 1 Timothy 2:8; James 1:19,20),

   b. the displeasure of human governments (Romans 13:4,5),

   c. the suffering of the Jews at the hands of the Gentiles (Luke 21:23),

   d. what the Law brings about (Romans 4:15),

   e. "the anger" of the Lord Jesus (Mark 3:5),

   f. God's "anger" with Israel in the wilderness, in a quotation from the Old Testament (Hebrews 3:11; 4:3; see also Psalm 95:11),

   g. God's present "anger" with Jews who don't believe (Romans 9:22; 1 Thessalonians 2:14-16),

   h. his present "anger" with those who disobey the Lord Jesus in his Gospel (John 3:36), and

   i. God's purposes in judgment (Matthew 3:7; Luke 3:7; Romans 1:18; 2:5,8; 3:5; 5:9; 12:19; Ephesians 2:3; 5:6; Colossians 3:6; 1 Thessalonians 1:10; 5:9).

Thumos is another term for anger in the New Testament, for an even more agitated state than *orgē*. The word *thumos* is used 18 times in the New Testament, ten of which are in Revelation; seven of those ten refer to the wrath of God. Everywhere else it is used in a negative way.

2: *orgizō* (verb, Strong's #3710)

The verb *orgizō* means "to provoke, to arouse to anger," and in the eight places where it is found it is used in the Middle Voice (a Greek grammatical form), thus meaning "to be angry, incensed."

It is said of

   a. individuals (Matthew 5:22; 18:34; 22:7; Luke 14:21; 15:28; Ephesians 4:26),

   b. nations (Revelation 11:18), and

   c. Satan as the dragon (Revelation 12:17).

Quotes

"Explosions of anger may appear to be the fruit of a moment's waywardness, but in reality, they're usually the result of a history of ignoring warnings about an impending fire."

> —Max Lucado, *God Came Near: No Wonder They Call Him the Savior* (Sisters, OR: Multnomah, 1986), 106-107.

"We don't sit down and say, 'I think I will now experience anger.' Anger is a *response* to some event or situation in life that causes us irritation, frustration, pain, or other displeasure."

> —Gary Chapman, *Anger: Taming a Powerful Emotion* (Carol Stream, IL: Tyndale House Publishers, 2015), 18.

Anoint, Anointing

In the Old and New Testaments "anointing" was when one person poured or rubbed a substance such as ointment or oil on another, often on their head, but sometimes on other parts of the body. It symbolized setting someone apart for an important task, or appointing them to a position of authority, like that of a king, priest, or prophet. In the New Testament it is especially significant for Jesus, known by the title *Christ*, which means "Anointed One."

Definitions

1: *aleiphō* (verb, Strong's #218)

This verb is a general term for an "anointing" of any kind, whether of

a. physical refreshment after washing (see the Septuagint's Greek translation of Ruth 3:3; 2 Samuel 12:20; Daniel 10:3; Micah 6:15; in the New Testament, see Matthew 6:17; Luke 7:38,46; John 11:2; 12:3),

b. the sick (Mark 6:13; James 5:14), or

c. a dead body (Mark 16:1).

The material used was either oil or ointment.

In the Septuagint, it is used of anointing

a. a pillar (Genesis 31:13),

b. prisoners (2 Chronicles 28:15),

c. a wall with mortar (Ezekiel 13:10-12,14,15), and

d. priests, to ordain them for holy service (Exodus 40:15; Numbers 3:3).

2: *chriō* (verb, Strong's #5548)

This verb, related to the Greek word *christos* ("Anointed One" or "Christ"), is more limited in its use than *aleiphō* above. It's confined to "sacred and symbolic anointings," and specifically to Christ as the "Anointed" of God (Luke 4:18; Acts 4:27; 10:38). In Hebrews 1:9, it is used metaphorically in connection with the "oil of joy." It is used once of believers (2 Corinthians 1:21).

In the Septuagint, *chriō* is used very frequently, and it is used of

a. kings (1 Samuel 10:1),

b. priests (Exodus 28:41), and

c. prophets (1 Kings 19:16).

Among the Greeks it was used in other contexts than the ceremonial, but in the Scriptures it is not found in connection with secular matters.

Anointed One (see Christ)

Apostle

An "apostle" is a "sent one," specifically sent from God, through Jesus, to spread the gospel. The original twelve disciples were apostles because they were commissioned by Jesus, to "go and make disciples of all nations" (Matthew 28:19). Paul referred to himself as an apostle because he was "sent not from men nor by a man, but by Jesus Christ and God the Father, who raised him from the dead" (Galatians 1:1; see Acts 9).

Definitions

1: *apostolos* (masculine noun, Strong's #652)

Literally, an "apostle" is "one sent from" someone (*apo*, "from," *stellō*, "to send"). In the New Testament, it is usually one sent from God. It is used of Jesus to describe his relationship to God (Hebrews 3:1; see John 17:3). The twelve disciples chosen by Jesus for special training were also called apostles (Luke 6:13; 9:10). Paul, though he had seen the Lord Jesus (1 Corinthians 9:1; 15:8), had not "been with" the twelve "the whole time" of Jesus's earthly ministry, and as a result was not eligible for a place among them, according to Peter's description of the necessary qualifications (Acts 1:21-22). Paul was sent directly by the Lord himself, after his ascension, to carry the gospel to the Gentiles.

The word also has a wider reference. In Acts 14:4,14, it is used of Barnabas as well as of Paul, and in Romans 16:7, Andronicus and Junia are referred to as apostles. In 2 Corinthians 8:23, unnamed Christians are called (literally in the Greek) "apostles of the churches." Epaphroditus is also literally referred to as "your apostle" in Philippians 2:25. Paul, Silas, and Timothy call themselves "apostles of Christ" in 1 Thessalonians 2:6.

2: *apostolē* (feminine noun, Strong's #651)

This noun refers to a "sending, mission"—an apostleship (Acts 1:25; Romans 1:5; 1 Corinthians 9:2; Galatians 2:8).

Insight

Pseudapostoloi, "false apostles," occurs in 2 Corinthians 11:13.

Archangel

The only archangel ("chief angel") in the New Testament is the leader of the heavenly armies, Michael.

Definition

archangelos (masculine noun, Strong's #743)

This term is found nowhere in the Old Testament. The only two places in the New Testament where it appears are 1 Thessalonians 4:16 and Jude 1:9, where it is used of Michael, who in Daniel is called "one of the chief princes" and "the great prince" (10:13,21; 12:1; compare Revelation 12:7). There may be other exalted heavenly beings of this rank in Scripture, but the term is not attached to any other name. The phrase "one of the chief princes" in Daniel 10:13 lends support to the notion that Michael is one archangel among others.

Insights

- In Daniel 12:1, the Septuagint translates the Hebrew phrase referring to Michael, *hassar haggadōl* ("the great prince"), as *ho angelos ho megas*, "the great angel."
- The dictionary form of the word translated as "rule" in Ephesians 1:21 and as "rulers" in Colossians 1:16 is *archē*, the prefix of the word *archangelos*.

Ark

In the New Testament, "ark" only refers to two things: the boat Noah, his family, and certain animals sailed on, and the golden box known as the "ark of the covenant." An "ark" in both cases is really just a "box"—one used for the sea, and the other used to store important items such as the tablets of the covenant, the golden pot of manna, and Aaron's budded rod (see Hebrews 9:4). The ark of the covenant was in the Holy of Holies, the most holy space in the tabernacle and later in the temple.

Definition

kibōtos (feminine noun, Strong's #2787)
A *kibōtos* ("ark") is defined as a "wooden box or chest." This can refer either to

a. Noah's boat (Matthew 24:38; Luke 17:27; Hebrews 11:7),

b. the "ark" of the covenant in the tabernacle (Hebrews 9:4), or

c. the "ark" seen in the vision of the heavenly temple (Revelation 11:19).

Atonement

"Atonement" (or "atoning sacrifice, propitiation") has to do with making amends for, or covering over, sin. The verb for this is *hilaskomai* ("to appease or conciliate"). A corresponding noun, *hilastērion*, is also translated "mercy seat," as in the lid of the ark of the covenant, which was important for sacrifices offered for the atonement (or "covering over") of sins among the people of Israel. Another noun, *hilasmos*, refers to propitiation or atonement in general.

Definitions

1: *hilaskomai* (verb, Strong's #2433)

This verb, as used amongst the Greeks, had the significance "to appease the gods," since people believed the gods did not generally extend good will; it had to be earned. But this use of the word is foreign to both the Septuagint and the New Testament. It is never used of any act by which humanity brings God into a favorable attitude or gracious disposition. Through the provision God has made in the atoning sacrifice of Christ, he has so dealt with sin that he can show mercy to the believing sinner by removing guilt and forgiving sins.

Thus in Luke 18:13 it signifies "to be propitious;" that is, "to be merciful to," with the sinner as the object of the verb. In Hebrews 2:17 it means "to expiate, to make propitiation for," with sins as the object of the verb. Through the "propitiation" or atonement sacrifice of Christ, the person who believes in him is by God's own act delivered from justly deserved wrath and comes under the covenant of grace. Never is God said to be reconciled, which shows that the enmity exists on the side of humans alone. It is humanity which needs to be reconciled to God, and not God to humanity.

God is always the same; he never changes, but his relative attitude does change toward those who themselves change. He can act differently toward those who come to him by faith, and solely on the ground of the "propitiatory" (atoning) sacrifice of Christ; not because he has changed, but because he always acts according to his unchanging righteousness.

The atoning work of the cross is therefore the means whereby the barrier which sin places between God and humans is broken down. By the sacrificial giving up of his sinless life, Christ annulled the power of sin to separate the believer from God.

In the Old Testament, the Hebrew verb *kaphar* is connected with *kōpher*, "a covering" (as in the mercy seat or lid of the ark of the covenant—see below). It is used in connection with the burnt offering (as in Leviticus 1:4; 14:20; 16:24), the guilt offering (Leviticus 5:16,18), the sin offering (Leviticus 4:20,26,31,35), the sin offering and burnt offering together (Leviticus 5:10; 9:7), the grain offering and fellowship offering (Ezekiel 45:15,17), as well as in other respects. It is used of the ram offered at the consecration of the high priest (Exodus 29:33), and of the blood which God provided and required to make atonement for the souls of the people, because the life of a creature is in the blood (Leviticus 17:11)—that is, blood makes atonement because of the life. Humans have forfeited their lives on account of sin, and God has provided the one and only way by which eternal life can be given, namely, by the voluntary laying down of his life by his Son. The former sacrifices appointed by God were foreshadowings of this.

2: *hilastērion* (neuter noun, Strong's #2435)

Related to *hilaskomai* (see above), *hilastērion* is regarded as the neuter of an adjective signifying "propitiatory" or "atoning." In the Septuagint it is used adjectivally in connection with *epithema*, "a cover," referring to the lid of the ark (Exodus 25:17; 37:6), but it is used as a noun (without *epithema*) with reference to location (Exodus 25:18-22; 31:7; 35:12; 37:7-9; Leviticus 16:2,13-15; Numbers 7:89), and this is its use in Hebrews 9:5.

Elsewhere in the New Testament, it occurs in Romans 3:25, where it is used of Christ himself: "God presented him as a sacrifice of atonement, through the shedding of his blood—to be received by faith." The NIV translates the word for "propitiation" there, *hilastērion*, as "a sacrifice of atonement." The Greek phrase *en tō haimati autou* (literally, "by his blood" but translated by the NIV as "through the shedding of his blood") is to be taken in immediate connection with "a sacrifice of atonement." Christ, through his atoning death, is the personal means by whom God shows the mercy of his justifying grace to the sinner who believes. His "blood" stands for the voluntary giving up of his life, by the shedding of his blood in atoning sacrifice, under divine judgment righteously due to us as sinners, with faith as the sole condition on humanity's part.

3: *hilasmos* (masculine noun, Strong's #2434)

This word means "an atonement, a means by which sin is covered and remitted." It occurs in the New Testament with reference to Christ himself as "the atoning sacrifice" (1 John 2:2; 4:10), showing that he himself, through his death, is the personal means by which God shows mercy to the sinner who believes. The point about God sending his Son Jesus to be an atoning sacrifice for our sins in 1 John 4:10 supports John's point that believers are to love one another just as God loved us (1 John 4:7-12).

Quotes

"Why was it that God 'did not spare his own Son, but gave him up for all' (Rom 8:32)? Because of his grace. It was his own free decision to save which brought the atonement."

> —J.I. Packer, *Knowing God* (Downers Grove, IL: InterVarsity Press, 1993), 133-134.

"One life is forfeit; another life is sacrificed instead."

> —John Stott, *The Cross of Christ* (Downers Grove, IL: InterVarsity Press, 2006), 138, speaking of the atonement.

Authority

"Authority" is closely linked to power in the New Testament (see *Power*). Jesus's authority to forgive sins, for instance, is associated with his power to heal.

Definition

exousia (feminine noun, Strong's #1849)

This noun denotes "authority" (from the impersonal verb *exestin*, "it is lawful"). From the meaning of "permission" or "liberty to do what one pleases," it developed the meaning of "the ability or strength one has," and finally to the "power of authority," the right to exercise power (for example, see Matthew 9:6; 21:23; 2 Corinthians 10:8).

Quotes

"Jesus behaves from the start *both* with the sovereign authority of one who knows himself charged with the responsibility to inaugurate God's kingdom *and* with the recognition that this task will only be completed through his suffering and death."

> —N.T. Wright, *Simply Jesus* (New York: HarperCollins Publishers, 2011), 172.

"I am continually impressed today, as throughout my life, with the number of people who claim to have intellectual objections to the historic Christian faith (and some of them genuinely do), but if I converse with them long enough, their biggest barriers are existential ones. They want to remain in charge of their own beliefs and behaviors and not submit to any ultimate authority outside of themselves."

> —Craig Blomberg, *Can We Still Believe the Bible? An Evangelical Engagement with Contemporary Questions* (Grand Rapids, MI: Brazos Press, 2014), 144-145.

B

Bandit

There are two types of "bandits" in the New Testament: One was a robber who waited by the roadside, while the other was a revolutionary, someone who wanted to revolt against Rome. Barabbas is called a *lēstēs* ("bandit" or "insurrectionist") in John 18:40. He probably was an insurrectionist against Rome arrested for his participation in an uprising, likely similar to the two "bandits" crucified beside Jesus. The contrast in that scene is clear: Jesus was not a violent revolutionary; he had committed no crimes against Rome, but Pilate had him crucified anyway to satisfy the demands of the crowd.

Definition

lēstēs (masculine noun, Strong's #3027)

A *lēstēs* was a "bandit" or "robber," and perhaps in some cases an "insurrectionist" against Rome (see above). Such people could be in a group who waited by the side of the road to ambush someone, or the word could refer to a single person who stole from others. This is different from a *kleptēs*, which is better translated "thief." The "thief" or "robber" meaning of *lēstēs* fits well in certain contexts where cheating someone is implied (for example, Matthew 21:13). Jesus protested in Matthew 26:55 that those coming to arrest him were coming at him with weapons as they would a *lēstēs*, and perhaps here "insurrectionist" is meant. Barabbas is called a *lēstēs* in John 18:40 and the "insurrectionist" meaning is probably the one intended here too. The robbers crucified with Jesus are called *lēstai* (possibly "robbers," but could also be "insurrectionists"). In the Good Samaritan parable, the *lēstai* who overtake the man going down from Jerusalem to Jericho are undoubtedly meant to be understood as "robbers" (Luke 10:30,36).

Baptism, Baptist, Baptize

To "baptize" someone in the New Testament was usually to "immerse" them in water. This was symbolic of repentance. John, who prepared the way of Jesus, was a "baptist," that is, "one who baptizes." He would call for people to be baptized to show their repentance. Jesus's baptism, however, could not have been a sign of him repenting, as he was without sin. Instead, it was done "to fulfill all righteousness," as Jesus explained to a bewildered John when Jesus came to be baptized by him (Matthew 3:15). Paul was baptized after he put his faith in Jesus, a typical example of how a person's repentance from one path toward faith in Jesus was shown (Acts 9:18). But baptism with water, John's baptism, is said in Scripture to be inferior to the baptism Jesus offers, which is a baptism with the Holy Spirit and fire (Matthew 3:11).

Definitions

1: *baptisma* (neuter noun, Strong's #908)

A *baptisma*, that is, a "baptism," consists of the process of immersion, submersion, and emergence (from *baptō*, "to dip").

It is used of

a. John's "baptism," that which occurred before the cross,

b. Christian "baptism," such as Paul's own baptism demonstrating his faith,

c. the horrors Jesus submitted to on the cross (for example, Luke 12:50), and

d. the sufferings Jesus's followers would experience (Mark 10:38,39).

2: *baptismos* (masculine noun, Strong's #909)

A *baptismos* is distinct from a *baptisma* in that it refers to a "ceremonial washing" of articles (see Mark 7:4; Hebrews 6:2; 9:10).

3: *baptistēs* (masculine noun, Strong's #910)

This is the word for "baptist" (that is, "immerser" or "one who baptizes"), as in "John the Baptist" (*Iōannēs ho baptistēs*). This word occurs only 14 times, and only in the Synoptic Gospels (Matthew, Mark, and Luke).

4: *baptizō* (verb, Strong's #907)

Baptizō is the verb meaning "to immerse/baptize," related to the verb *baptō* ("to dip"). The Greeks used it to refer to the dyeing of a garment, or sometimes to the drawing of water by dipping one container into another.

In Luke 11:38 it is used of washing oneself (compare the Septuagint's use of the same verb in its translation of 2 Kings 5:14). In the early chapters of the four Gospels it refers to the rite performed by John the Baptist, who called on people to repent that they might receive forgiveness (see also Acts 1:5; 11:16; 19:4). Those who obeyed came "confessing their sins," thus admitting they did not qualify to be in the Messiah's coming kingdom. Distinct from this is the "baptism" enjoined by Christ (Matthew 28:19), a "baptism" for believers, showing their identification with him in death, burial, and resurrection (for examples, see Acts 19:5; Romans 6:3,4; 1 Corinthians 1:13-17; 12:13; Galatians 3:27; Colossians 2:12).

The verb is also used metaphorically with regard to "baptism" by the Holy Spirit, which took place on Pentecost (see Acts 2).

Insight

Baptism does not seem to be essential for salvation but rather is an outward sign of one's faith in Jesus. Paul did not want the divided Corinthians to form a faction under him and say they were "baptized" in Paul's name:

Is Christ divided? Was Paul crucified for you? Were you baptized in the name of Paul? I thank God that I did not baptize any of you except Crispus and Gaius, so no one can say that you were baptized in my name. (Yes, I also baptized the house of Stephanas; beyond that, I don't remember if I baptized anyone else.) For Christ did not send me to baptize, but to preach the gospel—not with wisdom and eloquence, lest the cross of Christ be emptied of its power (1 Corinthians 1:13-17).

Quotes

"Jesus appears to have been identified as the one upon whom the Spirit of God rested. The anointing of Jesus with the Spirit at the time of his baptism is of particular importance in this respect."

> —Alister McGrath, *Christian Theology: An Introduction* (Sixth Edition) (West Sussex: John Wiley & Sons Ltd, 2017), 232.

"Baptism is an important step in a new believer's new life, not a requirement for salvation from sin."

> —Chuck Swindoll, *Jesus: The Greatest Life of All* (Nashville, TN: Thomas Nelson, 2008), 276.

Bear (see Carry)

Belief, Believe, Believers

"Belief," "faith," "faithfulness," and "trust" all translate the same word in the New Testament—*pistis*. This is a fundamental concept in theology because it is about how we relate to God and how God relates to us. God is faithful, but he also requires people to trust in him. If they don't, they are on the road that leads to destruction. In the Bible people are often punished or chastised for their unbelief or lack of faith.

Definitions

1: *pisteuō* (verb, Strong's #4100)

The verb *pisteuō* means "to believe" or "to be persuaded of" (in this regard, it is associated with *peithō*, "to persuade"), and also "to place confidence in, to trust." Therefore, it denotes a "reliance upon" someone or something, not mere credence. It occurs most often in John's Gospel and his other writings. He does not use the noun form (see below). For Jesus's first use of the verb, see John 1:50.

This is how often each Gospel writer uses the verb:

a. Matthew: 10 times

b. Mark: 10 times

c. Luke: 9 times

d. John: 99 times

In Acts 5:14, the present participle of the verb is translated "believers" (ESV).

2: *pistis* (feminine noun, Strong's #4102)

As the noun for "faith" or "belief" or "faithfulness," *pistis* occurs 243 times in the New Testament and is a major theme in the New Testament (for example, Matthew 9:2; Romans 3:28; 10:17; Galatians 2:16; 5:22; 2 Thessalonians 2:13). As noted above, this noun does not appear in John's Gospel, but the verb *pisteuō* does.

Quotes

"We must go on to recognize the real Giver... But never, never pin your whole faith on any human being: not if he is the best and wisest in the whole world."

—C.S. Lewis, *Mere Christianity* (New York: HarperCollins Publishers, 1980), 191.

"For you who believe in Jesus Christ, the future is assured. Tomorrow belongs to you!"

> —Billy Graham, *Hope for Each Day: Morning and Evening Devotions* (Nashville, TN: Thomas Nelson, 2012), 55.

"Faith is the way believers jump on board with God and participate in countless wonderful things He has a mind to do."

> —Beth Moore, *Believing God* (Nashville, TN: B&H Publishing Group, 2004), ix.

Blaspheme, Blasphemy, Blasphemer, Blasphemous

To "blaspheme" God in the New Testament is to speak disrespectfully of him. Technically, one could "blaspheme" anyone or anything (in the sense of speaking disrespectfully), but in the New Testament, the word is almost always used with reference to disrespectful speech about God or other supernatural beings.

Definitions

1: *blasphēmia* (feminine noun, Strong's #988)

Probably from *blaptō* ("to injure") and *phēmē* ("speech"), *blasphēmia* is often translated as "blasphemy," meaning "injurious speech." This noun occurs 18 times in the New Testament and is practically confined to speech defamatory of God.

2: *blasphēmeō* (verb, Strong's #987)

Occuring 34 times in the New Testament, *blasphēmeō* means "to revile," and it is used

   a. in a general way, of any insulting speech or railings against someone, as of those who railed against Christ (for example, Matthew 27:39; Mark 15:29; Luke 22:65; 23:39), and

b. of those who speak contemptuously of God or sacred things (for example, Matthew 9:3; Mark 3:28; Romans 2:24; 1 Timothy 1:20; 6:1; Revelation 13:6; 16:9,11,21). The verb doesn't always need to be translated as "blaspheme," as several synonyms such as "revile," "rail at," "speak evil of," and so on can be used to represent its meaning. In Acts 19:37, the verb is in its present participial form and can be translated "blasphemers."

3: *blasphēmos* (adjective, Strong's #987)

This adjective, commonly translated as "blasphemous" (for example, Acts 6:11), means "abusive, speaking evil." Paul uses the adjective as a substantive in 1 Timothy 1:13 (literally, "a blasphemous [one]"), so it is translated as "blasphemer" there. See also 2 Timothy 3:2 and 2 Peter 2:11.

Quotes

"That the Jewish authorities would condemn Jesus of blasphemy...flows not from his claim to be Messiah but from his loftier claim to be Daniel's exalted Son of Man [in Daniel 7:13-14] coming on the clouds of heaven."

—Craig L. Blomberg, *The Historical Reliability of the New Testament: Countering the Challenges to Evangelical Christian Beliefs* (Nashville, TN: B&H Academic, 2016), 144-145.

"Jesus [by claiming to be the Son of Man in Daniel 7:13-14] in effect is claiming the right to go directly into God's presence and be seated with him in heaven. To Jewish ears this is highly offensive—worse than claiming the right to walk in and permanently reside in the 'Holy of Holies' at the temple, since the temple represented God's presence in heaven."

—Darrell Bock, *The NIV Application Commentary: Luke* (Grand Rapids, MI: Zondervan, 1996), 578.

Bless, Blessed, Blessedness, Blessing

To "bless" someone in the New Testament is to speak well of them (*eulogeō*), to pronounce someone as happy, or to mark them as privileged or favored (*makarizō*), depending on the Greek word used. Jesus declared those who fit anywhere in his list of attributes in the beatitudes to be "happy" or "favored" (*makarios*). In his song to God, Zacharias called God "praised" or "blessed" in Luke 1:68 (*eulogētos*).

Definitions

1: *eulogeō* (verb, Strong's #2127)

Literally "to speak well of" (*eu*, "well," *logos*, "a word"), *eulogeō* occurs 41 times in the New Testament and signifies

    a. "to praise," the object of which is God (Luke 1:64; 2:28; 24:51,53; James 3:9),

    b. "to invoke good favor upon a person" (for example, Luke 6:28; Romans 12:14),

    c. "to consecrate a thing with solemn prayers, to ask God's favor on a thing" (for example, Luke 9:16; 1 Corinthians 10:16), and

    d. "to cause to prosper, to make happy, to bestow good things on" (for example, Acts 3:26; Galatians 3:9; Ephesians 1:3). Compare the synonym *aineō*, "to praise." See *Praise.*

2: *makarizō* (verb, Strong's #3106)

Makarizō denotes "to pronounce happy, blessed" (Luke 1:48; James 5:11). Part of its root meaning has to do with "length;" so perhaps the word implies happiness sustained for a long period of time.

3: *eulogētos* (adjective, Strong's #2128)

Akin to the verb *eulogeō* (see above), *eulogētos* is an adjective applied only to God in the New Testament (Mark 14:61; Luke 1:68; Romans 1:25; 9:5; 2 Corinthians 1:3; 11:31; Ephesians 1:3; 1 Peter 1:3).

In the Septuagint, it is also applied to humans (Genesis 24:31; 26:29; Deuteronomy 7:14; Judges 17:2; Ruth 2:20; 1 Samuel 15:13).

4: *makarios* (adjective, Strong's #3107)

Akin to the verb *makarizō* (see above), *makarios* is an adjective used in the beatitudes in Matthew 5 and Luke 6, and it is especially frequent in the Gospel of Luke. It occurs seven times in Revelation (1:3; 14:13; 16:15; 19:9; 20:6; 22:7,14) and describes God twice (1 Timothy 1:11; 6:15). In the beatitudes (Matthew 5:3-12), Jesus indicated not only those who are "blessed" but also the nature of godly attitude, speech, and action.

5: *eulogia* (feminine noun, Strong's #2129)

Akin to *eulogeō* (see above), *eulogia* is a noun that literally means "good speaking, praise" and is used of

   a. God the Father and Christ (Revelation 5:12,13; 7:12),

   b. the seeking and invocation of blessing (Hebrews 12:17; James 3:10),

   c. the giving of thanks (1 Corinthians 10:16),

   d. a blessing or benefit bestowed (Romans 15:29; Galatians 3:14; Ephesians 1:3; Hebrews 6:7), such as a monetary gift sent to needy believers (2 Corinthians 9:5,6), and

   e. flattering speech, in a bad sense (Romans 16:18).

Quotes

"All our actions, as well as our thoughts and words, should tend to the praise of him who always blesses us."

        —C.H. Spurgeon, "Daily Blessings for God's People," preached at the Metropolitan Tabernacle on September 21, 1871.

"The contentment we desire comes from doing what is right in His sight. This, then, is 'true' happiness. It is an enduring, flowering plant that draws its life and beauty and fragrance not from the shifting ground of circum-stances but from being solidly, deeply rooted in a right relationship with God Himself."

—Kay Arthur, *Lord, Only You Can Change Me: A Devotional Study on Growing in Character from the Beatitudes* (Colorado Springs, CO: Waterbrook Press, 2000), 21-22.

Blood

"Blood" is doctrinally significant in the Bible as a whole; in the New Testament it is especially important with reference to the atoning death of Christ. Hebrews 9:18-22 indicates that blood was important for the first covenant, saying that "without the shedding of blood there is no forgiveness" (Hebrews 9:22—this is also the only place that *haimatekchusia*, a compound word meaning "shedding or pouring out of blood," is used in the New Testament). Even so, "it is impossible for the blood of bulls and goats to take away sins" (Hebrews 10:4), even though this is what was used to make atonement for sin in the Old Testament. Lamb's blood was also used in the first Passover to "cover" the doorposts and save the people of Israel from the slaying of every firstborn (see Exodus 12). Similarly, Jesus is the Passover "Lamb of God, who takes away the sin of the world" (John 1:29).

Definition

haima (neuter noun, Strong's #129)

The word for "blood," *haima*

a. often occurs with the word *sarx* ("flesh"), that is, "flesh and blood," another way of saying "human beings," stressing human limitations and two components essential to the makeup of the human body (see Matthew 16:17; 1 Corinthians 15:50; the literal Greek of Galatians 1:16; Ephesians 6:12; Hebrews 2:14; compare with "the life of the flesh is in the blood" in Leviticus 17:11 ESV),

b. describes human descent contrasted with becoming children of God (John 1:13 ESV),

c. is the sort shed by violence (for example, see Matthew 23:35; Revelation 17:6), and

d. describes the sort shed by sacrificial victims (see Hebrews 9:7), as well as the blood shed by Christ, which his disciples can "drink," meaning to appropriate its saving effects (see John 6:53).

Quotes

"For those who have received the most precious gift of Christ's redeeming blood...you have reason to look forward to the glories of Heaven, for you will be perfected, you will be joyful, you will once again be active, and right *now* you can be certain that you are *nearing home*."

—Billy Graham, *Nearing Home: Life, Faith, and Finishing Well* (Nashville, TN: Thomas Nelson, 2011), 180.

"How rich is God?...Everything that exists belongs to him. And when he gave the infinitely precious blood of Jesus to redeem us from death, he truly gave according to his infinite riches."

—Michael Youssef, *Leading the Way Through Ephesians* (Eugene, OR: Harvest House Publishers, 2012), 21.

Body

The New Testament uses the image of a "body" in three significant ways, all of which relate to the body of Jesus Christ. First, Jesus's physical body was offered on the cross, and when Jesus took bread to represent his body (as when he took the cup of wine to represent his blood), it was given as a reminder of his sacrifice. Second, he also "bodily" rose from the dead, which is how believers know they too will rise from the dead. And third, believers are said to make up the "body of Christ" in that they each are granted something to contribute—"spiritual gifts"—as members of his church (1 Corinthians 12:27; see also verses 12-31).

Definition

sōma (neuter noun, Strong's #4983)

The *sōma* is the "body as a whole," the "instrument of life." It can refer to

  a. a living person (for example, see Matthew 6:22),

  b. a dead person (Matthew 27:52),

  c. bodily resurrection into a "spiritual" body (1 Corinthians 15:44),

  d. animals (Hebrews 13:11),

  e. plants (1 Corinthians 15:37,38),

  f. heavenly beings (1 Corinthians 15:40), and

  g. "slaves" (the translation used in Revelation 18:13).

A person can exist apart from their *sōma* (2 Corinthians 12:2,3), but somewhat paradoxically, the *sōma* is an essential part of the human being; therefore, it must one day be made perfect (Hebrews 11:40). No human beings will be without their bodies in their final state (John 5:28,29; Revelation 20:13).

The word is also used for physical nature, as contrasted with *pneuma* ("spirit" or the spiritual nature) in passages like 1 Corinthians 5:3 ESV). It is contrasted with both *pneuma* ("spirit") and *psuchē* ("soul") in 1 Thessalonians 5:23.

Sōma is also used metaphorically to describe the church as the body of Christ (1 Corinthians 12:27; Ephesians 1:23; Colossians 1:18,24).

Quotes

"Christians are Christ's body, the organism through which He works."
> —C.S. Lewis, *Mere Christianity* (New York: HarperCollins Publishers, 1980), 110.

"The site of Jesus's tomb was known to both Christian and Jew alike, so it could have been checked by skeptics. In fact, nobody, not even the Roman authorities or Jewish leaders, ever claimed that the tomb still contained Jesus's body. Instead they were forced to invent the absurd story that the disciples, despite having no motive or opportunity, had stolen the body—a theory that not even the most skeptical critic believes today."

> —Lee Strobel, *The Case for Christ: A Journalist's Personal Investigation of the Evidence for Jesus* (Grand Rapids, MI: Zondervan, 1998), 263.

Book

A "book" in New Testament times would have been a composition written on a scroll, a rolled-up document on papyrus. The two most prominent words for "book" in the New Testament (see below) can refer to large or small written works.

Definitions

1: *biblos* (feminine noun, Strong's #976)

This is the Greek noun for what was known in New Testament times as a written "book, roll, scroll, or volume." Matthew used the term to refer to his own Gospel (Matthew 1:1). In Mark 12:26, Jesus used the term to describe the Pentateuch as the "Book of Moses." Luke cited the "book of the words of Isaiah the prophet" in Luke 3:4. Jesus (Luke 20:42) and Peter (Acts 1:20) made reference to the "Book of Psalms." During Stephen's recounting of the story of the people of Israel, he cited "the prophets" collectively as a "book" (Acts 7:42). This term also describes the "book of life," which records the names of the redeemed (Philippians 4:3; Revelation 3:5; 20:15). Only once is the term used with reference to pagan documents (Acts 19:19, "scrolls").

2: *biblion* (neuter noun, Strong's #975)

A diminutive form of *biblos* (see above), *biblion* describes a "scroll or small book."

It is used to describe

a. the "book" of Isaiah (Luke 4:17,20),

b. the Gospel of John (John 20:30),

c. the entire Torah (Galatians 3:10) and the whole Old Testament (Hebrews 10:7),

d. a "scroll" written by Moses (Hebrews 9:19),

e. the "scroll" of Revelation (Revelation 1:11; 22:7,9,10,18,19),

f. "books" or "scrolls" in general (John 21:25; 2 Timothy 4:13),

g. the "book" of life (Revelation 13:8; 17:8; 20:12; 21:27),

h. other "books" to be opened at the final judgment, presumably containing records of the deeds of humans (Revelation 20:12),

i. a "scroll" representing the revelation of God's plans for judgement upon the world (Revelation 5:1-9; so also with the "scroll" of Revelation 10:8),

j. a "scroll" being rolled up, a metaphor for the heavens receding (Revelation 6:14), and

k. a "certificate" of divorce (Matthew 19:7; Mark 10:4).

Insight

Our modern English word *Bible* comes from the Greek word *biblos*.

Born, Bear

Giving birth, becoming the parent of a child, or simply being "born" are all key concepts in the New Testament. Jesus was "born" into this world as God made flesh. When God "becomes our Father," we are "born again," coming into his kingdom. Mary was a virgin when she "gave birth" to Jesus, and Jesus's genealogy demonstrates his messianic credentials as the Son of David, shows his Jewish identity as a son of Abraham (Matthew's genealogy), and reveals his line of descent back to the original created humans and even God himself (Luke's genealogy).

Definitions

1: *gennaō* (Strong's #1080)

A verb meaning "to beget" (or, in its passive form, "to be born"), *gennaō* refers to

a. chiefly men "begetting" children (Matthew 1:2-16),

b. more rarely women "begetting" children (Luke 1:13,17),

c. allegorical contrasting between birth from Hagar and Sarah (Galatians 4:22-24),

d. conception (Matthew 1:20), and

e. the act of God in the birth of Christ (Acts 13:33; Hebrews 1:5; 5:5).

It also refers metaphorically to

a. the gracious act of God granting spiritual life and status as his "children," those who believe in him, in John's writings (John 3:3,5,7; 1 John 2:29; 3:9; 4:7; 5:1,4,18),

b. spiritual fathers of those to whom they preach eternal life (1 Corinthians 4:15; Philemon 1:10),

c. evil people said to be born like animals (2 Peter 2:12), and

d. stupid arguments producing quarrels (2 Timothy 2:23).

2: *tiktō* (Strong's #5088)

This verb can mean

a. "to give birth" (Luke 1:57; John 16:21; Hebrews 11:11; Revelation 12:2,4),

b. "to be born," referring to the child Jesus (Matthew 2:2; Luke 2:11), and

    c. "to give birth" or "to produce" in a metaphorical sense (James 1:15).

Insight

In John 3 when Jesus talked to Nicodemus about how someone can be "born again," the word for "again" in Greek in that passage is *anōthen*, which can actually mean either "again" or "from above."

Bread

"Bread" was a common food long before, and during, the time of Jesus. It is biblically significant in many ways. Jesus is the "bread" of life (John 6:35). Bread serves as the symbol of Jesus's body, broken for believers (see Matthew 26:26). It can be leavened, often symbolizing something bad or corrupting, or it can be unleavened, symbolizing purity.

Definitions

1: *artos* (masculine noun, Strong's #740)

Artos can refer to

    a. a small loaf of bread, such as the consecrated bread in the house of God (Matthew 12:4),

    b. the piece of bread at the Last Supper (Matthew 26:26),

    c. bread that is broken to commemorate the Last Supper (Acts 2:42; 20:7; 1 Corinthians 10:17; 11:23),

    d. ordinary bread (Matthew 16:11),

    e. Christ, metaphorically, as the bread of life (John 6:33,35), and

    f. food in general, necessary to sustain life (Matthew 6:11).

2: *azumos* (adjective, Strong's #106)

This word refers to "unleavened" bread, that is, bread without yeast (leaven). Metaphorically, it can refer to a holy, spiritual condition (1 Corinthians 5:7) and to sincerity and truth (1 Corinthians 5:8). With the definite article, it denotes the Feast of the Unleavened Bread (Matthew 26:17; Mark 14:1,12; Luke 22:1,7; Acts 12:3; 20:6).

Brother

Although primarily the word for "brother" in the New Testament, *adelphos* can refer to any sibling, regardless of gender. Paul frequently addressed fellow believers as *adelphoi*, and while "brothers" is acceptable as a translation of this term, Paul certainly didn't mean to *only* refer to male Christians. It is an important word for kinship in the New Testament, both literally and with reference to the "kinship" between followers of Jesus who share devotion to him.

Definition

adelphos (masculine noun, Strong's #80)

An *adelphos* is a "brother or near kinsman." In the plural, this word means "a community based on identity of origin."

It is used of

a. male children of the same parents (Matthew 1:2; 14:3),

b. male descendants of a common ancestor (Acts 7:23,26; Hebrews 7:5),

c. male children of the same mother (Matthew 13:55; 1 Corinthians 9:5; Galatians 1:19),

d. people of the same nationality (Acts 3:17,22; Romans 9:3),

e. people being addressed with *anēr* ("man") prefixed, with this particular compound version of the word used only in such addresses (Acts 2:29,37, etc.),

   f. any person, a neighbor (Luke 10:29; Matthew 5:22; 7:3),

   g. persons united by a common interest or identity (Matthew 5:47),

   h. persons united by a common calling (Revelation 22:9),

   i. mankind (Matthew 25:40; Hebrews 2:17),

   j. the disciples, and so, by implication, all believers (Matthew 28:10; John 20:17), and

   k. believers, apart from gender (Matthew 23:8; Acts 1:15; Romans 1:13; 1 Thessalonians 1:4; Revelation 19:10).

Insight

There is a word *adelphē* (feminine noun), meaning specifically "sister." In a rare instance, it appears explicitly in the text alongside *adelphos* (James 2:15). Otherwise, sisters are meant to be included in certain contexts that clearly would apply to both genders but only use the word *adelphos*.

Carry

"Carrying, bearing, or lifting up" is a common image in the New Testament. One might "carry" an object, or "bear" a burden (whether a physical, emotional, task-oriented, daily, or even legal burden).

Definition

1: *bastazō* (verb, Strong's #941)

This verb means "to support as a burden." It is used with the meaning

a. "to take up," as in picking up objects, like stones (John 10:31),

b. "to carry" something (Matthew 3:11; Mark 14:13; Luke 7:14; 22:10; Acts 3:2; 21:35; Revelation 17:7),

c. "to carry" on one's person (Luke 10:4; Galatians 6:17),

d. of carrying a baby in one's body (Luke 11:27),

e. "to bear" a name in testimony (Acts 9:15),

f. "supporting" branches from a root, metaphorically speaking (Romans 11:18),

g. "carrying" a burden, whether physically, as of the cross (John

19:17), or metaphorically, with respect to the sufferings endured in the cause of Christ (Luke 14:27),

h. of physical endurance (Matthew 20:12),

i. "bearing" suffering on behalf of others (Matthew 8:17; Romans 15:1; Galatians 6:2),

j. of spiritual truths one cannot "bear" (John 16:12),

k. of tolerating wicked people, which one should not do (Revelation 2:2),

l. "bearing" oppressive religious regulations (Acts 15:10),

m. of suffering the penalty of God's judgment (Galatians 5:10), and

n. to take or carry away (John 12:6; 20:15).

2: *airō* (verb, Strong's #142)

This verb means either

a. "to raise up, to lift, to take upon oneself and carry what has been raised, physically" (its most frequent use), or

b. "to take away what is attached to anything, to remove," as of Christ, in "taking away" the sin of the world (John 1:29).

Christ

The title *Christ* (Greek: *christos*) actually means "Anointed One," which is also the translation of the word "Messiah" (capitalized in English when referring to Jesus). So it is not Jesus's last name but rather his title—he is "anointed" (see *Anointed*), or set aside to be the true King of the Jews who would deliver them from their sin. Jesus was *the* Christ, but the term *christos* is actually an adjective, meaning "anointed." In Jesus's case, it is used like a noun, thus Jesus's "Anointed One." Many kings, priests, and prophets were anointed through Israel's history, and Jesus is the pinnacle of those offices.

Definition

christos (adjective, Strong's #5547)

Meaning "anointed," this adjective is used to translate the Hebrew word *mashiach* (from which the term "Messiah" comes) in the Old Testament, a term applied to the priests who were anointed with holy oil, particularly the high priest (see Leviticus 4:3,5,16). The prophets were called *hoi christoi theou*, "the anointed ones of God" (see the Septuagint's translation of Psalm 105:15). A king of Israel was described upon occasion as the Lord's *christos*, the Lord's "anointed" (see the Septuagint's translation of the following verses: 1 Samuel 2:10,35; 2 Samuel 1:14; Psalm 2:2; 18:50; Habakkuk 3:13). Even King Cyrus of Persia was called the Lord's *christos* (see the Septuagint of Isaiah 45:1).

The title *ho christos*, "the Christ," however, is not used of Jesus in the Septuagint's translation of the Old Testament. In the New Testament, the word is frequently used in conjunction with the name *Jesus*, as in "Jesus Christ" (for example, John 17:3; Acts 9:34; 1 Corinthians 3:11; 1 John 5:6).

Quotes

"John knew that the phrase *Son of God* was tainted with misleading associations in the minds of his readers. Jewish theology used it as a title for the expected (human) Messiah."

> —J.I. Packer, *Knowing God* (Downer's Grove, IL: InterVarsity Press, 1993), 55.

"The sign [of turning water into wine, for example,] backed up the claim that Jesus was the one who would bring in this new order. He was the Messiah. As he was soon to say to the Samaritan woman, 'I am he.'"

> —John Stott, *Basic Christianity* (Downers Grove, IL: Inter-Varsity Press, 2008), 46.

Christian

It is surprising to many people to learn that the word *Christian* (Greek: *christianos*) only appears three times in the entire New Testament (Acts 11:26; 26:28; 1 Peter 4:16). Early in the history of the church, believers in Jesus were known as belonging to *hē hodos*, "the Way" (see Acts 9:2). The first time the word *Christian* appears, in Acts 11:26, it is said that it was in Antioch where the disciples of Jesus were first called "Christians," suggesting this was not a name they gave themselves. Perhaps other Greek-speaking persons heard them talking about "Christ" and how they followed him, and so they called them "those associated with or adhering to Christ" or "Christians" (similar to how "Herodians" were "those associated with or adhering to Herod").

Definition

christianos (masculine noun, Strong's #5546)

A *christianos* ("Christian") means "an adherent of Christ," namely, Jesus (similar to how "Herodian" was "an adherent of Herod"). It was first applied to such by the Gentiles and is found in Acts 11:26.

Though the word rendered "were called" in Acts 11:26 might be used of a name adopted by oneself or given by others, the "Christians" do not seem to have adopted it for themselves in the time of the apostles. In 1 Peter 4:16, the writer is speaking of one who might "suffer as a Christian" in the sense that the one causing the suffering is doing so because of the victim's devotion to Christ. Agrippa's use of "Christian" in Acts 26:28 was no doubt meant derisively. Tacitus, writing near the end of the first century, said, "The vulgar call them Christians. The author or origin of this denomination, Christus, had, in the reign of Tiberius, been executed by the procurator, Pontius Pilate" (*The Annals of Tacitus*, Book 15, Section 44).

Quotes

"When the Christian says the first clause of the Creed, he will put all this together and confess his Creator as both the Father of his Savior and his own Father through Christ—a Father who now loves him no less than he loves his own begotten Son."

> —J.I. Packer, *Growing in Christ* (Wheaton, IL: Crossway Books, 1994), 29.

"Christians are Christ's body, the organism through which He works."

> —C.S. Lewis, *Mere Christianity* (New York: HarperCollins Publishers, 1980), 110.

Church

In the time of Jesus and the apostles the Greek word for "church" (*ekklēsia*) could be applied to any assembly or community of people. But in the New Testament *ekklēsia* usually describes either a local "assembly" or "community" of believers in Jesus, or all followers of Jesus everywhere, collectively. Jesus told Peter, whose name means "rock," that "on this rock" (meaning, on the foundation of early disciples like Peter) he would build his *ekklēsia*, the universal community of all who believe in him.

Definition

ekklēsia (feminine noun, Strong's #1577)

From *ek* ("out of") and *klēsis* ("a calling"), *ekklēsia* was used among the Greeks to denote a body of citizens "gathered" to discuss the affairs of the state (Acts 19:39). In the Septuagint it is used to designate a "gathering" of Israel, summoned for any definite purpose, or a "gathering" regarded as representative of the whole nation. In Acts 7:38 it is used of Israel; in Acts 19:32,41, of a riotous mob.

It has two applications to groups of Christians:

a. *Ekklēsia* can refer to the whole company of the redeemed. Christ said he would build his "church" (Matthew 16:18); this is further described as "the church which is his body" (Ephesians 1:22-23) or "the church, his body" (Ephesians 5:23).

b. An *ekklēsia* can be a specific congregation or community of believers (Acts 20:28; 1 Corinthians 1:2; Galatians 1:13; 1 Thessalonians 1:1; 2 Thessalonians 1:1; 1 Timothy 3:5).

Quotes

"The purpose of the church is to make disciples, not just add names to the roll or increase small-group Bible study attendance."

—Tony Evans, *Kingdom Disciples: Heaven's Representatives on Earth* (Chicago, IL: Moody Publishers, 2017), 20.

"In today's culture, *church* is most often thought of as a building or an organization. But that is far from what the disciples and apostles understood after Pentecost. Once the Holy Spirit filled them they understood the concept—the church was God's people. The church was Christ's agent to spread the kingdom message. The church was the visible representation of Christ himself."

—Josh McDowell and Sean McDowell, *The Unshakable Truth: How You Can Experience the 12 Essentials of a Relevant Faith* (Eugene, OR: Harvest House Publishers, 2010), 379.

Clay

"Clay" was an earthen substance used in biblical times to fashion pottery or other useful items. The word is often used to illustrate God's shaping influence over humans.

Definition

pēlos (masculine noun, Strong's #4081)

Pēlos can refer in the New Testament to

   a. moist clay (John 9:6,11,14-15, in connection with Jesus healing the blind man), or

   b. potter's clay, as with the potter's right over it as an illustration of the prerogatives of God in his dealings with humans (Romans 9:21).

The significance of a "colt" or "foal" was that it was a humble animal (the foal of a donkey) upon which Jesus chose to ride (along with its mother, according to Matthew 21:2) during his triumphal entry into Jerusalem.

Definition

pōlos (masculine noun, Strong's #4454)

A *pōlos* could be a "young creature" or "foal" of any animal, but in Matthew 21:2 (and parallel passages), it was a donkey's colt. This is what Jesus rode during his triumphal entry into Jerusalem.

Insights

   • Of the synoptic accounts of the triumphal entry, only in Matthew 21:2 did Jesus specify that the disciples bring him a donkey's colt and the donkey itself (compare with Jesus's instructions in Mark 11:2 and Luke 19:30). In John 12:14-15, Jesus rode on a "young donkey," specified as a donkey's "colt."

   • In Mark's and Luke's account of the story, Jesus said the colt he wanted the disciples to bring to him had never been ridden before.

- Zechariah 9:9 is the base text for the triumphal entry story in all four Gospels. Jesus, as the "king" of the Jews, the Messiah, fulfilled this passage by riding into Jerusalem on "a donkey, on a colt, the foal of a donkey."

Quote

"God called Israel, so that through Israel he might redeem the world; but Israel itself needs redeeming as well. Hence God comes to Israel riding on a donkey, in fulfillment of Zechariah's prophecy of the coming peaceful kingdom, announcing judgment on the system and the city that have turned their vocation in upon themselves and going off to take the weight of the world's evil and hostility onto himself, so that by dying under them he might exhaust their power."

—N.T. Wright, *Simply Jesus* (New York: HarperCollins Publishers, 2011), 38-39.

Condemn, Condemnation

To "condemn" someone in the New Testament is to pronounce some kind of judgment on them—to sentence them. To be "condemned" by God is to be consigned to everlasting punishment, the fate of those who do not believe in Jesus whom God has sent (see John 3:16-17).

Definitions

1: *krinō* (verb, Strong's #2919)
This verb means "to distinguish, choose, give an opinion upon, judge." It sometimes denotes "to condemn" (for example, Acts 13:27; Romans 2:27).

In other places, "to judge" may be a better way to translate the verb (for example, Matthew 7:1-2). (See *Judge, Judging, Judgment*.)

2: *katakrinō* (verb, Strong's #2632)

This verb is a strengthened form of *krinō* (see above). It signifies "to give judgment against, pass sentence upon," implying

a. a crime or sin has taken place (see Romans 2:1; 14:23; 2 Peter 2:6), or

b. the claim of a crime or sin, such as the "condemnation" of Christ by those who called for his execution (Matthew 20:18; Mark 14:64).

This verb also is used with reference to the "condemning" that some historical figures will be allowed to pronounce on others (Matthew 12:41,42; Luke 11:31,32; Hebrews 11:7). Romans 8:3 says our sin was "condemned," as Jesus came in the likeness of sinful flesh and became a sin offering, taking on the judgment the sin demanded.

3: *krima* (neuter noun, Strong's #2917)

This noun denotes

a. "a sentence pronounced, a verdict, a condemnation, the decision resulting from an investigation" (for example, Mark 12:40; Luke 23:40; 1 Timothy 3:6; Jude 1:4) or

b. "the process of judgment leading to a decision" (see 1 Peter 4:17).

In Luke 24:20, the phrase *eis krima* (literally, "into judgment") is translated "to be sentenced." Sometimes the single word "judgment" is appropriate (for example, Romans 11:33; 1 Corinthians 11:34; Galatians 5:10 NASB; James 3:1 NASB).

Quote

"The doctrines of hell and eternal punishment have become increasingly unpopular in our day, even among some Christian pastors and theologians. Those who question the doctrine ought to consider that some of our clearest statements on it come from the Lord Jesus Himself."

> —Ron Rhodes, *What Happens After Life?* (Eugene, OR: Harvest House Publishers, 2014), 138.

Confess, Confession

"Confessing" in the New Testament can be admitting guilt to something (like confessing a sinful action), or declaring a conviction or belief in someone or something (like confessing that Jesus is Lord).

Definitions

1: *homologeō* (verb, Strong's #3670)

Literally, *homologeō* means "to speak the same thing" (*homos*, "same," *legō*, "to speak") or "to assent, accord, agree with." It denotes

   a. "to confess, declare, admit" (for example, John 1:20; Acts 24:14; Hebrews 11:13),

   b. "to confess by way of admitting oneself guilty of what one is accused of, the result of inner conviction" (see 1 John 1:9),

   c. "to declare openly by way of speaking out freely, such confession being the effect of deep conviction of facts" (Matthew 7:23; 10:32; Luke 12:8; John 9:22; 12:42; Acts 23:8; Romans 10:9,10; 1 Timothy 6:12; Titus 1:16; 1 John 2:23; 4:2,15; 2 John 1:7),

   d. "to confess by way of celebrating with praise" (see Hebrews 13:15), and

   e. "to promise" (see Matthew 14:7).

2: *exomologeō* (verb, Strong's #1843)

The word *ek* ("out of, from") and *homologeō* ("to confess") combine to form this verb. It is a stronger form than *homologeō* (above).

It can mean

a. "a public acknowledgment or confession of sins" (Matthew 3:6; Mark 1:5; Acts 19:18; James 5:16),

b. "to profess or acknowledge openly" (Philippians 2:11), or

c. "to confess by way of celebrating, giving praise" (Romans 14:11; 15:9).

In Matthew 11:25 and Luke 10:21 it is translated "praise," but *exomologeō* is the underlying word and "gladly acknowledge" is probably better in both instances.

3: *homologia* (feminine noun, Strong's #3671)

Akin to *homologeō* (see above), the noun denotes "confession, by acknowledgment of the truth" (see 2 Corinthians 9:13; 1 Timothy 6:12,13; Hebrews 3:1; 4:14; 10:23).

Quotes

"To confess and testify to the truth as it is in Jesus, and at the same time to love the enemies of that truth, his enemies and ours, and to love them with the infinite love of Jesus Christ, is indeed a narrow way."

> —Dietrich Bonhoeffer, *The Cost of Discipleship*, translated by R.H. Fuller, with some revision by Irmgard Booth (New York: Touchstone Rockefeller Center, 1995), 190.

"Do you want freedom from sin's penalty? Believe that Christ died *for you.* He suffered *for you.* He won the battle over sin *for you.* He rose from the grave and was victorious over death so that *you* can live forever. But you must respond by receiving Him into your heart by faith and committing your life to Him without reserve. He is waiting for you to confess your sins, to surrender yourself to Him, and to make Him Lord and Master of your life."

> —Billy Graham, *The Heaven Answer Book* (Nashville, TN: Thomas Nelson, 2012), 131.

Conquer, Conqueror

"Conquering" or "overcoming" or "being victorious" is military language used in the New Testament to refer to victory in the spiritual realm as well as in the physical.

Definition

nikaō (verb, Strong's #3528)
This verb is used of

   a. God (Romans 3:4),

   b. Christ (John 16:33; Revelation 3:21; 5:5; 17:14),

   c. his followers (Romans 12:21; 1 John 2:13,14; 4:4; 5:4,5; Revelation 2:7,11,17,26; 3:5,12,21; 12:11; 15:2; 21:7),

   d. faith (1 John 5:4),

   e. evil (Romans 12:21), and

   f. predicted human powers (Revelation 6:2; 11:7; 13:7).

Correct, Correction, Corrector, Correcting

The New Testament word for correction is from the idea of making something "straight," like taking a crooked line and making it straight.

Definition

diorthōsis (feminine noun, Strong's #1357)
Literally meaning "a making straight" (*dia*, "through," *orthoō*, "straight"), *diorthōsis* means "a reform, amendment, correction" (for example, Acts 24:2; Hebrews 9:10).

Insights

- Instead of the noun *diorthōsis* or the verb *orthoō* (see above), Paul used the verb *paideuō* (literally, "to train up a child") in 2 Timothy 2:25, which is still rightly translated as "correcting."

- *Epanorthōsis* ("a restoration to an upright or right state"), related to *diorthōsis*, is the noun translated "correcting" in the famous passage 2 Timothy 3:16.

Corner, Cornerstone

A *gōnia* is an "angle" or "corner." Christ is said to be the "stone" (*lithos*) which the builders rejected, which became the "chief" (*kephalē*) "corner" (*gōnia*) stone. This word is important because of how crucial a "cornerstone" is to the structure of a building. It is laid to set the pattern for the walls on either side.

Definition

gōnia (feminine noun, Strong's #1137)

As noted above, a *gōnia* is an "angle" or "corner," and it signifies

a. "an external angle," as of the "corner" of a street (Matthew 6:5), or of a building (Matthew 21:42; Mark 12:10; Luke 20:17; Acts 4:11; 1 Peter 2:7; compare Psalm 118:22), or

b. "an internal corner," a secret place (Acts 26:26).

Insights

- The word *archē*, though it primarily means "beginning" or "principal," can also be used to denote the "corners" of a sheet (Acts 10:11; 11:5).

- The adjective *akrogōniaios* means "at the chief corner" and is used to describe the corner *lithos* ("stone") in Ephesians 2:20 and 1 Peter 2:6 (compare the Septuagint of Isaiah 28:16).

Covenant

A "covenant" is a contract between two or more parties. In both the Old and the New Testament, "covenant" usually refers to one authored by God to establish a relationship between himself and humans. There is an old covenant he made with the people of Israel after he brought them out of Egypt, and a "new covenant" (Luke 22:20; see also Jeremiah 31:31) represented by the blood of Jesus; in this covenant his blood washes away the sins of humanity and breaks down the barrier of the dividing wall between Jews and Gentiles (see Ephesians 2).

Definition

diathēkē (feminine noun, Strong's #1242)

A *diathēkē* is primarily "a disposition of property by will or otherwise." In the Septuagint it is used for the Hebrew word *bᵉrit*, meaning a covenant or agreement (often accompanying the Hebrew verb *karat*, signifying "to cut or divide," an allusion to a sacrificial custom in connection with covenant-making; see Genesis 15:10). The Greek word *diathēkē* has a similar use in the New Testament. Unlike the English word "covenant," which suggests mutual effort by two parties, the word *diathēkē* (like its Hebrew counterpart, *bᵉrit*) refers to a contract that obligates a single person (compare "promise" with "covenant" in Galatians 3:17). When God instituted the rite of circumcision with Abraham, God's promise to him, his "covenant," was not conditional upon Abraham's observance of circumcision. It instead required his faith, his belief that God would bring about what he promised.

The word *diathēkē* is used with reference to

a. a promise or undertaking, human or divine (see Galatians 3:15),

b. a promise or undertaking on the part of God (Luke 1:72; Acts 3:25; Romans 9:4; 11:27; Galatians 3:17; Ephesians 2:12; Hebrews 7:22; 8:6,8,10; 10:16),

c. an agreement, a mutual undertaking, between God and Israel (see Hebrews 8:9; 9:20; compare Deuteronomy 29; 30),

d. the promise made to Abraham (Acts 7:8),

e. the record of the covenant (2 Corinthians 3:14; Hebrews 9:4; compare Revelation 11:19), and

f. the basis, established by the death of Christ, on which our salvation is secured (Matthew 26:28; Mark 14:24; Luke 22:20; 1 Corinthians 11:25; 2 Corinthians 3:6; Hebrews 10:29; 12:24; 13:20).

The New Testament gets its name from the phrase *new covenant*, promised in Jeremiah (Jeremiah 31:31) and realized later with Jesus (*diathēkē* is sometimes also translated "testament"). The author of Hebrews calls the covenant established by Jesus the "new" (Hebrews 9:15), the "second" (Hebrews 8:7 ESV), and the "better" (Hebrews 7:22) covenant.

Quotes

"Yahweh revealed himself as Israel's covenant God."

> —John Stott, *The Cross of Christ* (Downers Grove, IL: InterVarsity Press, 2006), 140.

"Christians are not expected to express their loyalty to God by keeping the Old Testament law(s), since we are related to God under a new covenant."

> —Gordon D. Fee and Douglas Stuart, *How to Read the Bible for All Its Worth* (Grand Rapids, MI: Zondervan, 2003), 165.

Create, Creation, Creature

"Creation" is just as important a concept in the New Testament as in the Old. Jesus is said to be the "firstborn over all creation" (Colossians 1:15), for example. Paul wrote, "Creation waits in eager expectation for the children of God to be revealed" (Romans 8:19).

Definitions

1: *ktizō* (verb, Strong's #2936)

This verb was used among the Greeks to mean "the founding of a place, a city, or colony." In the New Testament it signifies "to create," always an act of God, whether

a. in the natural creation (Mark 13:19; Romans 1:25; 1 Corinthians 11:9; Ephesians 3:9; Colossians 1:16; 1 Timothy 4:3; Revelation 4:11; 10:6), or

b. in the spiritual creation (Ephesians 2:10,15; 4:24; Colossians 3:10).

2: *ktisis* (feminine noun, Strong's #2937)

This noun denotes primarily "the act of creating" or "the creative act in process" (see Romans 1:20; Galatians 6:15). Like the English word "creation," the Greek word *ktisis* also signifies the product of the created act, the creatures and other created things (as in Romans 1:25; 8:19; Colossians 1:15). In Galatians 6:15, it seems to be referring more to the creative act of God, whereas in 2 Corinthians 5:17, the "new creation" is a reference to the believer becoming a new creature in Christ.

Quotes

"The God of Genesis is the Creator, bringing order out of chaos, calling life into being by his word, making Adam from earth's dust and Eve from Adam's rib."

> —J.I. Packer, *Knowing God* (Downers Grove, IL: InterVarsity Press, 1993), 84.

"So then, everything in us that is attributeable to our creation in the image of God we gratefully affirm, while everything in us that is attributable to the Fall we must resolutely deny."

> —John Stott, *Why I Am Christian* (Downers Grove, IL: Inter-Varsity Press, 2003), 78.

Cross, Crucify

The Romans "crucified" criminals on "crosses," most familiar to us as two beams crossed somewhat like a *T*. Jesus, however, was not a criminal and was innocent of all charges brought against him. Through his death on the cross, salvation is available to all who believe.

Definitions

1: *stauros* (masculine noun, Strong's #4716)

This noun denotes, primarily, an "upright pale or stake." Criminals were nailed on such for execution. Both the noun and the verb *stauroō*, "to fasten to a stake or pale," are originally to be distinguished from the ecclesiastical form of a two-beamed "cross." The shape of the latter had its origin in ancient Chaldea, and was used as the symbol of the god Tammuz (being in the shape of the mystic *Tau*, the initial of his name), in that country and in adjacent lands, including Egypt. The method of execution was borrowed by the Greeks and Romans from the Phoenicians.

Stauros refers to

   a. "the cross, or stake itself" (for example, Matthew 27:32), and

   b. "the crucifixion suffered" (see 1 Corithians 1:17,18, where "the
      message of the cross" stands for the gospel; Galatians 5:11, where
      the "cross" has to do with salvation by grace instead of by law;
      Galatians 6:12,14; Ephesians 2:16; Philippians 3:18).

The judicial custom, by which the condemned person carried his stake to
the place of execution, was applied by the Lord to those sufferings by which
his faithful followers were to express their fellowship with him (see Matthew 10:38).

2: *stauroō* (verb, Strong's #4717)

This word signifies

   a. "the act of crucifixion" (Matthew 20:19), or

   b. metaphorically, "the putting off of the flesh with its passions and
      lusts," a condition fulfilled in the case of those who "belong to
      Christ Jesus" (Galatians 5:24), and so of the relationship between
      the believer and the world (Galatians 6:14).

3: *sustauroō* (verb, Strong's #4957)

This verb means "to crucify with" (*su*, "for," *sun*, "with") and is used

   a. of actual crucifixion in company with another (Matthew 27:44;
      Mark 15:32; John 19:32), and

   b. metaphorically, of spiritual identification with Christ in his
      death (Romans 6:6; Galatians 2:20).

4: *anastauroō* (verb, Strong's #388)

(*Ana*, "again"). This is used in Hebrews 6:6 of Hebrew apostates, merely
nominal Christians who turned back to Judaism and thereby were virtually
guilty of crucifying Christ again.

5: *prospēgnumi* (verb, Strong's #4362)

This means "to fix or fasten to anything" (*pros*, "to," *pegnumi*, "to fix") and is
used of the crucifixion of Christ (Acts 2:23).

"God, who needs nothing, loves into existence wholly superfluous creatures in order that He may love and perfect them. He creates the universe, already foreseeing—or should we say 'seeing'? there are no tenses in God—the buzzing cloud of flies about the cross, the flayed back pressed against the uneven stake, the nails driven through the mesial nerves, the repeated incipient suffocation as the body droops, the repeated torture of back and arms as it is time after time, for breath's sake, hitched up. If I may dare the biological image, God is a 'host'; who deliberately creates His own parasites; causes us to be that we may exploit and 'take advantage of' Him. Herein is love. This is the diagram of Love Himself, the inventor of all loves."

> —C.S. Lewis, *The Four Loves* (New York: HarperCollins, 1960), 162-163.

"Certainly God, whose existence I had denied for years, seemed extremely distant, and it became obvious to me that I needed the cross of Jesus to bridge that gulf."

> —Lee Strobel, *The Case for Christ: A Journalist's Personal Investigation of the Evidence for Jesus* (Grand Rapids, MI: Zondervan, 1998), 268.

Crown

A "crown," or circular garland for the head, denotes or symbolizes many things in the New Testament, among them victory (as in the Greco-Roman games), military triumph, and even life, honor, and celebration, especially at the coming of kings. The unsettling and simultaneously powerful image of the "crown of thorns" placed on Jesus's head by the soldiers was a humiliating gesture, mocking a "king" about to be executed. At the same time, it demonstrated the kind of king he was. No one at the time would have conceived of a king like Jesus, whose mission it was to suffer.

Definitions

1: *stephanos* (masculine noun, Strong's #4735)

A *stephanos* was primarily "that which surrounds" (from *stephō*, "to encircle"). It denotes

a. "the victor's crown" (the symbol of triumph in the games or some such context, thus a reward or prize), or

b. "a token of public honor" for distinguished service, military prowess, etc., or of nuptial joy, or celebratory gladness, especially at the coming of kings.

It was woven as a garland of oak, ivy, parsley, myrtle, or olive, or, in imitation of these materials, in gold. In some passages, the image of a crown worn in victory at the games is evoked (1 Corinthians 9:25; 2 Timothy 4:8). In 1 Peter 5:4, "the crown of glory" is contrasted with the fragile garlands of earth. In other passages, it stands as an emblem of life, joy, reward, and glory (Philippians 4:1; 1 Thessalonians 2:19; James 1:12; Revelation 2:10; 3:11; 4:4,10). It is also used with reference to triumph (Revelation 6:2; 9:7; 12:1; 14:14).

Stephanos is also the word used for the "crown" of thorns the soldiers put on Christ's head (Matthew 27:29; Mark 15:17; John 19:2,5). Though not the typical word for "kingly crown" in the New Testament (see below), the Roman emperor would have worn a *stephanos* or "laurel wreath," so the Roman soldiers were trying to cast Jesus as a parodied version of Caesar. As evangelical scholar Mark L. Strauss notes of this moment, "The scene as a whole resembles the Roman triumph, where Caesar would be hailed as emperor wearing a purple robe and a laurel wreath and holding a scepter."[2]

2: *diadēma* (neuter noun, Strong's #1238)

Diadēma is never used as *stephanos* is. Rather, it is always the symbol of kingly or imperial authority (it occurs, for example, in Revelation 12:3; 13:1; 19:12).

Crucifixion (see Cross)

Cup

A "cup" is significant in the New Testament as the drinking vessel filled with wine from which Jesus commanded his disciples at the Last Supper to drink, as a symbol of his blood "poured out for many for the forgiveness of sins" (Matthew 26:27). The image of a cup is also used as a vessel containing positive and negative experiences, sin, or the wrath of God to be poured out on the earth in judgment. This last image is also common in the Old Testament.

Definition

potērion (neuter noun, Strong's #4221)

As a diminutive version of the word *potēr*, the term *potērion* denotes primarily a "drinking vessel" or "cup."

It can be used

a. literally (as in Matthew 10:42; see also the "cup of thanksgiving" in 1 Corinthians 10:16, referring to the cup Jesus used while celebrating the Passover one final time with his disciples), and

b. figuratively, of one's experience, joyous or sorrowful (frequent in the Psalms, like in Psalm 116:13), of Christ's sufferings (Matthew 20:22,23; 26:39; Mark 10:38,39; 14:36; Luke 22:42; John 18:11), of the evil deeds of Babylon (Revelation 17:4; 18:6), of divine punishments to be inflicted (Revelation 14:10; 16:19). Compare Psalm 75:8; Isaiah 51:17; Jeremiah 25:15; Zechariah 12:2.

Daughter

A "daughter" in the New Testament can be a female child of another person, or of God. Sometimes the "daughter" of a city or region can be the inhabitants of that place, collectively.

Definition

thugatēr (feminine noun, Strong's #2364)

A *thugatēr* is "a daughter," and it is used of

a. the natural relationship between a female child and a parent (frequent in the Gospels),

b. a spiritual relationship to God (2 Corinthians 6:18),

c. the inhabitants of a city or region (Matthew 21:5; John 12:15),

d. the women who followed Christ to Calvary (Luke 23:28), and

e. a female descendant of Aaron (Luke 1:5), or of Abraham (Luke 13:16).

Dead, Death

The words for "death" are used in several ways in the New Testament. The most common associations are with physical death and spiritual death. Central to all Christian teaching is the fact that Jesus rose from the dead and thus conquered or defeated death.

Definitions

1: *nekros* (adjective, Strong's #3498)

This adjective is used of

a. the death of the body, its most frequent sense,

b. the spiritual condition of unsaved people (Matthew 8:22; John 5:25; Ephesians 2:1,5; 5:14; Colossians 2:13),

c. the ideal spiritual condition of believers in regard to sin (being "dead" to sin, as in Romans 6:11),

d. an inactive and barren church (Revelation 3:1),

e. sin, which apart from the law cannot produce a sense of guilt (Romans 7:8),

f. the body of the believer in contrast to his spirit (Romans 8:10),

g. the works of the Law, which, as good as they are in themselves (Romans 7:13), cannot produce life (Hebrews 6:1; 9:14), and

h. faith that does not produce works (James 2:17,26).

2: *thanatos* (masculine noun, Strong's #2288)

Thanatos, "death," is used in Scripture of

a. the separation of the soul (the spiritual part of humans) from the body (the material part), the latter ceasing to function and turning to dust (as in John 11:13; Hebrews 2:15; 5:7; 7:23), and

b. the separation of humans from God (Romans 5:12,14,17,21;

compare Genesis 2:17), from which, if they believe in Jesus, they are delivered (John 5:24; 1 John 3:14).

Death, in whichever of the above-mentioned senses, in Scripture, is always viewed as the consequence of sin. And because sinners alone are subject to death (Romans 5:12), Jesus submitted to bearing sin on the cross to save sinful humanity from death (1 Peter 2:24).

Quotes

"Can you imagine a world with no death, only life? If you can, you can imagine heaven. For citizens of heaven wear the crown of life."

—Max Lucado, *Beyond Heaven's Door* (Nashville, TN: Thomas Nelson, 2013), 63.

"Jesus behaves from the start *both* with the sovereign authority of one who knows himself charged with the responsibility to inaugurate God's kingdom *and* with the recognition that this task will only be completed through his suffering and death."

—N.T. Wright, *Simply Jesus* (New York: HarperCollins Publishers, 2011), 172.

"In order for someone's soul to become fully alive, it must first die to self. And it will need to die daily. The self-life, your selfish thoughts that dominate your mind and are in conflict with the will and Word of God, must die. Much more important is to save your soul, which remains forever, either in hell or heaven."

—Tony Evans, *Kingdom Disciples: Heaven's Representatives on Earth* (Chicago, IL: Moody Publishers, 2017), 21.

Deed

The Bible teaches that "deeds" (or "works") do not save a person. Only faith in Jesus saves, yet deeds nevertheless show a person's faith.

Definition

ergon (neuter noun, Strong's #2041)

This noun denotes either

a. "work, employment, task" (such as Mark 13:34; John 4:34; 17:4; Acts 13:2; Philippians 2:30; 1 Thessalonians 5:13; in Acts 5:38 with the idea of enterprise), or

b. "a deed, act"

  i. of God (such as John 6:28,29; 9:3; 10:37; 14:10; Acts 13:41; Romans 14:20; Hebrews 1:10; 3:9; 4:3,4,10; Revelation 15:3),

  ii. of Christ (such as Matthew 11:2; especially in John's writings, such as John 5:36; 7:3,21; 10:25,32,33,38; 14:11,12; 15:24; Revelation 2:26), and

  iii. of believers (as in Matthew 5:16; Mark 14:6; Acts 9:36; Romans 13:3; Colossians 1:10; 1 Thessalonians 1:3; frequently in James of deeds working together with faith, as in James 2:18-26).

Quotes

"Salvation is a gift to be received, not a reward to be earned."

> —Steve McVey, *Grace Walk* (Eugene, OR: Harvest House Publishers, 1995), 18.

"Why can't we earn our own salvation? Because we are dead in our sins. A corpse can't work. A corpse can't pay. A corpse can do nothing. That's why salvation is a free gift from God."

> —Michael Youssef, *Leading the Way Through Ephesians* (Eugene, OR: Harvest House Publishers, 2012), 41.

Defense

An *apologia* in the Bible is a "defense" for the hope that we have (1 Peter 3:15). Sometimes the faith of a person is unfairly attacked or maligned, and they need to stand up for, or defend, it.

Definition

apologia (feminine noun, Strong's #627)

This word means "a verbal defense, a speech in defense," or an "answer" (see Acts 22:1; 25:16; 1 Corinthians 9:3; 2 Timothy 4:16). In 1 Peter 3:15, it is probably best understood as an "answer." That is, Peter told the suffering believers to whom he was writing that they needed to be prepared to give an answer to anyone who asked them to give an account for the hope that was within them, with gentleness and respect. This is the word from which our modern term "apologetics" comes. Many early Christian apologists such as Justin Martyr spoke up in defense of the faith, particularly when it was unfairly maligned.

Quotes

"Maybe you too have been basing your spiritual outlook on the evidence you've observed around you or gleaned long ago from books, college professors, family members, or friends. But is your conclusion really the best possible explanation for the evidence? If you were to dig deeper—to confront your preconceptions and systematically seek out proof—what would you find?"

—Lee Strobel, *The Case for Christ: A Journalist's Personal Investigation of the Evidence for Jesus* (Grand Rapids, MI: Zondervan, 1998), 14.

"Peter clearly assumes [in 1 Peter 3:15] that Christian ideas are being misunderstood or misrepresented, and urges his readers to set the record straight—but to do so graciously and considerately. For Peter, apologetics is about defending the truth with gentleness and respect. The object of apologetics is not to antagonize or humiliate those outside the church, but to help open their eyes to the reality, reliability, and relevance of the Christian faith."

—Alister McGrath, *Mere Apologetics: How to Help Seekers and Skeptics Find Faith* (Grand Rapids, MI: Baker Books, 2012), 16.

"I am continually impressed today, as throughout my life, with the number of people who claim to have intellectual objections to the historic Christian faith (and some of them genuinely do), but if I converse with them long enough, their biggest barriers are existential ones. They want to remain in charge of their own beliefs and behaviors and not submit to any ultimate authority outside of themselves."

—Craig Blomberg, *Can We Still Believe the Bible? An Evangelical Engagement with Contemporary Questions* (Grand Rapids, MI: Brazos Press, 2014), 144-145.

Demon

The word "demon" in the New Testament can refer to a specific evil presence that can possess someone, or to the ungodly forces at work in the world against believers.

Definition

daimonion (neuter noun, Strong's #1140)

A *daimonion* is a "demon." In Acts 17:18 it denotes inferior pagan deities. "Demons" are the spiritual agents of idolatry. An idol is nothing itself, but every idol has a "demon" associated with it who induces idolatry, with its worship and sacrifices (1 Corinthians 10:20,21; Revelation 9:20). They spread errors among people and seek to seduce believers (1 Timothy 4:1). As seducing spirits they deceive people into the supposition that through mediums (such as those in Leviticus 20:6,27) they can converse with the dead, which is why spiritism is a destructive deception forbidden in Scripture (Leviticus 19:31; Deuteronomy 18:11; Isaiah 8:19). Demons "tremble" before God (James 2:19), and they recognize Christ as Lord and as their future judge (Matthew 8:29; Luke 4:41). Jesus cast them out of humans by the power of God (Luke 11:20). His disciples did so in his name, and by exercising faith (Luke 10:17).

Acting under Satan (compare Revelation 16:13,14), demons are permitted to afflict with bodily disease (Luke 13:16). Being unclean, they tempt human beings with unclean thoughts (Matthew 10:1; Mark 5:2; 7:25; Luke 8:27-29; Revelation 16:13; 18:2). They differ in degrees of wickedness (Matthew 12:45). At the end of the age they will instigate the rulers of the nations to make war against God and his Christ (Revelation 16:14).

Denarius

A "denarius" in New Testament times was a coin used to pay a day's wages.

Definition

dēnarion (neuter noun, Strong's #1220)

The word *dēnarion* occurs 16 times in the New Testament and refers to a "denarius," that is, a coin approximately equal in value to a day's wages. Jesus used the denarius in his parables (Matthew 18:28; 20:2,9,10,13; Luke 7:41; 10:35), and to make a point about giving to Caesar what is Caesar's and to God what is God's (Matthew 22:19; Mark 12:15; Luke 20:24). When Jesus told the disciples they were to give the people assembled to hear him something to eat, they replied it would take two hundred denarii ("more than half a year's wages") to do so (Mark 6:37; John 6:7). People expressed indignation at a woman who used a precious perfume to anoint Jesus, by saying it could have been sold for three hundred denarii ("more than a year's wages") and the money given to the poor (Mark 14:5; John 12:5). It occurs twice in Revelation 6:6 when John heard of coming economic disaster.

Desert

A "desert" may be a "barren region," a "wilderness," or an "uninhabited place." It is biblically significant in that the people of Israel wandered in the wilderness for 40 years after coming out of Egypt with Moses. Jesus was also tempted in the desert by the devil for 40 days and 40 nights.

Definitions

1: *erēmia* (feminine noun, Strong's #2047)

This word means primarily "a place of solitude, an uninhabited place" in contrast to a town or village. It is translated as "deserts" in Hebrews 11:38 and "remote place" in Matthew 15:33. It does not always denote a barren region, devoid of vegetation.

2: *erēmos* (noun/adjective, Strong's #2048)

Used as a noun, this word has the same meaning as *erēmia* (see Matthew 24:26; Luke 5:16; 8:29; John 6:31).

As an adjective, it denotes

a. deserted persons, those deprived of friends or family, such as a woman deserted by her husband (Galatians 4:27), and

b. a deserted city (Matthew 23:38) or uninhabited places (Matthew 14:13,15; Mark 1:35; Acts 8:26).

Desire

"Desire" in the New Testament can be positive or negative. The word *epithumia* often refers to negative or sinful desires, while *eudokia* is used for positive or godly desires, or good will.

Definitions

epithumia (feminine noun, Strong's #1939)

This is a "desire, craving, longing, mostly of evil desires," frequently translated as "lust." It can also be used of good desires, such as of Jesus's desire concerning the Passover (Luke 22:15), Paul's desire to be with Christ (Philippians 1:23), or his intense desire to see the saints at Thessalonica again (1 Thessalonians 2:17). But it often denotes evil desires (for example, Colossians 3:5; 1 Thessalonians 4:5).

Devil

Satan is not mentioned many times in the Old Testament. His most overt appearances are in the Garden of Eden and in the beginning of Job as "the Satan" or "the adversary." There he challenged the Lord that suffering could cause God's faithful servant Job to turn against him. In the New Testament, Satan (or, as he is commonly known, "the devil" or "the accuser") is far more prominent, active as the adversary of God and humans.

Definition

diabolos (adjective, Strong's #1228)

Technically an adjective, the word *diabolos* ("slanderous") is overwhelmingly treated as a noun in the New Testament ("slanderous one") and is a name of Satan. *Satanas*, a Greek transliteration of the Hebrew word for "adversary," also appears in the New Testament. "Devil" is a popular translation of *diabolos*, who is portrayed as a figure far more powerful than the demons (though certainly nowhere equal to God in power), and as the archenemy of God and humans. He accuses humans to God (Job 1:6-11; 2:1-5; Revelation 12:9,10) and even accuses God to humans (Genesis 3). He afflicts people with physical suffering (Acts 10:38). Being himself sinful (1 John 3:8), he tempted humans to sin in the first place (Genesis 3) and continues to tempt people to do evil things (Ephesians 4:27; 6:11). Satan had the power of death, but Jesus triumphed over him (Hebrews 2:14). Satan seeks to trap and devour believers as a roaring lion (1 Peter 5:8). But if believers resist, he will flee from them (James 4:7). God can save them from Satan's grasp (2 Timothy 2:26). His doom is the lake of fire (Matthew 25:41; Revelation 20:10).

Aside from its primary use about the devil, this word is also used of slanderers and false accusers (1 Timothy 3:11; 2 Timothy 3:3; Titus 2:3).

Disciple

A "disciple" is one who learns from a teacher. In New Testament times, many teachers and groups of teachers had disciples, but the most famous are the disciples of Jesus. The word is used both for the specific twelve disciples of Jesus's inner circle and his disciples more broadly—that is, all who choose to follow him.

Definition

mathētēs (masculine noun, Strong's #3101)

Literally "a learner" (from the verb *manthanō*, "to learn"), *mathētēs* refers to "one who follows the teaching of another," as in the disciples

  a. of John the Baptist (Matthew 9:14),

  b. of the Pharisees (Matthew 22:16),

  c. of Moses (John 9:28), and

  d. of Jesus,

> i. in a wide sense of Jews who became his followers (John 6:66; Luke 6:17, and some secretly, as in John 19:38),

> ii. especially the twelve disciples in his inner circle (Matthew 10:1; Luke 22:11), and

> iii. all who become his disciples by believing in him (frequently in the book of Acts).

Quotes

"The heart of the disciple must be set on Christ alone."

> —Dietrich Bonhoeffer, *The Cost of Discipleship*, translated by
> R.H. Fuller, with some revision by Irmgard Booth (New
> York: Touchstone Rockefeller Center, 1995), 174.

"The disciple must be as his Master—he that, would follow the Crucified,
must himself bear the cross."

> —Charles Haddon Spurgeon, "Up from the Country and
> Pressed into Service (Mark 15:21)," *Spurgeon's Sermons on
> the Cross of Christ* (Grand Rapids, MI: Kregel, 1993), 110.

Door

The word for "door" or "gate" in the New Testament is often used for those
actual items, but also used metaphorically to refer to humans entering the
kingdom of God, Jesus entering believers' hearts, or the like.

Definition

thura (feminine noun, Strong's #2374)

A *thura*, "door" or "gate," in the New Testament is either a literal door (as in
Matthew 6:6; 27:60) or a metaphorical word. For example, Jesus calls himself the "gate" for the sheep to enter to be saved (John 10:7,9). The image of
a *thura* is used in Acts 14:27 of faith. In 1 Corinthians 16:9, it is used of entry-
ways for preaching and teaching the Word of God (see also 2 Corinthians
2:12; Colossians 4:3; Revelation 3:8). It is used of the entrance to the kingdom of God (Matthew 25:10; Luke 13:24,25) and of Christ's entrance into
the metaphorical home of the repentant believer (Revelation 3:20). It is also
used of the nearness of Jesus's second advent (Matthew 24:33; Mark 13:29;
compare James 5:9) and of an entryway for John the apostle to see visions
about the purposes of God (Revelation 4:1).

Drunkenness

A "drunkard" is one who drinks too much alcohol and is inebriated. It can be used literally and metaphorically.

Definition

methuō (verb, Strong's #3184)

This verb means "to be drunk with wine." It refers to literal intoxication (Matthew 24:49; Acts 2:15; 1 Corinthians 11:21; 1 Thessalonians 5:7), and to metaphorical intoxication, such as the effect of humans joining in the abominations of the Babylonian system (Revelation 17:2).

E

Ear

The "ear" is the part of the body for listening. Having "an ear to hear" is an important phrase in the New Testament, as it refers to the need to pay attention to what is being said and to do something about it. "Ear" is also used in Paul's illustration of the church as a body with various parts, each with its own function (1 Corinthians 12:16).

Definition

ous (neuter noun, Strong's #3775)

Aside from its normal meaning as the auditory organ, *ous* refers to the metaphorical function of the ear, that is, listening, understanding, and perceiving correctly. For example, "Whoever has ears, let them hear" (Matthew 11:15; 13:9,43; Mark 4:9,23; Luke 8:8; 14:35; Revelation 2:7,11,17,29; 3:6,13,22; 13:9).

Earth

The word for "earth" in the New Testament is used various ways, such as to refer to land useful for agriculture, to the world in contrast to the heavens, or to inhabited lands.

Definition

gē (feminine noun, Strong's #1093)

More common and comprehensive than *oikoumenē* ("inhabited earth"), *gē* denotes

a. earth as arable land; soil (as in Matthew 13:5,8,23),

b. the earth as a whole, the whole world, in contrast to the heavens (as in Matthew 5:18,35), or in contrast to heaven, the residence of God (Matthew 6:19-20),

c. as a synonym of *oikoumenē* for the inhabited world (as in Luke 21:25; Acts 1:8),

d. a country or territory (Luke 4:25; John 3:22),

e. the ground (Matthew 10:29; Mark 4:26), and

f. land in general (Mark 4:1; John 21:8,9,11).

End

In the New Testament, an "end" can refer to a limit, a result, a goal, a purpose, an utmost degree of something, or even the last thing in a series. It is an important word for teaching about the end of history (see Matthew 24:14; 1 Peter 4:7).

Definition

telos (neuter noun, Strong's #5056)

The Greek word for "end" refers to

a. the limit of what a person or thing can do or be (see 2 Corinthians 3:13; 1 Peter 4:7),

b. the final result of a process (as in Luke 1:33; Romans 10:4),

c. a fulfillment (as in Luke 22:37),

d. the utmost degree of an act, as of Jesus's love toward his disciples (John 13:1),

e. the aim or purpose of a thing (1 Timothy 1:5), and

f. the last thing in a series (Revelation 21:6).

Envy (see Jealousy)

Evangelize (see Gospel; see also Preach)

Everlasting (see Forever)

Evil, Evildoer

"Evil" in the New Testament can describe persons, spirits, or actions. The word is also used to express that something is physically painful or in a bad condition.

Definition

ponēros (adjective, Strong's #4190)

As an adjective, this word denotes "evil that causes labor, pain, or sorrow; malignant evil." It carries the meaning of bad or worthless, in the physical sense (Matthew 7:17,18), and in the moral or ethical sense, such as with reference to evil people (Matthew 7:11; Luke 6:45; Acts 17:5; 2 Thessalonians 3:2; 2 Timothy 3:13), evil spirits (Matthew 12:45; Luke 7:21), or evil things (Matthew 5:11; 6:23; Galatians 1:4).

When used as a noun, it can refer to

a. Satan as the "evil one" (Matthew 5:37; 6:13; etc.),

b. humans (Luke 6:35; 1 Corinthians 5:13), and

c. evil things (Matthew 9:4; 12:35; Mark 7:23; Luke 3:19).

Quote

"It was wonderful when we first met someone who cared for our favorite poet. What we had hardly understood before now took clear shape. What we had been half ashamed of we now freely acknowledged. But it was no less delightful than when we first met someone who shared with us a secret evil. This too became far more palpable and explicit; of this too, we ceased to be ashamed. Even now, at whatever age, we all know the perilous charm of a shared hatred or grievance."

—C.S. Lewis, *The Four Loves* (New York: HarperCollins Publishers, 1960), 100-101.

Eye

The "eye" is the organ with which we see. In the New Testament, eyes see visions or perhaps regain sight. An eye might cause a person to sin.

Definition

ophthalmos (masculine noun, Strong's #3788)

This term refers to

a. the physical organ (Matthew 5:38),

b. God's power of vision (Hebrews 4:13; 1 Peter 3:12),

c. Jesus in a vision (Revelation 1:14; 2:18; 19:12),

d. ethical qualities such as evil in a metaphorical sense (Matthew 6:23; Mark 9:47; Luke 11:34; 1 John 2:16; 2 Peter 2:14), and

e. mental vision as a metaphor (Matthew 13:14; John 12:40; Romans 11:8; Galatians 3:1).

Insight

In Galatians 3:1 Paul rebukes the Galatians as foolish and asks who "bewitched" them. The Greek word behind the term "to bewitch" is *baskainō*, which means something like using an "evil eye" as a way to make a person fall under a spell. This is juxtaposed with the Galatians having seen with their "eyes" the portrayal of Jesus being crucified for them. Despite this, they still became bewitched by a false gospel, one requiring them to observe "the works of the Law" (verse 2) before they could truly become Christians. Paul insisted that salvation came only from believing in the true gospel message.

Faith, Faithfulness (see Believe)

Father

A "father" in the New Testament can be an earthly father, like Zacharias was to John the Baptist; an adoptive father, like Joseph was to Jesus; or an ancestor. God the Father is the ultimate example of fatherhood. Jesus modeled obedience to the Father by doing his will, even to the point of death on a cross.

Definition

patēr (masculine noun, Strong's #3962)

This comes from a root signifying "a nourisher, protector, upholder" (the Latin word is similar in sound: *pater*; the English "father" is related to these). The Greek word *patēr* refers to

a. the nearest ancestor (Matthew 2:22),

b. a more remote ancestor, a forefather (Matthew 3:9; 23:30; 1 Corinthians 10:1),

  c. one advanced in the knowledge of Christ (1 John 2:13),

  d. the originator of a family or company of persons, such as Abraham (Romans 4:11,16,17,18),

  e. one who, as a preacher of the gospel and as a teacher, stands in a "father's" place, caring for his spiritual "children" (1 Corinthians 4:15),

  f. members of the Sanhedrin, as those who exercised religious authority over others (Acts 7:2; 22:1), and

  g. God the Father (John 1:12,13; Matthew 11:27; John 20:17; Romans 15:6; 2 Corinthians 1:3; Hebrews 12:9; James 1:17).

Quotes

"God is the Creator of everyone, but only those who take Jesus as their Savior and Lord can claim God as their Father."

    —Michael Youssef, *Leading the Way Through Ephesians* (Eugene, OR: Harvest House Publishers, 2012), 54.

"The Son came to introduce and explain the Father."

    —David Eckman, *Knowing the Heart of the Father: Four Experiences with God That Will Change Your Life* (Eugene, OR: Harvest House Publishers, 2008), 24.

Fear, Fearfulness

"Fear" is an emotion, displayed in the New Testament, such as by the disciples when they thought they were going to drown in the Sea of Galilee, or when they thought Jesus was a ghost. "Fear" in the New Testament can also be reverential, as toward God.

phobos (masculine noun, Strong's #5401)

This term can be understood as

a. "fear, dread, terror," always with this significance in the Gospels (see also Acts 2:43; 19:17; 1 Corinthians 2:3; 1 Timothy 5:20), and

b. reverential fear of God (Romans 8:15; Ephesians 5:21; 1 Peter 1:17).

"Irrational fears either compel us to do that which is irresponsible or prevent us from doing that which is responsible."

—Neil T. Anderson and Rich Miller, *Freedom from Fear*
(Eugene, OR: Harvest House Publishers, 1999), 144.

Fire

Aside from its literal meaning, "fire" is used in the New Testament to indicate the holiness of God, fire in judgment, fire of the tongue, or fire in other metaphorical ways.

pur (neuter noun, Strong's #4442)

The word *pur*, aside from meaning "a literal fire," can refer to

a. the holiness of God as a consuming fire (Hebrews 10:27; 12:29),

b. the divine judgment of believers at the judgment seat of Christ (1 Corinthians 3:13),

c. the judgment against those who reject Jesus (Matthew 3:11),

d. judgments of God at the close of the present age (2 Thessalonians 1:8; Revelation 18:8),

e. the "fire" of hell, to be endured by the wicked (Matthew 5:22; 13:42,50; 18:8,9; 25:41; Mark 9:43,48; Luke 3:17),

f. the tongue, having a destructive potential (James 3:6), and

g. a symbol of danger and destruction.

Fish

Fish were important in the New Testament as food. Jesus even provided fish miraculously for his disciples after the resurrection (John 21).

Definition

ichthus (masculine noun, Strong's #2486)
An *ichthus* is a "fish" (Matthew 7:10; Mark 6:38; etc.). The only other place it occurs outside the Gospels is in 1 Corinthians 15:39.

Insight

The *ichthus* was an early symbol for Christians. It is from an acronym of the Greek words for "Jesus Christ, God's Son, Savior."

Fisher

Jesus's disciples were fishers by profession. Jesus told them that if they followed him, he would make them fishers of people (Matthew 4:19).

Definition

halieus (masculine noun, Strong's #231)

Meaning "a fisherman, fisher," *halieus* occurs in Matthew 4:18,19, Mark 1:16,17, and Luke 5:2.

Insight

In Matthew 4:19, the most well-known translation of the Greek phrase *halieis anthrōpōn* is "fishers of men," but women also joined the ministry of Jesus and in fact were the initial discoverers of the empty tomb, and the ones who first proclaimed it to the male disciples. Women have been disciples of Jesus since the earliest days. All twelve of Jesus's inner circle were men, but because the word *anthrōpos* can mean "person" as well as "man," and the twelve were called to minister to everyone and not just to men, "fishers of people" is also a viable translation.

Flesh

"Flesh" (*sarx*) in the New Testament is a multifaceted word. Aside from its literal meaning, it can work together with "blood" (*haima*) in the phrase "flesh and blood" to denote human beings. It can also describe the sinful tendency of humans. Jesus became flesh, with a physical human body (John 1:14), though without sin (Hebrews 4:15).

Definition

sarx (feminine noun, Strong's #4561)

This word has a wider range of meaning in the New Testament than in the Old Testament. Some of its uses in the New Testament:

   a. "the substance of the body," whether of animals or of people (see 1 Corinthians 15:39),

b. the human body (2 Corinthians 10:3 NASB; Galatians 2:20; Philippians 1:22),

c. humankind, in the totality of all that is essential to the human person, such as spirit, soul, and body (Matthew 24:22; John 1:13; Romans 3:20),

d. the holy humanity of Jesus (John 1:14; 1 Timothy 3:16; 1 John 4:2; 2 John 1:7),

e. a weaker element of human nature (Matthew 26:41),

f. the sinful state of humans (Romans 7:5; 8:8,9),

g. the seat of sin in humans (2 Peter 2:18),

h. the temporary element in the Christian (Galatians 3:3; 6:8), and

i. externals of life (2 Corinthians 7:1; Ephesians 6:5; Hebrews 9:13).

Quotes

"The city [of Bethlehem] hums. The merchants are unaware that God has visited their planet. The innkeeper would never believe that he had just sent God into the cold."

—Max Lucado, *God Came Near: No Wonder They Call Him the Savior* (Sisters, OR: Multnomah Publishers, 1986), 21.

"How are we to think of the Incarnation? The New Testament does not encourage us to puzzle our heads over the physical and psychological problems that it raises, but to worship God for the love that was shown in it."

—J.I. Packer, *Knowing God* (Downers Grove, IL: InterVarsity Press, 1993), 58.

Follow

In the Gospels Jesus asked his disciples to "follow" him. Following was to be in a posture of action, cooperation, and imitation. To follow Jesus is to go with him and to live in his way.

Definition

akoloutheō (verb, Strong's #190)

This verb means "to be a follower or companion," or "going in the same way." It is used

a. frequently in the literal sense (as in Matthew 4:25), and

b. metaphorically of discipleship (as in Mark 8:34; 9:38; 10:21).

Quotes

"Jesus made it very clear: If you want to be His disciple, then you must deny yourself, take up your cross, and follow Him."

—Kay Arthur, *The Call to Follow Jesus: Luke* (Eugene, OR: Harvest House Publishers, 2002), 15.

"One only has to look through the Gospels to see Christ's great compassion for the broken, hurting, and hopeless. As followers and imitators of Christ, we can do no less. Not only does He care about our own needs. He demands that we follow His example and care about others who feel neglected, unloved, useless."

—Chuck Colson, *Loving God* (Grand Rapids, MI: Zondervan, 1996), 302.

Foot

"Foot" in the Bible, aside from the literal meaning, can be a metaphor related to going in motion. In Jesus's day one might wash another's feet as part of hospitality.

Definition

pous (masculine noun, Strong's #4228)

Aside from its literal meaning, *pous* can be used to describe a person in motion (Luke 1:79; Acts 5:9; Romans 3:15; 10:15; Hebrews 12:13). It can express the idea of subjection (1 Corinthians 15:27), humility, and receptivity of discipleship (Luke 10:39; Acts 22:3). It can also refer to a gesture of worship (Matthew 28:9) or of scornful rejection (Matthew 10:14; Acts 13:51). Washing the feet of another demonstrated the humility of the host in serving and making the guest comfortable (Luke 7:38; John 13:5; 1 Timothy 5:10).

Quote

"After a few moments, Jesus stands and removes his outer garments. He wraps a servant's girdle around his waist, takes up the basin, and kneels before one of the disciples. He unlaces the sandal and gently lifts the foot and places it in the basin, covers it with water, and begins to bathe it. One by one, one grimy foot after another, Jesus works his way down the row."

—Max Lucado, *Just Like Jesus: Learning to Have a Heart Like His* (Nashville, TN: Thomas Nelson, 2003), 17.

Footstool

A "footstool" is literally a stool to support the foot. It is often used in the New Testament to indicate subjection.

hupopodion (neuter noun, Strong's #5286)

From *hupo* ("under") and *pous* ("foot"), *hupopodion* is used

a. literally in James 2:3 NASB, and

b. metaphorically of the earth as God's "footstool" (Matthew 5:35) and of God's enemies (Luke 20:43; Acts 2:35; 7:49; Hebrews 1:13; 10:13).

Forever

The Greek words we translate as "eternal" or "forever" do not always mean a period of time without end, but can sometimes describe an undefined duration of time.

Definitions

1: *aiōn* (masculine noun, Strong's #165)

An *aiōn* is simply an "age," endless or not. It is still common to use words like "forever" or "eternal" to express it, as in Ephesians 3:11, where it is translated with the word "eternal."

2: *aiōnios* (adjective, Strong's #166)

The word *aiōnios* describes duration, either undefined but not endless (as in Romans 16:25; 2 Timothy 1:9; Titus 1:2), or undefined with no end in sight (Luke 18:30 and many other places in the New Testament).

"Messiah will come from Heaven to Earth, not to take us away from Earth to Heaven, but to restore Earth to what he intended so he can live with us here forever."

> —Randy Alcorn, *Heaven* (Carol Stream, IL: Tyndale House Publishers, 2004), 90.

Forgive, Forgiveness

"Forgiveness" means sending something away, and usually in the New Testament that something is sin or a debt. God is said to be full of forgiveness, and Jesus's own blood was poured out for the forgiveness of sins (Matthew 26:28). Because God is forgiving we also are to be forgiving of one another.

Definitions

1: *aphiēmi* (verb, Strong's #863)

A verb meaning primarily "to send forth, send away," *aphiēmi* signifies (in addition to its other meanings) "to remit or forgive"

   a. debts, these being completely canceled (Matthew 6:12; 18:27,32), and

   b. sins (Matthew 9:2,5,6; 12:31,32; Acts 8:22; Romans 4:7; James 5:15). In this latter respect, the word means the deliverance of the sinner from the divine penalty that would otherwise fall on the person. Forgiveness is closely associated with the cross and therefore with the concept of propitiation or atonement, the act by which God forgives sin.

2: *aphesis* (feminine noun, Strong's #859)

Similar to its related verb *aphiēmi* (see above), the noun *aphesis* denotes "a dismissal, release." It refers to the remission of sins, forgiveness (Mark 3:29;

Ephesians 1:7; Colossians 1:14). Eleven times it is followed by "of sins" and once by "of trespasses."

Quotes

"[Joseph] is one who deliberately chose to overlook unfair offenses, to overcome enormous obstacles, and model a virtue that is fast becoming lost in our hostile age—*forgiveness.*"

> —Chuck Swindoll, *Joseph: A Man of Integrity and Forgiveness* (Nashville, TN: Thomas Nelson, 1998), xi.

"Forgiveness is good for us as a salve on open wounds and as corrective surgery for a broken heart."

> —June Hunt, *How to Forgive...When You Don't Feel Like It* (Eugene, OR: Harvest House Publishers, 2007), 61.

Forsake

To "forsake" someone in the New Testament is to leave them, to abandon them. Martha used the term with regard to her sister Mary (Luke 10:40). Jesus also cried out from the cross, using another word meaning "to forsake," saying, "My God, my God, why have you forsaken me?" (Matthew 27:46; Mark 15:34), an allusion to Psalm 22.

Definitions

1: *kataleipō* (verb, Strong's #2641)
As a strengthened form of *leipō* ("to leave"), *kataleipō* refers to

- a. leaving, leaving behind (as in Matthew 4:13),
- b. leaving someone remaining, as in what Martha accused Mary of doing, leaving her alone to do work (Luke 10:40), and

c. forsaking or abandoning (Luke 5:28; Acts 6:2; Hebrews 11:27).

2: *egkataleipō* (verb, Strong's #1459)

This term denotes

a. leaving behind or leaving surviving (Romans 9:29), or

b. forsaking or abandoning (Matthew 27:46; Mark 15:34; Acts 2:27,31; 2 Corinthians 4:9; 2 Timothy 4:10,16; Hebrews 13:5).

Insight

In some instances, the verb for forgiving, *aphiēmi*, can mean "forsaking" (see Mark 1:18; 14:50; Luke 5:11).

Fruit

"Fruit" is the product of trees, bushes, and other plants, but that is not its only meaning in the New Testament. Children are the "fruit of the womb." If people "bear fruit," it means they are showing growth and character in their deeds, reflecting the content of their hearts. The Spirit produces such metaphorical "fruit" perhaps most famously in Galatians 5:22-23, good characteristics which come from a person who is "walking in the Spirit" and not carrying out the desires of the flesh.

Definition

karpos (masculine noun, Strong's #2590)

Karpos, "fruit," is used of natural fruit from trees or produce from the ground (Matthew 7:17; James 5:7,18), and also of "fruit" from the human body, that is, children (Luke 1:42; Acts 2:30).

Frequently, it has a metaphorical meaning. It can refer to

a. works or deeds, such "fruit" demonstrating the power of the one producing it (Matthew 7:16),

b. the "fruit" produced by the Spirit in the life of the believer, namely, the characteristics that grow in the life of such a person (Galatians 5:22-23), and

c. "fruit" as related to righteousness (Hebrews 12:11; James 3:18).

Generosity

"Generosity" in the New Testament is most often expressed through alms-giving or kindness to those in need.

Definition

eleēmosunē (feminine noun, Strong's #1654)

Connected with *eleēmon* ("merciful"), *eleēmosunē* means

a. mercy, pity, particularly in giving alms (Matthew 6:1-4; Acts 10:2; 24:17), and

b. the gift itself (Luke 11:41; 12:33; Acts 3:2,3,10; 9:36).

Gentile (see Nation)

Gentle, Gentleness

"Gentle" speaks of a sensitive attitude or mild behavior, or of one who is caring, kind, and gracious. That God views this as an important trait is evident from the fact "gentleness" is among the fruit of the Spirit (Galatians 5:22-23).

Definitions

1: *praüs* (adjective, Strong's #4239)

This adjective denotes "gentle, mild, meek." For its significance, see the corresponding noun listed below. Christ used it of his own disposition (Matthew 11:29), and mentioned it in his beatitudes (Matthew 5:5). It describes his character even as the messianic king (Matthew 21:5; cf. Zechariah 9:9). It is an attribute Christian women should adorn themselves with (1 Peter 3:4). This word is similar in meaning to the Greek word *epios*, meaning "gentle, of a soothing disposition" (1 Thessalonians 2:7; 2 Timothy 2:24).

2: *praütēs* (feminine noun, Strong's #4240)

This noun denotes "meekness." In the Bible it has a fuller, deeper significance than in nonscriptural Greek writings. That is, it does not refer to outward behavior only, in how one relates to others; it is a grace worked within the soul, and when a person puts it into practice, it is first and foremost directed toward God. It is that type of spirit where we accept his dealings with us as good, without disputing or resisting. It is closely linked with *tapeinophrosunē*, the word for "humility." See, for example, Ephesians 4:2 and Colossians 3:12 (see also the Septuagint's Greek translation of the Hebrew terms for "meekness" and "lowliness" in Zephaniah 3:12). The humble in heart are also the gentle or meek. "Gentleness" (*praütēs*) is also one of the fruit of the Spirit listed in Galatians 5:22-23, notably alongside self-control (*enkrateia*).

Praütēs has no perfect equivalent in English. Here are three translations often suggested for the term, but they are imperfect:

   a. "Meekness." The problem with this term is that it often suggests "weakness" in English. *Praütēs* implies dependence on an infinite source of strength.

b. "Gentleness." This word is used in English translations of Paul's list of the fruit of the Spirit in Galatians 5:22-23, but it is also flawed because in English, "gentleness" generally relates to actions. *Praütēs* relates to a condition of the mind and heart.

c. "Humility." This translation choice does express the aspect of this word that relates to dependence on God, but "humility" already (and more closely) is used to translate the related word *tapeinophrosunē.*

In the end, however one translates this word, *praütēs* is a disposition that is a fruit of power. As a fruit of the Spirit, it is an attribute that comes from a place of strength.

Quotes

"When people think of Jesus Christ, they often imagine a man with stringy hair, a pale complexion, and a wispy build, moving about with faraway eyes and a passive, feeble demeanor. Or they think of him as a combination of Mister Rogers, Clark Kent, and Santa Claus dressed in a robe and sandals. These notions usually come from a faulty understanding of the term 'meek.' Jesus described his temperament as 'gentle and humble in heart' (Matt. 11:29). The King James Version of the Bible renders it 'meek and lowly in heart.' While he was meek, that in no way means that he was weak. Jesus was commenting on his behavior and attitude, not his capability. Comparatively, a prized stallion could have a gentle spirit, making him a hospitable ride for inexperienced riders. The quality of meekness might be thought of as strength under control."

—Chuck Swindoll, *Swindoll's Living Insights New Testament Commentary: Insights on Mark* (Carol Stream, IL: Tyndale House Publishers, 2016), 296.

"In all its constant stress on the reality of God's personal concern for his people, and on the gentleness, tenderness, sympathy, patience and yearning compassion that he shows toward them, the Bible never lets us lose sight of his majesty and his unlimited dominion over all his creatures."

> —J.I. Packer, *Knowing God* (Downers Grove, IL: InterVarsity Press, 1973), 83.

Give

"Giving" in the New Testament can refer to a variety of things, depending on the context. Someone can "give" another person a blow (as in striking them), "give" a ring onto a finger (in the sense of putting the ring on the finger), or "give oneself" into a place (meaning, venturing into it).

Definition

didōmi (verb, Strong's #1325)

This verb means "to give" and occurs with various meanings according to the context. For example, a seed can be said to "bear" (literally, "give") fruit (Mark 4:7,8). Someone can "try hard" (literally, "give effort") to do something (Luke 12:58). Jesus is said to "punish" (literally, "give vengeance") those who do not know God or obey the gospel (2 Thessalonians 1:8). The soldiers who mocked Jesus "slapped him in the face" (literally, "gave him blows"; see John 19:3). Paul was also warned not to "give himself" (that is, "venture") into a theater (Acts 19:31).

Gladness (see Joy)

Glory

"Glory" (*doxa*) in the New Testament denotes brightness, but its meaning goes beyond anything perceived by the eyes. Depending on the context, it may include honor, power, or grace. The "glory" of God is understood in a variety of ways in Scripture, but it all has to do with his amazing attributes, such as his power over, and love toward, creation.

Definition

doxa (feminine noun, Strong's #1391)

A noun meaning "glory," *doxa* refers to a shining or bright quality, but also perhaps to honor, greatness of some kind, fame, or renown.

It occurs with reference to

a. brightness or splendor, as that emanating from God, as in his Shekinah glory (Luke 2:9; Acts 22:11; Romans 9:4; 2 Corinthians 3:7; James 2:1; compare Exodus 16:10; 25:22), or natural light from heavenly bodies (1 Corinthians 15:40,41),

b. God's identity and activities, particularly in the person of Jesus Christ (John 17:5,24; Romans 6:4; Hebrews 1:3),

c. the character and ways of God as shown through Christ, and to and through believers (2 Corinthians 3:18; 4:6),

d. the state and blessedness into which believers will enter after being made like Christ (Romans 8:18,21; Philippians 3:21; 1 Peter 5:1,10; Revelation 21:11), and

e. good reputation, praise, or honor (Luke 14:10; John 5:41; 7:18; 8:50; 12:43; 2 Corinthians 6:8; 11:7; Philippians 3:19; Hebrews 3:3).

"Glory, as Christianity teaches me to hope for it, turns out to satisfy my original desire and indeed to reveal an element in that desire which I had not noticed."

> —C.S. Lewis, *The Weight of Glory* (New York: HarperCollins Publishers, 1980), Kindle edition.

"There is power in reflecting and representing Christ in all we do because Christ is the image and replication of God Himself. Through Him, we not only enter into a deeper level of intimacy with God and each other, but we also reflect His glory, something we have been created and called to do."

> —Tony Evans, *Kingdom Disciples: Heaven's Representatives on Earth* (Chicago, IL: Moody Publishers, 2017), 237.

God

In the New Testament, *theos* usually refers to the one true "God." The same word is used in other Greek documents for other deities, but the writers of the New Testament (like the Septuagint translators before them) had no problem using it to refer to God himself. The absence or presence of the Greek definite article does not in itself determine whether the word refers to *the* one true God or *a* god. Context is often the key. Sometimes there is no definite article accompanying the word *theos*, but it still refers to the one true God, as in John 1:1.

Definition

theos (masculine/feminine noun, Strong's #2316)

This word can mean "a god or deity," as in the polytheism of the Greeks, but the Jewish translators who compiled the Septuagint used *theos* for the "God" of the Old Testament (in addition to using it to refer to other gods). The New Testament writers in turn used the term this way. As in the Septuagint, the New Testament uses *theos* primarily to refer to the one true God, though sometimes to refer to a pagan deity.

Insight

Sometimes there is confusion about this word in John 1:1. Because there is no definite article in the Greek with *theos* in this verse, those responsible for the Jehovah's Witnesses' *New World Translation* erroneously render this verse as: "In the beginning was the Word, and the Word was with God, and the Word was a god." A footnote next to "a god" says "was divine," suggesting the word can be understood adjectivally.

While it is true that *theos* can refer to "a god" (as in a pagan deity), the mere absence of the article in John 1:1 is actually an insufficient reason to render the phrase *kai theos ēn ho logos* as "and the Word was a god." John was clearly alluding to Genesis 1 by starting his Gospel with the words *en archē* ("in the beginning"). Also, calling Jesus *ho logos* ("the Word") suggests he was present at creation, as the *logos* language recalls the divine speech that spoke the universe into existence. Taking the wider theology of John's Gospel into account, remembering, for example, Jesus's claim to being equal with God through an "I am" statement (John 8:58; compare this with Exodus 3:14), it makes little sense to see John 1:1 to be about "a god" distinct from the God of Moses. Daniel Wallace argues for a qualitative understanding of this occurrence of *theos*, suggesting that John means to say something like, "What God was, the Word was." He supports the option of the translation "was divine," but only if these divine qualities are understood in relation to the one true God. But in modern English, "divine" has too many meanings aside from this, so it is distracting and unhelpful.[3] Ron Rhodes points out that the "a god" translation uses a principle that doesn't work in other contexts where *theos* doesn't have the article, citing many examples, such as in Matthew 5:9, where peacemakers would nonsensically be called "sons of *a* god" rather than the contextually sensible "sons of God." Like Wallace, Rhodes (along with most New Testament scholars) agrees that this use of *theos* in John 1:1 is indeed "qualitative"—that is, as Rhodes explains with a quote from Robert Bowman, qualitative nouns express the qualities or nature of something.[4]

Quotes

"Certainly God, whose existence I had denied for years, seemed extremely distant, and it became obvious to me that I needed the cross of Jesus to bridge that gulf."

> —Lee Strobel, *The Case for Christ: A Journalist's Personal Investigation of the Evidence for Jesus* (Grand Rapids, MI: Zondervan, 1998), 268.

"The answer to the child's question 'Who made God?' is simply that God did not need to be made, for He was always there. He exists forever, and He is always the same. He does not grow older. His life does not wax or wane. He does not gain new powers nor lose those that He once had. He does not mature or develop. He does not get stronger, or weaker, or wiser, as time goes by."

> —J.I. Packer, *Knowing God* (Downers Grove, IL: InterVarsity Press, 1993), 77.

"God is the only comfort, He is also the supreme terror: the thing we most need and the thing we most want to hide from."

> —C.S. Lewis, *Mere Christianity* (New York: HarperCollins Publishers, 1980), 52.

Godliness

"Godliness" in the New Testament has to do with devotion to God and fearing him (in the sense of reverence). A person can do godly acts (that is, actions that show one's faith and reverence for God) or have godly character which produces such acts.

Definition

eusebeia (feminine noun, Strong's #2150)

From *eu* ("good") and *sebomai* ("devout"), *eusebia* denotes that piety which does what is well-pleasing to God, characterized by an attitude oriented toward him. This and the corresponding verb and adverb (see below) are frequent in 1 Timothy, 2 Timothy, and Titus (1 Timothy 2:2; 3:16; 4:7,8; 6:3,5,6,11; 2 Timothy 3:5; Titus 1:1), but they don't occur in the other letters of Paul. The noun occurs four times in 2 Peter (1:3,6,7; 3:11) and once in Acts 3:12. In 2 Peter 3:11, the word is plural, literally signifying "acts of godliness."

Gospel

The "gospel" or "good news" is an announcement of the arrival of the kingdom of God as realized in Jesus Christ, the Son of God, with the news that through believing in him we can receive salvation, forgiveness of sins, and eternal life—on the basis of his atoning death, burial, and resurrection. It is "good news" because it is an announcement of God's actions in Jesus to redeem us, Jew and Gentile alike.

Definitions

1: *euaggelion* (neuter noun, Strong's #2098)

The term *euaggelion* means "good news," or "gospel," as it is also commonly known in English. In the New Testament it refers to the good news of the kingdom of God and of salvation through Christ, to be received by faith, on the basis of his expiatory death, burial, resurrection, and ascension (see Acts 15:7; 20:24; 1 Peter 4:17).

Apart from those references, its occurrences in the Gospels of Matthew and Mark and Revelation 14:6, the noun is confined to Paul's letters. Paul used the word as a shorthand for two associated yet distinct items:

   a. the basic facts of the death, burial, and resurrection of Christ (for example, 1 Corinthians 15:1-3), and

   b. the interpretation of these facts (as in Romans 2:16; Galatians 1:7,11; 2:2).

The word *euaggelion* is used in Mark 1:1 to describe Mark's entire book about Jesus, suggesting that the definition of this term is simply the announcement of the good news about the kingdom of God having come in Jesus, and what his death, burial, resurrection, and ascension mean for those who believe in him.

2: *euaggelizō* (verb, Strong's #2097)

Related to the word *euangelion* (see above), this verb simply means "to evangelize" or "to preach good news."

It is used regarding

a. matters proclaimed as good news (Luke 16:16; Galatians 1:11; 1 Peter 1:25),

b. persons to whom the proclamation is made (Matthew 11:5; Luke 7:22; Hebrews 4:2,6; 1 Peter 4:6), and

c. the message of salvation (Acts 5:42; 11:20; Galatians 1:16).

Quotes

"It is not fashionable in the twenty-first century to preach a gospel that demands repentance."

—John MacArthur, *The Gospel According to Jesus* (Grand Rapids, MI: Zondervan, 1994), 175.

"Our BreakPoint ministry focuses on teaching a biblical worldview so that the Church once again can be salt and light as God intended, so that we live out the truth of the Gospel in such a way as to have a significant influence in reforming the moral values of our culture."

—Chuck Colson, *Born Again* (Grand Rapids, MI: Baker Publishing Group, 2008), 375.

"Our spiritual gifts equip us to be whole and to take the gospel of wholeness to a broken world."

—Michael Youssef, *Leading the Way Through Ephesians* (Eugene, OR: Harvest House Publishers, 2012), 77.

Good, Goodness

"Good" or "goodness" in the New Testament is about the things that are beneficial or pleasing to God.

Definitions

1: *agathos* (adjective, Strong's #18)

This term describes that which is beneficial in its effect. It is used of

a. physical things, such as a tree (Matthew 7:17), or ground (Luke 8:8),

b. persons and things in a moral sense, such as of God, who is absolutely good (Matthew 19:17; Mark 10:18; Luke 18:19).

2: *agathōsunē* (feminine noun, Strong's #19)

Meaning "goodness," this word signifies that moral quality which is described by the adjective *agathos* (see above). In the New Testament it occurs with relation to redeemed persons (Romans 15:14; Galatians 5:22; Ephesians 5:9; 2 Thessalonians 1:11).

Quote

"You can do good for the mere sake of goodness: you cannot be bad for the mere sake of badness. You can do a kind action when you are not feeling kind and when it gives you no pleasure, simply because kindness is right; but no one ever did a cruel action simply because cruelty is wrong—only because cruelty was pleasant or useful to him."

—C.S. Lewis, *Mere Christianity* (New York: HarperCollins Publishers, 1980), 74.

Grace

Because of God's "grace," we can be redeemed through the atoning sacrifice of Jesus's death on the cross (see *Atonement*). "Grace" is unmerited favor—specifically, favor granted freely to us from God the Father through the death and resurrection of his Son, that by believing in him, we can be saved.

Definitions

1: *charis* (feminine noun, Strong's #5485)

This word has various uses, such as

a. objective: that which bestows or occasions pleasure or delight, or causes favorable regard. It is applied, for example, to beauty, or gracefulness of a person (Luke 2:40); of an act (2 Corinthians 8:6), or of speech (see Luke 4:22, which contains the literal Greek phrase "words of grace"; Colossians 4:6); and

b. subjective:

   i. on the part of the bestower, the friendly disposition from which the kindly act proceeds; graciousness, lovingkindness, goodwill generally (Acts 7:10); especially with reference to the Divine favor or "grace" (Acts 14:26). In this respect there is stress on its freeness and generosity, its spontaneous character, as in the case of God's redemptive mercy, and the pleasure or joy he intends for the recipient. Thus it is set in contrast with debt (Romans 4:4,16), with works (Romans 11:6), and with law (John 1:17; see also Romans 6:14,15; Galatians 5:4);

   ii. on the part of the receiver, a sense of the favor bestowed, a feeling of gratitude (Romans 6:15-17).

Note: The corresponding verb *charitoō*, "to grant divine favor or grace," is used in Luke 1:28 and Ephesians 1:6.

2: *euprepeia* (feminine noun, Strong's #2143)

Meaning "pleasant of appearance, beautiful," it is said of the outward appearance of the blossom of a plant (James 1:11).

Quotes

"The redeemed have all from the grace of God. It was of mere grace that God gave us his only-begotten Son. The grace is great in proportion to the excellency of what was given. The gift was infinitely precious, because it was of a person infinitely worthy, a person of infinite glory; and also because it was of a person infinitely near and dear to God."

> —Jonathan Edwards, "God Glorified in the Work of Redemption, by the Greatness of Man's Dependence upon Him in the Whole of It," in *Sermons of Jonathan Edwards* (Peabody, MA: Hendrickson Publishers, 2005), 6.

"By the righteousness of Christ, believers...are made partakers of a divine nature; and from Jesus Christ, they receive grace for grace; and every grace that is in Christ is copied and transcribed onto their souls."

> —George Whitefield, "Christ the Believer's Wisdom, Righteousness, Sanctification, and Redemption," in *Sermons on Important Subjects* (London: Henry Fisher, Son, 1828), 503.

Greed

"Greed" in the New Testament is the driving desire to have more than one needs. The word can also have the sense of extortion. In one place it is even associated with idolatry.

Definition

pleonexia (feminine noun, Strong's #4124)

Pleonexia is literally "a desire to have more" (*pleon*, "more," *echō*, "to have") and is always used in a bad sense in the New Testament. It is used

a. in a general way (Mark 7:22; Romans 1:29; Ephesians 5:3; 1 Thessalonians 2:5),

b. related to sensuality (Ephesians 4:19), and

c. in association with idolatry (Colossians 3:5).

Quote

"The experts on the world hunger problem say that there is enough to go around right now. We don't have a production problem. We have the agricultural capability to produce enough food. We have the transportation technology to distribute the food. But we have a greed problem: If I don't grab mine while I can, I might not be happy. The hunger problem is not going to be solved by government or by industry but in church, among Christians who learn a different way to pursue happiness."

—Eugene Peterson, *A Long Obedience in the Same Direction: Discipleship in an Instant Society* (Downers Grove, IL: Inter-Varsity Press, 2000), 118-119.

Hades (see Hell)

Hallelujah

Our English word "hallelujah" comes from the Hebrew *hallelu Yah* (used in the Psalms), literally meaning "Praise Yah!" (where *Yah* is shorthand for *Yahweh*). After being transliterated to Greek, *hallelu Yah* becomes *hallēlouïa*, which in the New Testament is only used in Revelation.

Definition

hallēlouïa (interjection, Strong's #239)

This word literally means "Praise Yah!" It comes from the Hebrew *hallelu Yah*, a phrase used in the Psalms (such as Psalms 106; 111; 112; 146–150). In the New Testament it occurs only in Revelation 19:1,3,4,6 as the keynote in the song of the great multitude in heaven.

Hand

Aside from its literal meaning, "hand" often refers to the power or agency of someone.

Definition

cheir (feminine noun, Strong's #5495)

Referring to the human "hand," aside from this literal meaning, *cheir* occurs

    a. in idiomatic phrases like "by the hand of" or "at the hand of" to communicate something like "by the agency of" (see NASB of Acts 5:12; 7:35; 17:25; 14:3; Galatians 3:19; Revelation 19:2; including the footnotes),

    b. metaphorically for the power of God (such as in Luke 1:66; 23:46; John 10:28,29; Acts 11:21; 13:11; Hebrews 1:10; 2:7; 10:31), and

    c. as a word representing power in general (Matthew 17:22; Luke 24:7; John 10:39; Acts 12:11).

Head

Aside from its literal meaning, the "head" in the New Testament can be the chief or authority over someone or something. It is also used in other idiomatic expressions.

Definition

kephalē (feminine noun, Strong's #2776)

Aside from literally meaning the part of the body that is the "head," *kephalē* occurs

    a. figuratively, both of heaping coals on a person's "head" (Romans 12:20; from Proverbs 25:21-22), signifying a just response of kindness, and of having blood on one's own head (Acts 18:6), meaning letting the blood-guiltiness of a person rest on their own person, or

b. metaphorically, of authority, source, or direction in general (1 Corinthians 11:3,10; Ephesians 1:22; 4:15; 5:23; Colossians 1:18; 2:19; etc.).

Heal

The miracle of "healing" in the New Testament is a sign the Messiah has come, according to Jesus's interpretation of Isaiah 61 in his public reading of it in the synagogue in Luke 4. The word *iaomai* ("to heal") is not just used in reference to the physical body. For example, in 1 Peter 2:24 (evoking Isaiah 53:5) those who are redeemed by Jesus's suffering on the cross are "healed" by his wounds.

Definitions

1: *therapeuō* (verb, Strong's #2323)
This verb primarily means "to serve as an attendant," but also "to care for the sick, to treat, cure, heal." It occurs mostly in Matthew, Luke, and Acts; once in John (John 5:10), and then also in Revelation 13:3,12.

2: *iaomai* (verb, Strong's #2390)
This verb means "to heal" and is used of

a. physical treatment 22 times (examples include Matthew 15:28 and Acts 9:34), and

b. spiritual healing (Matthew 13:15; John 12:40; Acts 28:27; Hebrews 12:13; 1 Peter 2:24).

3: *sōzō* (verb, Strong's #4982)
As the verb primarily meaning "to save," *sōzō* occurs in Mark 5:23 and Luke 8:36 to mean "to heal."

Quotes

"God certainly does heal today, and there's no doubt about it. To render any other verdict would be to ignore both the clear witness of God's Word and the heartfelt testimonies of many grateful and exultant brothers and sisters around the world who want nothing more than to bring glory to their Savior and Healer."

> —Joni Eareckson Tada, *A Place of Healing: Wrestling with the Mysteries of Suffering, Pain, and God's Sovereignty* (Colorado Springs, CO: David C. Cook, 2010), 18.

"At some point, we have to come back to the realization that God, once again, is in charge of how we heal and when we heal and what the end result will be."

> —Emilie Barnes, *Heal My Heart, Lord* (Eugene, OR: Harvest House Publishers, 1996), 18.

Hear

"Hearing" in the New Testament has much to do with listening. It is the first word of the famous Old Testament declaration called the Shema: "Hear O Israel, the LORD our God, the LORD is one. Love the LORD your God with all your heart and with all your soul and with all your strength" (Deuteronomy 6:4-5), which Jesus quoted as the first and greatest commandment (Mark 12:29-30). God also "hears" prayer in the sense that he receives and answers it.

Definition

akouó (feminine noun, Strong's #191)

The usual word meaning "to hear," *akouō*, is used

   a. without a direct object accompanying it, which is to say that it simply occurs as "to hear" and not "to hear [something]" (Matthew 11:15; Mark 4:23), or

b. with a direct object accompanying it, as in Acts 9:7, referring there to hearing a voice.

God is said in the New Testament to "hear" prayer, in that he answers it (as in John 9:31). In Mark 12:29-30, Jesus quoted the famous passage from Deuteronomy 6:4-5, known as the Shema, that opens with the declaration, "Hear!" As in the Septuagint, Mark used the word *akoue* (the command form of *akouō*) to translate *shᵉma* ("hear") from Deuteronomy 6:4.

Heart

Perhaps because of its central importance in the human body, in the New Testament the "heart" came to represent all mental and moral activity of a human individual. Thus the "heart" in the biblical sense is the real person within a human being, the person's true character.

Definition

kardia (feminine noun, Strong's #2588)

In the New Testament, "heart" or *kardia* (like its Old Testament equivalent *lev*) came to stand for much more than the physical organ. It refers to the entire inner life, the mental and moral activity of human beings. It is used figuratively for the hidden springs of the personal life. It is the center of a person's true life, which is why the Bible says sin comes from the "heart" (see Matthew 15:19,20). On the positive side, Scripture also regards the "heart" as the sphere of divine influence (Romans 2:15; Acts 15:9). Thus the "heart" refers to the real person.

In the New Testament, *kardia* denotes

a. the seat of physical life (Acts 14:17; James 5:5),

b. the seat of moral nature and spiritual life, or the seat of the emotions (John 14:1; Romans 9:2; 2 Corinthians 2:4), among various other things, such as

c. desires (Matthew 5:28) or intentions (Hebrews 4:12).

Quote

"We are all trying to let our mind or heart go their own way—centered on money or pleasure or ambition—and hoping, in spite of this, to behave honestly and chastely and humbly."

> —C.S. Lewis, *Mere Christianity* (New York: HarperCollins Publishers, 1980), 339.

Heaven

"Heaven" or "the heavens" can in both Old and New Testaments refer to the skies (which, from the ancient perspective, would include "heavenly bodies" such as the sun, moon, and stars, all of which God made), or to the place where God resides.

Definition

ouranos (Strong's #3772)

This is the word in the New Testament translated as "heaven" or "sky" (which can also occur in the plural). It can refer to

a. the sky (Matthew 6:26; 8:20; Acts 10:12; 11:6; James 5:18),

b. the location of the sun, moon, planets, stars, etc. (Matthew 24:29,35; Mark 13:25,31),

c. the eternal dwelling place of God (Matthew 5:16; 12:50; Revelation 3:12; 11:13; 16:11; 20:9),

d. the present "heavens," which humans can see, that will pass away (2 Peter 3:10,12; Revelation 20:11), and

e. the new "heavens" along with a new earth that will be established in the age to come (2 Peter 3:13; Revelation 21:1).

Quotes

"Messiah will come from Heaven to Earth, not to take us away from Earth to Heaven, but to restore Earth to what he intended so he can live with us here forever."

> —Randy Alcorn, *Heaven* (Carol Stream, IL: Tyndale House Publishers, 2004), 90.

"The new [Narnia] was a deeper country: every rock and flower and blade of grass looked as if it meant more. I can't describe it any better than that: if you ever get there you will know what I mean."

> —C.S. Lewis, *The Last Battle* (New York: HarperCollins Publishers, 1984), 196.

Hell

There are a few different words translated as "hell" in the New Testament: *Gehenna*, *Hades*, and *Tartarus*. They each have their own specific connotations, but they all seem to follow the same theological theme of judgment in the afterlife for those condemned in their sin, those who did not receive salvation through faith in Jesus.

Definitions

1: *geenna* (feminine noun, Strong's #1067)

The word *geenna*, or, as it is more commonly represented in English, "Gehenna," actually refers to the Hebrew *Gey-ben-Hinnom* ("Valley of the Son of Hinnom") and a corresponding Aramaic word. The Valley of the Son of Hinnom is associated in the Old Testament with human sacrificial burnings detestable to God (see 2 Chronicles 28:3; 2 Kings 23:10; Jeremiah 32:35), and a place whose inhabitants would be judged for their evil practice of burning their sons and daughters there (Jeremiah 7:30-32; 19:5-6). The word for "Gehenna" occurs twelve times in the New Testament, eleven of which are in the Synoptic Gospels and spoken by Jesus. He said that whoever calls their brother a fool would be in danger of the fire of "Gehenna" (Matthew 5:22), and that it is better to pluck out an eye or cut off a hand or foot that causes a person to stumble than for the whole body to end up in "Gehenna" (Matthew 5:29-30; 18:8,9).

Jesus also said God has the power to cast people into "hell" after they die (Luke 12:5; compare Matthew 10:28). Jesus denounced the scribes and Pharisees in Matthew 23, who after proselytizing a person, "make them twice as much a child of hell ['Gehenna']" as themselves (Matthew 23:15), wondering aloud how they would escape the fires of "Gehenna" (Matthew 23:33). In James 3:6, "Gehenna" is described as the source of the evil done by the misuse of the tongue.

2: *hadēs* (masculine noun, Strong's #86)

To the ancient Greeks, "Hades" (*hadēs*) was the underworld, the place of the dead. It corresponded to the ancient Hebrew concept of Sheol (*sheōl*). In the New Testament, "Hades" occurs only 10 times and refers to "the region of the departed spirits of the lost." The NIV uses "Hades" when the word appears in Matthew or Luke, where it has only a negative connotation as a place of judgment, or the place with gates that might strive to prevail against Jesus's church but will not be able to (see Matthew 11:23; 16:18; Luke 10:15; 16:23). When the term occurs in Acts 2:27,31, concerning the Messiah not seeing decay or being abandoned by the Father in "Hades," the NIV renders it as "the realm of the dead." So in that passage "Hades" is a vague, shadowy place for the dead, like Sheol in the Old Testament. In Revelation 1:18, Jesus said he had the keys to death and "Hades." Revelation 6:8 personifies "Hades" (along with death), and in Revelation 20:13-14, John said he saw in his vision that "Hades," along with death, "gave up the dead that were in them, and each person was judged according to what they had done. Then death and Hades were thrown into the lake of fire. The lake of fire is the second death."

Those references show why translators often avoid translating *hadēs* strictly as "hell" (which they generally reserve as the word for *geenna*). Also, the "lake of fire" in Revelation 19–20 is another image for hell. Both of the related concepts of death and Hades are thrown into this "lake of fire," which suggests that "Hades" is something other than "the lake of fire" itself. Still, fire is associated with the rich man's experience when he died and went to "Hades," in Jesus's parable of Lazarus and the rich man (see Luke 16:23-24). Since death and Hades will be cast into the "lake of fire," and since this is called the "second death," and since those whose names are not found in the book of life will also be cast into the lake of fire (Revelation 20:15), this all suggests that death and Hades hold the souls of the departed until the second and final death will consume everything.

3: *tartaroō* (verb, Strong's #5020)

The Greek noun *tartaros* ("Tartarus") does not occur in the New Testament, but the verb *tartaroō* ("to hold captive in Tartarus" or "to put in chains of darkness") does. It only occurs in 2 Peter 2:4, and refers to a holding place for angels who have sinned and await judgment. "Tartarus" was, in the words of New Testament scholar Douglas J. Moo, the underground place in ancient Greek mythology "to which disobedient gods and rebellious humans were consigned." To Peter, as Moo goes on to say, Tartarus "appears not so much to represent a place of final and endless punishment (as our 'hell' often does), but the limitation on sphere of influence that God imposed on the angels who fell."[5]

Insight

There is no one word for "hell" in the New Testament. "Hades" and "Tartarus" seem to overlap with the use of "Gehenna" and "the lake of fire" in some contexts, but in other contexts seem to be somewhat different concepts. "Tartarus" is only mentioned once, and "Hades," while sometimes depicting a place of judgment like "Gehenna," is also sometimes just depicted like Sheol, a place for the dead.

Quotes

"In order for someone's soul to become fully alive, it must first die to self. And it will need to die daily. The self-life, your selfish thoughts that dominate your mind and are in conflict with the will and Word of God, must die.

Much more important is to save your soul, which remains forever, either in hell or heaven."

> —Tony Evans, *Kingdom Disciples: Heaven's Representatives on Earth* (Chicago, IL: Moody Publishers, 2017), 21.

"The doctrines of hell and eternal punishment have become increasingly unpopular in our day, even among some Christian pastors and theologians. Those who question the doctrine ought to consider that some of our clearest statements on it come from the Lord Jesus Himself."

> —Ron Rhodes, *What Happens After Life?* (Eugene, OR: Harvest House Publishers, 2014), 138.

High Priest (see Priest)

Holy

In the Bible, if something is "holy," it is set apart from sin. The Holy Spirit, the third Person of the Trinity, is an example of God himself being distinct from sin—that is, holy. The Holy Place and the Holy of Holies are also areas set apart for God. Redeemed persons are often called "holy ones" or "saints." Sainthood is not earned—it is something God calls a person to, and grants.

Definition

hagios (adjective, Strong's #40)

This word refers to being "separated." The Greeks used it with reference to devotion to the gods, so its use in Scripture is parallel to this: what is "holy" is separated from sin and therefore consecrated to God. The New Testament calls God "holy." For example, it uses this word of the Father (Luke 1:49; John 17:11; 1 Peter 1:15,16; Revelation 4:8; 6:10), the Son (Luke 1:35; Acts

3:14; 4:27,30; 1 John 2:20), and the Spirit (frequently throughout the Gospels and many of the epistles).

People and things devoted to God, such as believers, are called *hagioi* ("holy ones" or "saints"). Even though sainthood is something given graciously to people by God and not earned, the Bible calls believers to "sanctify" or "make holy" themselves (as in 2 Timothy 1:9, consistent with their calling), cleansing themselves from all defilement and forsaking sin by living a "holy" manner of life (1 Peter 1:15; 2 Peter 3:11). The New Testament speaks of the saints figuratively as "a holy temple" (1 Corinthians 3:17; Ephesians 2:21; compare Ephesians 5:27). They are also collectively called "a holy priesthood" (1 Peter 2:5) and "a holy nation" (1 Peter 2:9).

The adjective is also used of the outer part of the tabernacle, the "Holy Place" (Hebrews 9:2) and of the inner part, the "Holy of Holies" or "Most Holy Place" (Hebrews 9:3). It also refers to the city of Jerusalem (Revelation 11:2), its temple (Acts 6:13), the faith (Jude 1:20), the greetings of the saints (1 Corinthians 16:20), angels (such as in Mark 8:38), the apostles and prophets (Ephesians 3:5), and the future heavenly Jerusalem (Revelation 21:2,10; 22:19).

Quote

"God, the Holy One of Israel, expects holy behavior from His sons, His children, His servants, His covenant partners."

> —Kay Arthur and Pete De Lacy, *Face-to-Face with a Holy God: Isaiah* (Eugene, OR: Harvest House Publishers, 2008), 20.

Holy Spirit (see Spirit)

Hope

"Hope" in the New Testament is "favorable and confident expectation". It has to do with the unseen and the future. It is anticipation of good, such as the promises of God, or it may refer to hope given by the gospel.

Definition

elpis (feminine noun, Strong's #1680)

Elpis ("hope") is a "favorable and confident expectation" concerning things unseen and the future.

Various phrases are used with the word *elpis*:

   a. "the hope of the resurrection of the dead" (Acts 23:6),

   b. "hope in what God has promised our ancestors" (Acts 26:6,7),

   c. "the hope of righteousness" (Galatians 5:5 ESV), and

   d. "the hope of the gospel" (Colossians 1:23 ESV), among others.

Hosanna

When Jesus rode into Jerusalem, he was greeted by crowds waving palm branches and shouting, "Hosanna!" This word in the New Testament comes from the Aramaic *hōsha na'*, corresponding to the Hebrew *hōshia na'* ("save!"), implying the request, "Save us!" The crowds recognized him as the Messiah, the Anointed One they were expecting to deliver them, perhaps from Rome—though his actual goal was greater: to deliver them from sin and death.

Definition

hōsanna (interjection, Strong's #5614)

In its original Aramaic (*hōsha na'*) and Hebrew (*hōshia na'*) forms, "hosanna" means "save!" The implication is, "Save us!" The word seems to have become an utterance of praise rather than of prayer, though probably it was originally a cry for help. The people's cry at Jesus's triumphal entry into Jerusalem (Matthew 21:9,15; Mark 11:9,10; John 12:13) was taken from Psalm 118, which was recited at the Feast of Tabernacles in what was known as the great Hallel (that is, Psalms 113–118) in responses with the priest, accompanied by the waving of palm and willow branches. "The last day of the feast" was called "the great Hosanna"; the branches also were called "hosannas."

Hospitality

"Hospitality" in the New Testament refers to loving or caring for strangers, or receiving a stranger or guest into the home.

Definitions

1: *xenizō* (verb, Strong's #3579)

This verb means either "to welcome a guest into one's home" (from *xenos*, "guest," also the word for "host" but primarily for "stranger"), as in Acts 28:7, Hebrews 13:2, and elsewhere. It can also mean "to be astonished at the strangeness of a thing" (see 1 Peter 4:12), but its primary meaning has to do with receiving someone into one's home—that is, showing hospitality (Acts 10:6,18,23,32; 21:16; 28:7; Hebrews 13:2).

2: *philoxenia* (feminine noun, Strong's #5381)

Literally meaning "love of strangers," *philoxenia* ("hospitality") is used in Romans 12:13 and Hebrews 13:2. In Hebrews 13:2, the writer reminded the recipients of the letter not to forget to show love to the stranger—that is, hospitality.

3: *philoxenos* (adjective, Strong's #5382)

Meaning "hospitable" or "loving the stranger," *philoxenos* occurs only in three places (1 Timothy 3:2; Titus 1:8; 1 Peter 4:9). In 1 Peter 4:9, Peter urged the believers to whom he is writing to be hospitable (*philoxenos*) to one another without grumbling.

Humanity

The word *anthrōpos*, while often meaning "man," can also simply refer to "a human being." The relationship between God and humans, the pinnacle of his creation, is the main subject of the entire Bible. When Jesus called himself the *huios tou anthrōpou* ("Son of Man"), on one level, he was calling himself the son of human beings, but on another, he was calling himself *the* human being, particularly in a divine sense, as it is an allusion to the divine figure "like a son of man" in Daniel 7:13-14. Apart from Jesus, all of humanity is sinful and in need of a Savior, found in the one human being who did not sin and is also fully God.

Definition

anthrōpos (masculine noun, Strong's #444)

This term can refer to

   a. a human being, male or female, without reference to sex or nationality (as in Matthew 4:4; 12:35; John 2:25),

   b. a human person as distinct from God (as in Matthew 19:6; John 10:33; Galatians 1:11; Colossians 3:23),

   c. humans in distinction from animals (as in Luke 5:10),

   d. people, whether male or female (Matthew 5:13,16),

   e. human frailty (1 Corinthians 2:5; Acts 14:15),

   f. the practices of fallen humanity (1 Corinthians 3:3),

   g. anything of human origin (Galatians 1:11), and so on.

The Hebrew word *'adam* (from which Adam, the first man, gets his name) can also refer to humans in general, though sometimes it refers to a male.

Humility

"Humility" in both Old and New Testaments is about being lowly in a positive sense, not estimating oneself too highly. It is contrasted with pride, which God opposes (1 Peter 5:5; from Proverbs 3:34). Jesus called himself humble in heart (Matthew 11:29), and said that those who exalt themselves will be humbled, while those who humble themselves will be exalted (Matthew 23:12).

Definitions

1: *tapeinos* (adjective, Strong's #5011)

Tapeinos primarily means "low-lying," but it is always used in a positive sense in the New Testament, and can denote

a. "of low degree, brought low" (as in Luke 1:52; Romans 12:16; 2 Corinthians 7:6),

b. "of low degree" (James 1:9), and

c. humble or lowly in spirit (Matthew 11:29; 2 Corinthians 10:1; James 4:6; 1 Peter 5:5).

2: *tapeinoō* (verb, Strong's #5013)

This verb means "to make low" or "to humble." It is used somewhat literally in Luke 3:5 regarding mountains and hills, but it is often used in the sense of humbling oneself or being humbled (Matthew 18:4; 23:12; Luke 14:11; 2 Corinthians 11:7; 12:21; Philippians 2:8; James 4:10; 1 Peter 5:6).

3: *tapeinophrosunē* (feminine noun, Strong's #5012)

This noun, usually translated "humility," refers to "a lowliness or humility of mind." It occurs seven times in the New Testament (Acts 20:19; Ephesians 4:2; Philippians 2:3; Colossians 2:18; 2:23; 3:12; 1 Peter 5:5).

Quote

"Humility doesn't mean you think less of yourself but that you think of yourself less."

> —Max Lucado, *Life Loved: Experiencing God's Presence in Everyday Life* (Nashville, TN: Thomas Nelson, 2011), 128.

Husband (see Man)

Hypocrite

A "hypocrite" was a mask-wearer, someone who wasn't for real, a play actor. Jesus often accused the scribes and Pharisees of being "hypocrites" (see Matthew 23).

Definition

hupokritēs (masculine noun, Strong's #5273)

The noun *hupokritēs* denotes "a play-actor." It was a custom for Greek and Roman actors to use large masks with mechanical devices for augmenting the force of the voice; as a result, the word became used metaphorically of what in English we call a "hypocrite." It is found only in the synoptics, and always by Jesus. It occurs frequently in Matthew, and also in Mark 7:6; Luke 6:42; 12:56; 13:15.

Quotes

"Some Christians invite disdain on themselves—and the God they claim to represent—with despicable behavior that contradicts any notion that God is love."

> —Bruce Bickel and Stan Jantz, *I'm Fine with God...It's Christians I Can't Stand* (Eugene, OR: Harvest House Publishers, 2008), 9.

"If you're still too turned off by hypocrites in the church to even consider Christianity, think about this question: Does the presence of counterfeits nullify the genuine? In other words, because there are hypocritical Christians in the church, can none be authentic or genuine?"

> —Ben Young, *Why Mike's Not a Christian* (Eugene, OR: Harvest House Publishers, 2006), 50.

Idol, Idolatry

"Idolatry" is the worship of "idols" (images or likenesses of false gods), but can refer to anything that moves our attention away from God and puts us in the service of, or in devotion to, other things.

Definitions

1: *eidōlon* (neuter noun, Strong's #1497)

An *eidōlon* ("idol"), mentioned eleven times in the New Testament, denotes

a. an image to represent a false god (Acts 7:41; 1 Corinthians 12:2; Revelation 9:20), and

b. the false god itself, worshiped in the image (Acts 15:20; Romans 2:22; 1 Corinthians 8:4,7; 10:19; 2 Corinthians 6:16; 1 Thessalonians 1:9; 1 John 5:21).

2: *eidōlolatria* (feminine noun, Strong's #1495)

The word *eidōlolatria* (from *eidōlon*, "idol," and *latreia*, "service") means "idolatry" or "serving a graven image representing a deity" or anything, such as greed (Colossians 3:5), that a person serves instead of God.

This word is used four times in the New Testament. Paul warned believers to flee from idolatry (1 Corinthians 10:14), listed it as one of the "works of the flesh" (see Galatians 5:19-20), and considered greed a form of idolatry, part of a person's "earthly nature" that needs to be "put to death" (Colossians 3:5). Peter reminded the recipients of his letter that they used to participate in *eidōlolatria*, which is "what pagans choose to do" (1 Peter 4:3).

Quotes

"There are many times when the church needs to recognize quite other 'forces' at work in the great movements of ideas and beliefs, forces that worship the idols of money, military power, blood and soil, and not least the supposed 'life force' of sex itself."

> —N.T. Wright, *Simply Jesus* (New York: HarperCollins Publishers, 2011), 209.

"Licentious behavior and greed were key characteristics of all forms of *gnosticism*. That was a deadly brand of false religion that flourished in the second century and often infiltrated the church, masquerading as Christianity."

> —John MacArthur, *The Truth War* (Nashville, TN: Thomas Nelson, 2007), 42.

Impure (see Unclean)

Iniquity (see Lawlessness)

Israel

The nation of "Israel," descended from Jacob, is of central importance in the New Testament. Jesus, a Jew, was a member of the nation of Israel, and his mission during his earthly ministry primarily related to it, though Gentiles (non-Jews) were always on the horizon. Some of the people of Israel believed in Jesus, but not all. Paul lamented this in Romans 10:1, longing for the salvation of the people of Israel who rejected the gospel.

Definition

Israēl (masculine proper noun, Strong's #2474)

When Jacob was wrestling a man who turned out to be a likely manifestation of God in Genesis 32:24-30, he was renamed "Israel" because, as the man told him, "Your name will no longer be Jacob, but Israel, because you have struggled with God and with humans and have overcome." The name "Israel," meaning "he contends" in Hebrew, came to be used for all of Jacob's descendants, the nation of "Israel," God's chosen people (Deuteronomy 7:6). It was through this people, as a light to the nations (Isaiah 51:4), God would reach the whole world. Jesus, a part of Israel as a descendant of Abraham, Isaac, and Jacob, initially limited the disciples' mission to "the lost sheep of Israel" (Matthew 10:5-6). He also ignored a Gentile woman seeking his help, as he said he was "sent only to the lost sheep of Israel" (Matthew 15:24), though he ended up healing her because of her faith, foreshadowing the full inclusion of the Gentiles (verse 28). Paul believed that one day "all Israel" would be saved (Romans 11:26). Precisely what he meant by "all Israel" here is debated, as also with when he spoke of the "Israel of God" (Galatians 6:16), since at that point some of Israel believed in the gospel but many did not, and Gentiles had been grafted in.

"God called Israel, so that through Israel he might redeem the world; but Israel itself needs redeeming as well. Hence God comes to Israel riding on a donkey, in fulfillment of Zechariah's prophecy of the coming peaceful kingdom, announcing judgment on the system and the city that have turned their vocation in upon themselves and going off to take the weight of the world's evil and hostility onto himself, so that by dying under them he might exhaust their power."

> —N.T. Wright, *Simply Jesus* (New York: HarperCollins Publishers, 2011), 38-39.

"Yahweh revealed himself as Israel's covenant God."

> —John Stott, *The Cross of Christ* (Downers Grove, IL: Inter-Varsity Press, 2006), 140.

Jealousy

Human "jealousy" is different from God's "jealousy." The difference is that humans might long for what is not rightfully theirs (though at least once, Paul expressed godly "jealousy" for the Corinthians, that they might belong to Christ), whereas God has *zēlos,* "jealousy," for what *is* rightfully his. God can be "jealous" of other gods who get humans' attention, whereas humans should be focused on God and not have *phthonos* ("envy") and the negative sense of *zēlos* for what their neighbor has that they desire.

Definitions

1: *zēlos* (masculine/neuter noun, Strong's #2205)

Also the word for "zeal" (see *Zeal*), *zēlos* can occur in negative contexts, such as "jealousy" among humans (Acts 5:17; 13:45; Romans 13:13; 1 Corinthians 3:3; Galatians 5:20; James 3:14,16). Paul used it once of himself in the sense of godly jealously, of his desire that the Corinthians might belong to Christ and no other (2 Corinthians 11:2), similar to how God is "jealous" in a righteous way, as in Exodus 20:5, for example (with the Hebrew *qana',* translated in the Septuagint by the similar Greek word *zēlōtēs*).

2: *phthonos* (masculine noun, Strong's #5355)

Unlike the "jealousy" meaning of *zēlos* (see above), *phthonos* ("envy") always occurs in a negative context, and refers to the feeling of displeasure produced by witnessing or hearing of the advantage or prosperity of others, wishing to deprive them of what they have. It occurs nine times in the New Testament (Matthew 17:18; Mark 15:10; Romans 1:29; Galatians 5:21; Philippians 1:15; 1 Timothy 6:4; Titus 3:3; James 4:5; 1 Peter 2:1).

Quote

"Can you recall a time when you made detracting remarks about someone? What was your motive in doing so? Why did you feel the need to diminish that person's character in the eyes of another? Were you speaking out of the pain of being hurt by her? Did you envy her accomplishments? If so, have you not learned how to let your envy motivate you to achieve your own goals rather than cause you to defame another? It is likely you grudgingly admire and desire something the other person possesses."

—Deborah Smith Pegues, *30 Days to Taming Your Tongue*
(Eugene, OR: Harvest House Publishers, 2005), 43.

Jesus

Above all, the New Testament is about "Jesus." His name in Hebrew, *Yeshua*, an alternate form of the name *Yᵉhōshua* (meaning "Joshua"), is transliterated as *Iēsous* in the New Testament and means "Yahweh is salvation," explained as follows: "You are to give him the name 'Jesus,' because he will save his people from their sins" (Matthew 1:21). He is God the Son, the second Person of the Trinity. Though he is God, he became flesh and made his dwelling among us (John 1:14), conducted his earthly ministry, was crucified for the sins of humanity, and rose on the third day, so that our Christian faith, as Paul said, is not in vain (1 Corinthians 15:14).

Definition

Iēsous (masculine proper name, Strong's #2424)

Iēsous is a transliteration of the Hebrew *Yeshua*, an alternate form of the word *Yᵉhōshua* ("Joshua"), meaning "Yahweh is salvation." It was a common Jewish name, and Jesus's parents, Mary and Joseph (who was only an adoptive father, as Mary conceived Jesus through the Holy Spirit) gave him that name in obedience to the angel who commanded this to Joseph (Matthew 1:21).

Jesus is the central figure of the New Testament. Without him becoming a human being, living among us, dying, and rising again, there would be no Christianity. Those who believe in him have eternal life (John 3:16) because of what was accomplished by his death on the cross for our sins (Matthew 26:26-28), and his resurrection from the dead on the third day (see Matthew 28; see also Mark 16). As Paul said of Jesus in 2 Corinthians 5:21, "God made him who knew no sin to be sin for us, so that in him we might become the righteousness of God."

Quotes

"Messiah will come from Heaven to Earth, not to take us away from Earth to Heaven, but to restore Earth to what he intended so he can live with us here forever."

> —Randy Alcorn, *Heaven* (Carol Stream, IL: Tyndale House Publishers, 2004), 90.

"Why was it that God 'did not spare his own Son, but gave him up for all' (Rom 8:32)? Because of his grace. It was his own free decision to save which brought the atonement."

> —J.I. Packer, *Knowing God* (Downers Grove, IL: InterVarsity Press, 1993), 133-134.

Jew

The word "Jew" or "Judean" (Greek *Ioudaios*) comes from "Judah," the name of one of the sons of Jacob and one of the 12 tribes of Israel. Anyone who was a member of the people of Israel eventually came to be known as a Jew, though for a time the kingdom of "Israel" was separate from the kingdom of "Judah." Jesus was a Jew, as were all his disciples. Paul, who wrote much of the New Testament, was also a Jew, and a Pharisee (see Acts 23:6; Philippians 3:5), trained under Rabbi Gamaliel (Acts 22:3).

Definition

Ioudaios (adjective, sometimes used like a noun, Strong's #2453)

This word occurs either

a. adjectivally, "Jewish," usually describing a person (such as in Acts 10:28; 22:3), or country (John 3:22), or

b. as a noun like "Jew, Jews," as it occurs frequently throughout the Gospel of John, as well as in places such as Matthew 2:2 and Mark 7:3. The noun in Hebrew, *Yᵉhudi*, first occurs in 2 Kings 16:6 as the plural *Yᵉhudim*, to mean "Judeans," or people from the southern kingdom of Judah (as distinct from the northern kingdom of Israel). After the Babylonian exile, the word was used to distinguish descendants of Abraham, Isaac, and Jacob from everyone else (eventually called "the nations" or "Gentiles"). "Jews" are distinguished from Samaritans (John 4:9) and from proselytes, that is, Gentiles who converted to faith in the God of the Jews (Acts 2:11). Jesus and his disciples were Jews, as was Paul. Many early believers were Jews. In fact, passages like Acts 15 and Paul's letter to the Galatians dealt with the controversy about whether Gentiles who came to faith in Christ had to essentially become Jews religiously before they could be real believers in Jesus. Paul powerfully declared in Galatians 5:6, "In Christ Jesus neither circumcision nor uncircumcision counts for anything, but only faith working through love." Paul also expressed longing for his fellow Jews, the majority of whom had rejected the gospel, that they would come to faith in Jesus (Romans 9:1-4).

Quote

"The Jews knew intimately the many Old Testament promises of future blessing, deliverance, and prosperity. They knew God had promised to vanquish all the enemies of His chosen people and to establish His eternal kingdom of righteousness and justice on earth. They knew that the Lord's Anointed One—His Messiah, or Christ—would come and establish the rule and reign of David again on earth, a reign of peace, prosperity, and safety that would never end. Their great longing was to see that day when God restored the kingdom as He had promised."

—John MacArthur, *The New Testament Commentary, Matthew 24–28* (Chicago: Moody Publishers, 1989), 3.

Joy

"Joy" in the New Testament is immense happiness, exultation, or delight in something, particularly of spiritual relevance in the life of a believer.

Definitions

1: *chara* (feminine noun, Strong's #5479)

As the word for "joy" or "happiness" (related to the verb *chairō*, "to rejoice"—see below) *chara* is found frequently in Matthew and Luke, even more often in John, and once in Mark (Mark 4:16). *Chara* is absent from 1 Corinthians (though the verb *chairō* is used in that book three times), but it shows up frequently in 2 Corinthians, possibly revealing Paul's feelings of relief, in comparison with the unhappy circumstances that called for him to write 1 Corinthians. The word is sometimes used for an occasion of great gladness, as in "good news of great joy" (Luke 2:10 ESV). Other times, recipients of a letter were described as "the joy" of the letter's author (as in 1 Thessalonians 2:19,20). James urged the recipients of his letter to consider it "joy" when they faced trials (James 1:2).

2: *chairō* (verb, Strong's #5463)

While some other verbs can also be translated as "to rejoice, express joy," *chairō* is a common one, and is related to *chara* above. Examples of its use include "rejoicing" at the birth of Jesus (Luke 1:14), the call to "rejoice at the names written" in heaven (Luke 10:20), and Paul's rejoicing at meeting other believers (1 Corinthians 16:17).

Quotes

"Joy was not a deception. Its visitations were rather the moments of clearest consciousness we had."

—C.S. Lewis, *Surprised by Joy* (Orlando, FL: Harcourt, Inc., 1955), 222.

"We may be successful in putting our personal affairs in place, but if we do it at the sacrifice of the more important—putting our spiritual affairs in order—we miss the joy and purpose of life."

—Billy Graham, *Nearing Home: Life, Faith, and Finishing Well* (Nashville, TN: Thomas Nelson, 2011), 92.

Judge, Judging, Judgment

"Judging" has both positive and negative connotations in the New Testament. On the one hand, one can "judge" or "issue a judgment" in a legal context or from a place of authority (such as when God issues a "judgment," as in Romans 2:2), but on the other hand, Jesus warned his disciples against "judging" another, as they would themselves be judged with the same measure (Matthew 7:1-2; see also Romans 2:1).

Definitions

1: *krinō* (verb, Strong's #2919)

As a verb that means "to condemn" (see *Condemn, Condemnation*), *krinō* also means "to judge, pronounce judgment" or "to separate, select, determine." The verb has many uses in the New Testament; *krinō* can mean

    a. to assume the office of a judge (as in Matthew 7:1; John 3:17),

    b. to undergo the process of a trial (John 3:18; 16:11; 18:31; James 2:12),

    c. to deliver a sentence (Acts 15:19; 16:4; 21:25),

    d. to condemn (John 12:48; Acts 13:27; Romans 2:27),

    e. to execute judgment upon (2 Thessalonians 2:12; Acts 7:7),

    f. to be involved in a lawsuit, whether as a plaintiff (Matthew 5:40; 1 Corinthians 6:1) or as a defendant (Acts 23:6),

    g. to administer affairs, to govern (Matthew 19:28; compare Judges 3:10),

    h. to form an opinion (Luke 7:43; John 7:24; Acts 4:19; Romans 14:5), and

    i. to resolve or decide to do something (Acts 3:13; 20:16; 1 Corinthians 2:2).

2: *kritēs* (masculine noun, Strong's #2923)

The noun *kritēs*, "judge," occurs in the New Testament with reference to

    a. God (Hebrews 12:23; James 4:12),

    b. Christ (Acts 10:42; 2 Timothy 4:8; James 5:9),

    c. a ruler in Israel in the times of the Judges (Acts 13:20),

    d. a Roman governor (Acts 24:10),

    e. those whose conduct puts them in the place of "judging" (Matthew 12:27; Luke 11:19),

    f. one who tries and decides a case (Matthew 5:25; Luke 12:14,58; 18:2,6; Acts 18:15), and

g. one who makes a judgment on anything or anyone wrongly
    (James 2:4; 4:11).

3: *krisis* (feminine noun, Strong's #2920)

A *krisis* is "a separating" or "a decision, judgment," most frequently in a
forensic sense, especially of the divine judgment. It denotes

a. "the process of investigation, the act of distinguishing or separat-
    ing," suggesting judicial authority (John 5:22,27), justice (Acts
    8:33; James 2:13), a tribunal (Matthew 5:21,22), a trial (John
    5:24; 2 Peter 2:4), a judgment (2 Peter 2:11; Jude 1:9), the stan-
    dard of judgment, just dealing (Matthew 12:18,20; 23:23; Luke
    11:42), and divine judgment executed (2 Thessalonians 1:5; Rev-
    elation 16:7).

b. Sometimes it has the meaning "condemnation," and is virtually
    equivalent to *krima* (see *Condemn, Condemnation*). (See Mat-
    thew 23:33; John 3:19; James 5:12.)

Quotes

"God must and will judge sinners; if He ignored their sin, He would not be
holy, righteous, and true to His nature."
> —John MacArthur, *The MacArthur New Testament Commen-
> tary, Revelation 12–22* (Chicago: Moody Publishers, 2000),
> 131.

"The doctrines of hell and eternal punishment have become increasingly
unpopular in our day, even among some Christian pastors and theologians.
Those who question the doctrine ought to consider that some of our clearest statements on it come from the Lord Jesus Himself."
> —Ron Rhodes, *What Happens After Life?* (Eugene, OR: Har-
> vest House Publishers, 2014), 138.

Judgment Seat

In New Testament times a "bema" (Greek: *bēma*) was a raised platform on which a Roman magistrate or official would make a judgment in a tribunal. Pilate was on one when trying Jesus (see Matthew 27:19), and Paul used the word regarding God's judgment of believers in the afterlife (Romans 14:10; 2 Corinthians 5:10).

Definition

bēma (neuter noun, Strong's #968)

Primarily meaning "a step," as in a walking movement forward (combined with *pous*, "foot," to mean "ground to set foot on" in Acts 7:5), *bēma* came to describe a raised place or platform, reached by steps—originally one such platform at Athens in the Pnyx Hill, where it was the place of assembly. From that *bēma* or platform, people would make speeches. By the time of the New Testament, the word also came to refer to a platform to which a tribune would ascend via steps, to lead a trial. Pilate used this "judgment seat" at the trial of Jesus (Matthew 27:19; John 19:13).

The NIV translates *bēma* as "throne" in Acts 12:21 and "place of judgment" in Acts 18:12. *Bēma* occurs once in Acts 18:16 (literally, "he drove them away from the judgment seat"), though the NIV obscures this by saying only, "he drove them off." In Acts 18:17, the NIV translates the phrase *emprosthen tou bēmatos* (literally, "in front of the judgment seat") as "in front of the proconsul" to clarify that Sosthenes the synagogue leader was being beaten in front of Gallio the proconsul, who would have been sitting on the *bēma*. Twice the NIV translates the phrase *kathisas epi tou bēmatos* (literally, "sitting on the judgment seat") as Festus having "convened the court" (Acts 25:6,17). Once the NIV translates the phrase *epi tou bēmatos Kaisaros estōs eimi* (literally, "before the judgment seat of Ceasar standing am I") as "I am now standing before Caesar's court" (Acts 25:10). Paul, whom Luke records as saying this, also used the term *bēma* twice in his letters, once calling it "God's judgment seat" (Romans 14:10) and another time calling it "the judgment seat of Christ" (2 Corinthians 5:10). Both times Paul was referring to the time when all believers will stand before this judgment seat for their deeds to be judged.

Justice (see Righteousness)

Kindness

The word for "kindness" in the New Testament does not merely have to do with being "nice" but with interacting with others in a way that reflects the goodness of one's heart.

Definition

chrēstotēs (feminine noun, Strong's #5544)

This word means "goodness of heart, kindness," and it occurs ten times in the New Testament. The NIV translates it as "kindness" nine of those times (Romans 2:4; three times in 11:22; 2 Corinthians 6:6; Galatians 5:22; Colossians 3:12; Titus 3:4). In Romans 3:12 (quoting passages like Psalm 14:1-3; 53:1-3; Ecclesiastes 7:20), the NIV translates the phrase *poiōn chrēstotēta* (literally, "one who does kind/good things") as "one who does good."

Insight

In Romans 3:9-20, Paul did not quote from passages like the above, that say there is no *poiōn chrēstotēta* ("one who does good"), in order to claim that no one ever does any good at all or is ever kind. Clearly, people do kind or good things for others on a regular basis. Instead, he quoted from those passages as part of his argument that because of the sinfulness of humans, not even one person can be "declared righteous in God's sight" through the works of the Law (Romans 3:20). This only happens through faith (verse 22).

Quote

"You can do good for the mere sake of goodness: you cannot be bad for the mere sake of badness. You can do a kind action when you are not feeling kind and when it gives you no pleasure, simply because kindness is right; but no one ever did a cruel action simply because cruelty is wrong—only because cruelty was pleasant or useful to him."

> —C.S. Lewis, *Mere Christianity* (New York: HarperCollins Publishers, 1980), 74.

King

"King" in the New Testament could either refer to an earthly ruler, as in Herod or the Roman emperor (1 Peter 2:13,17), or to the "King of kings," as in Jesus (see Revelation 17:14; 19:16). In his capacity as the Messiah or Anointed One, Jesus was considered the "king of the Jews" (for example, Matthew 2:2; 27:11,29,37).

Definition

basileus (masculine noun, Strong's #935)

A *basileus* is a "king." Peter used this word to refer to the emperor of Rome (1 Peter 2:13,17) in a context exhorting the recipients of his letter to be subservient to the emperor and his governors so that no one would be able to say that followers of Jesus did not do good. The word also describes Herod the Tetrarch (Matthew 14:9), and Christ as the "king of the Jews" (as in Matthew 2:2; 27:11,29,37) or as the "king of Israel" (Mark 15:32; John 1:49; 12:13) and the "King of kings" (Revelation 17:14; 19:16). God is called "the Great King"

(Matthew 5:35) and the "King of kings" (1 Timothy 6:15). Jesus's kingship was predicted in the Old Testament (see Psalm 2:6) and in the New Testament (Luke 1:32,33). He came as a king (Matthew 2:2; John 18:37), was rejected and died as such (Luke 19:14; Matthew 27:37), and is now a king-priest, in the order of Melchizedek (Hebrews 5:6; 7:1,2,17; see *Melchizedek*).

Kingdom

A "kingdom" is a dominion or territory ruled by a king. "The kingdom of God" (known in Matthew's Gospel as "the kingdom of heaven") is another way of talking about God's rule (his dominion), and is most frequently used in that way.

Definition

basileia (feminine noun, Strong's #932)

This is primarily an abstract noun, denoting "sovereignty, royal power, or dominion" (as in Revelation 17:18). Sometimes it denotes a territory or people over whom a king rules (as in Matthew 4:8; Mark 3:24).

The kingdom of God is

a. God's rule over the earth (Psalm 22:28; 145:13; Daniel 4:25; Luke 1:52; Romans 13:1,2). But because the earth is the scene of universal rebellion against God (as in Luke 4:5,6; 1 John 5:19; Revelation 11:15-18), God's kingdom is also

b. wherever God's rule is acknowledged, and God intends to establish it in spite of sinful humanity's failure to acknowledge his rule (Daniel 2:44; 7:14; 1 Corinthians 15:24,25). Still, in the meantime (in order to receive obedience), he gave his law to a nation (Israel) and appointed earthly kings over it (1 Chronicles 28:5). Israel, however, rebelled (Isaiah 1:2-4), most of Israel rejected God's Son (John 1:11), and as a result, those who did were cast away (Romans 11:15,20,25). Therefore God calls upon people everywhere, without distinction of race or nationality, to submit to his rule. Jesus called people to repent because the "kingdom of God has come near" in Mark 1:15. See also Matthew 4:17, where the phrase "kingdom of heaven" is used as a synonym for the "kingdom of God" as it is throughout the rest of Matthew's Gospel.

Know, Knowledge

"Knowledge" in the New Testament particularly pertains to understanding spiritual truth, to knowing Jesus and making him known.

Definitions

1: *ginōskō* (verb, Strong's #1097)

Meaning "to be taking in knowledge, to come to know, recognize, or understand," *ginōskō* is a very frequent word in the New Testament. It often indicates a relationship between the person "knowing" and the object being known. In this respect, what is known is important to the one who knows, such as God knowing those who love him (1 Corinthians 8:3; see also Galatians 4:9).

2: *gnōrizō* (verb, Strong's #1107)

Related to *ginōskō* (see above), *gnōrizō* means

   a. "to come to know, discover, know" (as in Philippians 1:22), and

   b. "to make known," whether communicating things before unknown (Luke 2:15,17; John 15:15; etc.), or reasserting things already known (as in 1 Corinthians 12:3).

3: *eidō* (verb, Strong's #1492)

From the same root as *eidon* ("to see"), *oida* primarily means "to have seen or perceived" and therefore also "to know, have knowledge of," whether this is divine knowledge (for example, Matthew 6:8,32; John 6:6,64;

2 Corinthians 11:31) or human knowledge, which would come from observation (for example, 1 Thessalonians 1;4,5).

The primary difference between *ginōskō* (see above) and *oida* is that *ginōskō* often suggests progress in knowledge, while *oida* suggests fullness of knowledge.

4: *gnōsis* (feminine noun, Strong's #1108)

Primarily "a seeking to know, investigation" (related to *ginōskō* above), *gnōsis* means "knowledge" in the New Testament, especially regarding spiritual truth. It is used

a. in a general, absolute way, simply as "knowledge" (for example, see Luke 11:52; 1 Corinthians 1:5), and

b. with a direct object, such as knowledge of God (2 Corinthians 2:14), knowledge of God's glory (2 Corinthians 4:6), knowledge of Christ (Philippians 3:8; 2 Peter 3:18), and knowledge of salvation (Luke 1:77).

Insight

When the New Testament was being written there was a movement that we know as "Gnosticism," which claimed to have secret "knowledge" (*gnōsis*) about important spiritual matters. One of the things they claimed was that physical things are bad or evil, which the church has rejected as heresy.

Quote

"Paul's concerns at Corinth were complex. The church was in danger of being influenced by early forms of Gnosticism, which held that individuals were saved by a secret, arcane knowledge. Others at Corinth prized intellectual sophistication and were not prepared to tolerate anything that seemed to lack this or any other mark of cultural erudition. Paul rightly rejects any such notions, insisting the Christian gospel must be taken on its own terms, even if it counters prevailing cultural notions of acceptability at Corinth. Yet this is about challenging secular notions of wisdom, not abandoning human notions of rationality!"

> —Alister McGrath, *Mere Apologetics: How to Help Seekers and Skeptics Find Faith* (Grand Rapids, MI: Baker Books, 2012), 90.

L

Lake of Fire (see Hell)

Lamb

At the first Passover in Egypt, a spotless lamb was to be killed and its blood smeared on the doorposts of those who feared God so that the angel of death, God's final and deadliest plague against Egypt, would pass over the dwelling and not kill the firstborn in the house. Jesus is known as the Passover Lamb of God, sometimes simply "the Lamb of God, who takes away the sin of the world" (John 1:29,36).

Definitions

1: *arnion* (neuter noun, Strong's #721)

This is the most frequent word for "lamb," and it only occurs in the writings of the apostle John. He used it once in his Gospel (in the plural) when Jesus asked Peter to feed his *arnia* or "lambs" (John 21:15). Every other time this word occurs is in Revelation, often referring to Jesus as the "Lamb" of God, in reference to his sacrificial atonement for sin, though he is then seen in his exalted state. The second beast in Revelation 13:11 is also described "like a lamb," evoking his status as a false messiah.

2: *amnos* (masculine noun, Strong's #286)

Amnos ("lamb") occurs only four times in the whole New Testament. Jesus is called the *amnos* who takes away the sin of the world (John 1:29,36). *Amnos* is also paralleled with *probaton* (the common word for "sheep"; see *Sheep*) in Acts 8:32 as it is the Septuagint's translation of Isaiah 53:7. Peter used *amnos* when he wrote of "the precious blood of Christ, a lamb without blemish or defect" (1 Peter 1:19), by which Christians are redeemed (verse 18). This recalls Exodus 12:5-8, where blood from lambs without blemish or defect was to be used on the doorposts to keep the angel of death from killing the firstborn in that house.

The difference between *arnion* and *amnos* as to their use as imagery of Jesus, is that *amnos* denotes Jesus as the sacrificial Lamb, while *arnion* describes Jesus in his majesty as well as in his sacrifice (in Revelation).

Law

The "Law" refers to that which was given by Moses at Sinai or to the books that contain the Law—the Pentateuch or Torah (Genesis, Exodus, Leviticus, Numbers, and Deuteronomy). Sometimes "Law" even functions as a shorthand for Old Testament Scripture in general. But it can also simply refer to any kind of "law" made by God or humans. Paul frequently stressed that one is saved by grace through faith and not through the works of the "Law," referring to the Law of Moses.

Definition

nomos (masculine noun, Strong's #3551)

Nomos means "law," which in Greco-Roman society was decreed by the state and set up as the standard administration of justice. The New Testament uses it of

a. law in general (Romans 2:14; 3:27),

b. a force or influence compelling one to wrong action (Romans 7:21,23),

c. the Mosaic Law, the one given at Sinai (for example, Matthew 5:18; John 1:17; Romans 2:15,18,20,26,27; 3:19; Galatians 3:10; 5:3; etc.), and

d. the books containing the Law, as in the Pentateuch (such as Matthew 5:17; 12:5; Luke 16:16; 24:44; John 1:45; Romans 3:21; Galatians 3:10), the Psalms (John 10:34; 15:25), the Psalms with Isaiah, Ezekiel, and Daniel (John 12:34), the Psalms and Isaiah (Romans 3:10-18,19), or just Isaiah (1 Corinthians 14:21). From all this we see that sometimes "the Law" in its most comprehensive sense was an alternative title to "the Scriptures." Sometimes "the Law and the Prophets" refers to the Old Testament as a whole (for example, Matthew 7:12).

Insight

The Hebrew word *tōrah*, which is the Old Testament word corresponding to the New Testament word *nomos*, means not just "law" but "teaching" (*tōrah* comes from the root *yarah*, "to teach"). In this regard, what the Old Testament calls God's *tōrah* is his "teaching." For example, a psalmist may say, "Oh how I love your law" (Psalm 119:97), and literally, the word for "law" means "teaching." The Greek *nomos* does not have this same meaning, but it is worthwhile to notice this aspect of the word in the Old Testament that corresponds to it.

Quotes

"Any standard is a law, and adherence to any law in order to attain, gain, or maintain God's acceptance is in direct violation of grace. It is legalism."

> —Neil T. Anderson, Rich Miller, and Paul Travis, *Grace That Breaks the Chains: Freedom from Guilt, Shame, and Trying Too Hard* (Eugene, OR: Harvest House Publishers, 2003), 31.

"Circumcision and life under the law do not restrain the flesh. The only way to overcome the flesh, according to Paul, is to live by the Spirit."

> —Thomas R. Schreiner, *Zondervan Exegetical Commentary on the New Testament: Galatians*, ed. Clinton E. Arnold (Grand Rapids, MI: Zondervan, 2010), 47.

Lawlessness

"Lawlessness" in the New Testament is another term for talking about sin, though the Greek words translated "lawlessness," "wrongdoing," "unrighteousness," or "misdeed" (all of these are very similar to each another) do not have the same sense of "missing the mark" as with *hamartia* ("sin").

Definitions

1: *anomia* (feminine noun, Strong's #458)
This word literally means "without lawfulness," and it is used in a way which indicates the meaning "lawlessness or wickedness," though it is translated with a variety of English synonyms for these words. It occurs 15 times in the New Testament (see Matthew 7:23; 13:41; 23:28; 24:12; Romans 4:7; 6:19; 2 Corinthians 6:14; 2 Thessalonians 2:3,7; Hebrews 1:9; 10:17; 1 John 3:4).

2: *adikia* (feminine noun, Strong's #93)
Literally meaning "unrighteousness," *adikia* appears 25 times in the New

Testament. One example has to do with the "unjust judge" in Luke 18:6 (literally, "the judge of unrighteousness"). Paul also told the Romans that the wrath of God is revealed against all ungodliness and "unrighteousness" (Romans 1:18).

3: *adikēma* (neuter noun, Strong's #92)

A "wrongdoing," "misdeed," "crime," or "misdemeanor," *adikēma* occurs only a few times in the New Testament (see Acts 24:20; Revelation 18:5).

Leaven

"Leaven" is yeast, the component of bread that makes it rise. In the New Testament (as in the Old Testament) it is often associated with impurity; no leaven was allowed in the bread eaten at the Passover.

Definition

zumē (feminine noun, Strong's #2219)

Meaning "leaven, sour dough, in a high state of fermentation," *zumē* occurs in the New Testament generally with reference to making bread. Most of the time leaven was required in the process, but sometimes bread had to be prepared quickly; in those situations, people would use *unleavened* bread. The Israelites were forbidden to use "leaven" (Hebrew: *chametz*) for seven days at the time of the Passover so they would be reminded that Yahweh had brought them out of Egypt "in haste" (Deuteronomy 16:3; see also Exodus 12:11). Deuteronomy 16:3 also calls unleavened bread "the bread of affliction," perhaps a reference to its taste, a reminder of the affliction they faced under slavery in Egypt.

Leaven was forbidden in all offerings to Yahweh by fire (Leviticus 2:11; 6:17). Linked to the idea of corruption, and because of how it spreads through a mass of dough, leaven also symbolized the pervasive character of evil and therefore was not appropriate for an offering to Yahweh.

In the Old Testament, "leaven" is *not* used in a metaphorical sense. But in the New Testament, *zumē* occurs

a. metaphorically, referring to corrupt teaching (Matthew 16:6,11; Mark 8:15; Luke 12:1), or to corrupt practices (Mark 8:15; 1 Corinthians 5:7,8). In its only positive sense, it is compared to the kingdom of God, because of how leaven expands and becomes pervasive (Luke 13:21). It can also occur

b. literally (Matthew 16:12; 1 Corinthians 5:6; Galatians 5:9).

Leper, Leprosy

"Lepers" had a skin disease (often translated as "leprosy") that made them considered untouchable according to Jewish law. Jesus healed lepers, touching them even though they were considered unclean.

Definition

lepros (adjective, Strong's #3015)

This is an adjective that is primarily used of a debilitating skin disease, characterized by an eruption of rough, scaly patches. It is chiefly used as a noun meaning "leper" or "one who has leprosy." It occurs nine times in the New Testament (Matthew 8:2; 10:8; 26:6; 11:5; Mark 1:40; 14:3; Luke 4:27; 7:22; 17:12).

Life

John 1:4 says that in Jesus "was life, and that life was the light of all mankind." It occurs frequently in the New Testament with reference to the "eternal life" that is given for believing in Jesus.

Definition

zōē (feminine noun, Strong's #2222)

This term is used in the New Testament of "life as a principle, life in the absolute sense"—that is, it refers to life as God has it, as that which the Father has in himself and which he gave to the Incarnate Son to have in himself (John 1:4; 5:26).

Eternal *zōē* ("life") is promised to the believer in Jesus in John 3:16 and many other passages, and it is associated with the promise of resurrection for believers (see 2 Corinthians 5:4; 2 Timothy 1:10) because of Jesus's resurrection, without which our faith is useless (see 1 Corinthians 15:14). This life is not merely a principle of power and mobility, however. It also has moral connotations to things like holiness and righteousness. The New Testament frequently contrasts death and sin with life and holiness.

Insight

Death came through sin (Romans 5:12), which is rebellion against God. Sin, therefore, involves the forfeiting of life. As Leviticus 17:11 says, "The life of the flesh is in the blood." So the giving of "life" to the sinner must come by a death with the shedding of blood, that element which is the life of the flesh. Because Christ had no sins of his own to die for, his death served as life-giving atonement (John 10:15; 2 Corinthians 5:21; see also Isaiah 53:5,10,12).

Quotes

"Salvation is a gift to be received, not a reward to be earned."

> —Steve McVey, *Grace Walk* (Eugene, OR: Harvest House Publishers, 1995), 18.

"Why can't we earn our own salvation? Because we are dead in our sins. A corpse can't work. A corpse can't pay. A corpse can do nothing. That's why salvation is a free gift from God."

> —Michael Youssef, *Leading the Way Through Ephesians* (Eugene, OR: Harvest House Publishers, 2012), 41.

Lord, Master

A "lord" (*kurios*) could be a "master" to a slave. Sometimes the disciples would address Jesus as "Lord," a term of respect for someone who was their superior. "Sir" occasionally would be a good translation as a term of respect. *Kurios* is the word the Septuagint uses to translate the Hebrew word for "lord" or "master," *'adōn*. It is also the word the Septuagint uses to translate two words used of God in the Old Testament: *'Adōnai* (translated as "Lord"), and the divine name itself, *YHWH* (thought to be pronounced *"Yahweh"*). So this link to the God of the Old Testament is significant when "Lord" occurs with reference to the Father, Son, or Holy Spirit in the New Testament. Sometimes the disciples also addressed Jesus as *Epistata* (the form of address of the word *epistatēs*), meaning "master." Another word for "master" is *despotēs*.

Definitions

1: *kurios* (masculine noun, Strong's #2962)

Kurios can be translated in the New Testament in various ways, such as "Lord," "master," "sir," or "owner." It can also appear as an adjective with the meaning "having power or authority." It is a title occurring in every New Testament book except Titus and the letters of John.

It occurs with reference to

a. an owner (as in Matthew 12:8; Luke 19:33; Acts 16:16; Galatians 4:1),

b. a master, that is, one to whom another owes service (Matthew 6:24; 24:50; Ephesians 6:5),

c. an emperor or king (Acts 25:26; Revelation 17:14),

d. idols, in an ironic sense (1 Corinthians 8:5; compare Isaiah 26:13),

e. a title of respect, as addressed to a father (Matthew 21:30), a husband (1 Peter 3:6), a master (Matthew 13:27; Luke 13:8), a ruler (Matthew 27:63), or an angel (Acts 10:4; Revelation 7:14), and

f. as a title of courtesy addressed to a stranger (John 12:21; 20:15; Acts 16:30).

g. Jesus was called "Lord" throughout his ministry (Matthew 8:2,25; Luke 5:8; John 4:11; 6:68).

h. *Kurios* in the Septuagint and New Testament also functions as a translation of two words used of God in the Old Testament: *'Adōnai* (literally "my lords," but translated as "Lord" when referring to Yahweh), or the divine name itself, *YHWH* (thought to be pronounced *"Yahweh"*). For example, see Matthew 1:22 and James 5:11.

2: *epistates* (masculine noun, Strong's #1988)

This word means "a chief, commander, overseer, master." In the form of address, *Epistata* ("Master"), it was the term the disciples used for Jesus as a way of recognizing his authority, rather than his instruction (for the latter, they would call him *Didaskale*, "Teacher"; see *Teach, Teacher, Teaching*).

3: *despotēs* (masculine noun, Strong's #1203)

A *despotēs* is a "master or lord" or "one who possess supreme authority." It occurs in personal address to God (Luke 2:29; Acts 4:24; Revelation 6:10), and to Christ (2 Timothy 2:21; 2 Peter 2:1; Jude 1:4). Elsewhere it refers to human masters (1 Timothy 6:1,2; Titus 2:9; 1 Peter 2:18).

Love

"Love" is a characteristic essential to who God is. The New Testament primarily uses two verbs for "love"—*agapaō* and *phileō*. Peter denied Jesus three times during Jesus's trial. After his resurrection, Jesus used both of these terms when reinstating Peter, repeatedly asking him, "Do you love me?" (see John 21:15-17). The apostle John also went so far as to identify God with the noun *agapē* ("love") in the statement *ho theos agapē estin*, meaning "God is love" (1 John 4:8,16).

Definitions

1: *agapaō* (verb, Strong's #25)

The verb *agapaō*, meaning "to love," and the corresponding noun *agapē* (feminine noun, Strong's #26), meaning "love," represent the action meant to characterize the life of a follower of Jesus: love. In the Septuagint, *agapaō* serves to translate the corresponding Hebrew verb *ahav* in both Deuteronomy 6:5 and Leviticus 19:18, passages Jesus called the greatest commandments (see Matthew 22:35-40). The first two times Jesus asked Peter if he loved him, Jesus used the verb *agapaō* (John 21:15-16). God is also said to have "loved" (using the aorist tense of the verb *agapaō*) the world (John 3:16), which is why he gave his only Son so that whoever believes in him shall have eternal life. God is also said to be *agapē* in 1 John 4:8,16, and Paul lists *agapē* as one of the fruit of the Spirit in Galatians 5:22-23.

2: *phileō* (verb, Strong's #5368)

Unlike *agapaō* (see above), the verb *phileō* (also meaning "to love") is closer to intimate affection, which may relate to the fact that it can also mean "to kiss" (Matthew 26:48; Mark 14:44; Luke 22:47,48). Also, the first two times Jesus asked Peter if he loved him he used *agapaō* (John 21:15-16); the third time he used *phileō* (John 21:17). It could suggest an appeal of Jesus to Peter to cherish Jesus above all else.

Quotes

"There is no disguising the fact that this means goodness, patience, self-denial, humility, and the continual intervention of a far higher sort of love than Affection, in itself, can ever be. That is the whole point. If we try to live by Affection alone, Affection will 'go bad on us.'"

  —C.S. Lewis, *The Four Loves* (New York: Harcourt, Brace, 1988), 55.

"God, who needs nothing, loves into existence wholly superfluous creatures in order that He may love and perfect them. He creates the universe, already foreseeing—or should we say 'seeing'? There are no tenses in God—the buzzing cloud of flies about the cross, the flayed back pressed against the uneven stake, the nails driven through the mesial nerves, the repeated incipient suffocation as the body droops, the repeated torture of back and arms as it is time after time, for breath's sake, hitched up. If I may dare the biological image, God is a 'host'; who deliberately creates His own parasites; causes us to be that we may exploit and 'take advantage of' Him. Herein is love. This is the diagram of Love Himself, the inventor of all loves."

—C.S. Lewis, *The Four Loves* (New York: HarperCollins, 1960), 162-163.

"Selfless, forbearing, Christlike *agape-love* is the umbrella trait that encompasses all other virtues. If you truly love God and love others, you will be humble, gentle, patient, and forbearing with everyone around you."

—Michael Youssef, *Leading the Way Through Ephesians* (Eugene, OR: Harvest House Publishers, 2012), 67.

Mammon

"Mammon," *mamōnas*, is a Greek transliteration of an Aramaic word meaning "riches." Jesus said in Matthew 6:24, "No one can serve two masters. Either you will hate the one and love the other, or you will be devoted to the one and despise the other. You cannot serve both God and money." That last word, "money," translates *mamōnas*.

Definition

mamōnas (masculine noun, Strong's #3126)

This word occurs four times in the New Testament, and in all four instances Jesus personified it. Two times the NIV translates the term as "money" (Matthew 6:24; Luke 16:13), and in the other two, it renders the word as "worldly wealth" (Luke 16:9,11).

"We are all trying to let our mind or heart go their own way—centered on money or pleasure or ambition—and hoping, in spite of this, to behave honestly and chastely and humbly."

> —C.S. Lewis, *Mere Christianity* (New York: HarperCollins Publishers, 1980), 339.

Man

In the New Testament, the word for "man" that is only used of a male is *anēr*. The word *athrōpos* can refer to a male person, but is frequently used to refer to people regardless of sex (see *Humanity*).

Definition

anēr (masculine noun, Strong's #435)

This term never occurs with reference to the female sex—it occurs

   a. for man in distinction from woman (Acts 8:12; 1 Timothy 2:12) and as the term for "husband" (Matthew 1:16; John 4:16; Romans 7:2; Titus 1:6),

   b. for an adult as against a boy or infant male (1 Corinthians 13:11; Ephesians 4:13),

   c. in conjunction with an adjective or noun (as in "a sinful man" in Luke 5:8), and

   d. with the meaning "a man, a male person," as in Luke 8:41. It occurs in the plural with this meaning in Acts 6:11.

Marana-tha

Marana-tha is a Greek transliteration of an Aramaic expression used in 1 Corinthians 16:22. Paul likely used the Greek word *anathema* (meaning "cursed") and juxtaposed it with the Aramaic phrase *marana-tha*, which sounds similar. There is some debate as to precisely what this means. The NIV translates it this way: "Come, Lord!" This would break up the word as *marana-tha*.

Definition

marana-tha (a phrase used as an interjection, Strong's #3134)

This expression appears in 1 Corinthians 16:22 and is the Greek spelling for two Aramaic words, formerly supposed by some to be a curse (*anathema*) reinforced by a prayer (*marana-tha*). But this idea is contrary to its positive use in early Christian documents.

The first part (broken up as *maran*) may mean "Lord." As to the second part (broken up as *atha*), the apostolic fathers regarded it as a past tense: "has come." Modern scholars regard the first part consisting of *marana* (still meaning "Lord" or "O Lord") and the last part as consisting of *tha* ("come!"), and thus regard the phrase as an interjection: "O Lord, come!" It is also possible Paul used it in the sense previously mentioned ("the Lord has come").

As to the reason why it was used, most likely it was a current saying among early Christians, expressing their ultimate desire.

Master (see Lord, Master)

Melchizedek

The author of Hebrews argued that Jesus is a high priest, not in the order of Levi, but "in the order of Melchizedek" (see Psalm 110:4 and the discussion of Melchizedek in Hebrews 5:6,10; 6:20; 7:1,10,11,15,17). Melchizedek appeared as king of Salem (meaning "peace") who was also a priest of "God Most High," in Genesis 14:18-20. He brought out bread and wine for Abram, and blessed him, after Abram's successful rescue of his nephew Lot and his family from evil kings. The writer of Hebrews likely noticed the "bread and wine" imagery, which are also the components of communion (representing Jesus's body and blood), in addition to the reference to David's Lord as being "in the order of Melchizedek" in Psalm 110:4.

Definition

Melchisedek (masculine proper noun, Strong's #3198)

Melchisedek is the Greek transliteration of the Hebrew *Malki-Tzedeq*, literally "king of righteousness" (with the "s" sound made by the Greek letter *sigma* standing in for the Hebrew letter *tzade*, which makes a "tz" sound as in the English word *ritz*). The name originally appears after the story of Abram's rescue of Lot and his family from evil kings. When Abram returned, he was greeted by a man named Melchizedek:

> Then Melchizedek king of Salem brought out bread and wine. He was priest of God Most High, and he blessed Abram, saying, "Blessed be Abram by God Most High, Creator of heaven and earth, and praise be to God Most High, who delivered your enemies into your hand." Then Abram gave him a tenth of everything (Genesis 14:18-20).

In Psalm 110:4, the one David called his Lord (see verse 1) is said to be "a priest forever in the order of Melchizedek." Normally, priests were in the order of Levi, because they were descended from Aaron the Levite. But the author of Hebrews used the messianic statement in Psalm 110:4 to cast Jesus as the new high priest of believers (see Hebrews 5:6,10; 6:20; 7:1,10,11,15,17), since the Levitical priesthood could only atone for the sins of the people once a year with blood that was not theirs, whereas Jesus used his own blood once and for all to take away sins (Hebrews 9). The author of Hebrews used the figure of Melchizedek, who is both a priest and a king (and who notably gave Abram "bread and wine" and "blessed" him), to describe the kind of perpetual high priest Jesus is—because Melchizedek showed up in Genesis 14:18-20 "without father or mother, without genealogy, without beginning of days or end of life" and therefore "resembling the Son of God, he remains a priest forever" (Hebrews 7:3).

Messiah (see Christ)

Merciful, Mercy

Being "merciful" in the New Testament is about seeing a need and meeting it, thus showing compassion. It can be about God's merciful act of providing salvation to anyone who will believe, but can also refer to mercy shown among human beings, such as the Good Samaritan's act of mercy in helping the man who was beaten and left for dead (see Luke 10:25-37).

Definition

eleos (neuter noun, Strong's #1656)
As the outward manifestation of compassion or "mercy" toward one in need, *eleos* occurs in the New Testament with reference to

a. God, who is rich in mercy (Ephesians 2:4),

b. his mercy to those who fear him (Luke 1:50), and, because of this,

c. human mercy one to another (Matthew 9:13; 12:7; Luke 10:37; James 2:13).

Quotes

"Destitution does not demand or deserve; it pleads for mercy and looks for grace."

—John Piper, *Future Grace* (Colorado Springs, CO: Multnomah Books, 2001), 246.

"Who, after all, would invent a religion that commands us to give up our lives for one another, to overcome evil with good, to love our enemies, to turn the other cheek, to give our possessions to the poor, to be just and merciful?"

—Chuck Colson and Nancy Pearcey, *How Now Shall We
Live?* (Wheaton, IL: Tyndale House Publishers, 1999), 271.

Mina

A "mina" was a coin worth about one hundred denarii, or about a hundred day's wages.

Definition

mna (feminine noun, Strong's #3414)

Of the *mna* ("mina"), David E. Garland writes, "The mina in Luke is worth about one-sixtieth of a talent (= one hundred denarii)."[6] A denarius was worth one day's wage, so a mina would be worth a hundred day's wages. In the New Testament the mina appears only in Jesus's Parable of the Minas (Luke 19:11-27).

Minister, Ministry (see Servant, Service)

Miracle

A "miracle" in the New Testament is a mighty work (*dunamis*, the same word for "power"—see *Power*), done in supernatural strength—feats done by God. The word *sēmeion* ("sign") is also used of miracles, showing that they were "signs" of God's authority.

Definitions

1: *dunamis* (feminine noun, Strong's #1411)

Dunamis means "power, inherent ability" and is often used to denote a powerful work, as in a miracle (for example, Matthew 13:58; Acts 8:13; 19:11; 1 Corinthians 12:10,28,29; Galatians 3:5).

2: *sēmeion* (neuter noun, Strong's #4592)

Sēmeion means "sign," used of miracles and wonders as symbols of God's divine authority. The Pharisees, for example, asked Jesus for a miraculous sign, but Jesus responded that no sign would be given to them except the sign of Jonah (Matthew 12:38,39), a way of referring to his resurrection: "As Jonah was three days and three nights in the belly of a huge fish, so the Son of Man will be three days and three nights in the heart of the earth" (Matthew 12:40).

Money

"Money" features frequently in Jesus's parables. One needs money to survive. It can be given in a spirit of generosity to meet the needs of others, or given to God, but it can also be something that one serves instead of God (see *Mammon*).

Definitions

1: *argurion* (neuter noun, Strong's #694)

Meaning "a piece of silver," *argurion* denotes

    a. silver (for example, Acts 3:6),

    b. a silver coin, often in the plural, referring to pieces of silver (as in Matthew 26:15), and

    c. money in general (as in Matthew 25:18,27; 28:15; Mark 14:11; Luke 9:3).

2: *chrēma* (neuter noun, Strong's #5536)

Literally "a thing that one uses," it can refer to

    a. wealth or riches (Mark 10:23,24; Luke 18:24), or

    b. money (Acts 4:37; 8:18,20; 24:26).

Insight

The word for "love of money" or "miserliness" in the New Testament is a compound word, *philarguria* (*philia*, "love, friendship," with *argurion*, "money"). Its only occurrence is in 1 Timothy 6:10, which says, "The love of money is a root of all kinds of evil."

Quotes

"Why did Jesus say more about how we are to view and handle money and possessions than about any other topic—including both Heaven and Hell, and prayer and faith? Because God wants us to recognize the powerful relationship between our true spiritual condition and our attitude and actions concerning money and possessions."

    —Randy Alcorn, *Managing God's Money* (Carol Stream, IL: Tyndale House Publishers, 2011), 5.

"Money reveals one's moral commitment, one's spiritual life. It is a good index on your character and your spirituality."

—John MacArthur, "The Biblical View of Money, Part 4," 2 Corinthians 8–9, https://www.gty.org/library/sermons-library/47-54/the-biblical-view-of-money-part-4.

Mother

The most important "mother" in the New Testament is Mary, the mother of Jesus. She conceived Jesus by being overshadowed by the Holy Spirit. The word for "mother" can also refer to one who takes a motherly role in a person's life, and it can have metaphorical uses too, as in Paul writing, "The Jerusalem that is above is free, and she is our mother" (Galatians 4:26).

Definition

mētēr (feminine noun, Strong's #3384)

In the New Testament, this word refers to

a. the natural relationship (Matthew 1:18; 2 Timothy 1:5),

b. one who takes on the role of a mother (Matthew 12:49,50; Mark 3:34,35; John 19:27; Romans 16:13; 1 Timothy 5:2),

c. Paul's allegorical usage of the free spiritual and heavenly Jerusalem as "our mother" (Galatians 4:26), and

d. Babylon in a symbolic sense, as the source of religious adultery, that is, syncretism (Revelation 17:5).

Mountain

Jesus referred to faith that can move a "mountain." That was a figurative way of saying one can accomplish great things with faith (see Matthew 17:20). But "mountains" can be literal in the New Testament too, and can serve as places on which important events take place—for example, the Mount of Olives, on which Jesus delivered a discourse about future judgments and his return (see Mark 13).

Definition

oros (neuter noun, Strong's #3735)

The word *oros* ("mountain") is used

a. without specification (as in Luke 3:5; John 4:20),

b. of the Mount of Transfiguration (Matthew 17:1,9; Mark 9:2,9; Luke 9:28,37; 2 Peter 1:18),

c. of Zion (Hebrews 12:22; Revelation 14:1),

d. of Sinai (Acts 7:30,38; Galatians 4:24,25; Hebrews 8:5; 12:20),

e. of the Mount of Olives (Matthew 21:1; 24:3; Mark 11:1; 13:3; Luke 19:29,37; 22:39; John 8:1; Acts 1:12),

f. of the hill districts as distinct from the lowlands, especially of the hills above the Sea of Galilee (as in Matthew 5:1; 8:1; 18:12; Mark 5:5),

g. of other mountains to the east of the Jordan valley, in the land of Ammon, and in the region of Petra (Matthew 24:16; Mark 13:14; Luke 21:21),

h. proverbially, of overcoming difficulties or accomplishing great things (1 Corinthians 13:2; compare Matthew 17:20; 21:21; Mark 11:23), and

i. symbolically (Revelation 17:9).

Murder

The sixth of the Ten Commandments in the Old Testament says, "You shall not murder" (Exodus 20:13), but Jesus raised the stakes and said that even if a person is angry toward their brother or sister to the point of treating them with contempt, they will be subject to judgment or even in danger of the fire of hell (Matthew 5:21-22). James cited "murder" in his explanation of how stumbling at any point of the Law can cause one to become a law-breaker (James 2:10-11).

Definitions

1: *phonos* (masculine noun, Strong's #5408)

This word, often meaning "murder," is used

   a. of a special act (Mark 15:7; Luke 23:19,25),

   b. in the plural, of murders in general (Matthew 15:19; Mark 7:21; Revelation 9:21),

   c. in the singular (Romans 1:29),

   d. in the sense of slaughter (Acts 9:1; Hebrews 11:37).

2: *phoneuō* (verb, Strong's #5407)

Meaning "to murder," the verb *phoneuō* occurs twelve times in the New Testament in

   a. passages referencing the sixth commandment (Matthew 5:21; 19:18; Mark 10:19; Luke 18:20; Romans 13:9; James 2:11; compare Exodus 20:13),

   b. references to those who kill the prophets or the innocent (Matthew 23:31,35; James 5:6), and

   c. a verse about those who kill to get what they want (James 4:2).

3: *phoneus* (masculine noun, Strong's #5406)

The word for "murderer," *phoneus* only occurs seven times in the New

Testament—in a parable (Matthew 22:7), with reference to Barabbas (Acts 3:14), regarding those who "betrayed and murdered" Jesus (literally, "you were traitors and murderers"—Acts 7:52), when residents on the island of Malta supposed Paul to be an escaped murderer (Acts 28:4), in a warning from Peter not to suffer as a murderer (1 Peter 4:15), and twice in Revelation in a list of people in hell (Revelation 21:8; 22:15).

Mustard Seed

Jesus compared the kingdom of God to a "mustard seed" (for example, Mark 4:31), a tiny seed that grows into a large plant, well-known in the Middle East. Jesus's parable is about the growth of God's kingdom. Jesus also talked in hyperbolic passages like Matthew 17:20 about what can be accomplished through faith even the size of a mustard seed.

Definition

sinapi (neuter noun, Strong's #4615)

The NIV translates *sinapi*, a word of Egyptian origin, as "mustard seed" in the New Testament. The mustard was a familiar plant, with a very small seed (Matthew 17:20; Luke 17:6), sown in the earth, that produced a plant that grew bigger than garden herbs (Matthew 13:31-32), with large branches (Mark 4:31-32), attractive to birds (Luke 13:19—for the occurrence of *dendron* here with the translation "tree" in the NIV, see *Tree*).

Name

"Names" carry a lot of significance in the Bible. In Western culture, some care a great deal about the meaning of the names they pick for their children, while others pick names for aesthetic reasons or because they occur somewhere in their family. In the New Testament, Jesus and John the Baptist received their names because of specific instructions (see Matthew 1:21; Luke 1:13). The Hebrew for "Jesus" is *Yeshua*, "Yahweh is salvation," appearing in the New Testament as the Greek *Iēsous*. The Hebrew for John is *Yōchanan*, "Yahweh is gracious," appearing in the New Testament as the Greek *Iōannēs*. Acts 4:12 says that there is no "name" other than Jesus by which we must be saved.

Definition

onoma (neuter noun, Strong's #3686)

This word for "name" appears in the New Testament in three primary ways:

a. in general, regarding the "name" by which a person or thing is called (as in Matthew 1:21; Luke 1:13), and especially when the "name" represents the title and dignity of God himself (Hebrews 1:4),

b. relating to all that a name implies, as in authority, character, rank, power, and excellence (for example, Romans 15:9; 1 Timothy 6:1), and

c. where plural forms of *onoma* stand in for a group of people. See Acts 1:15, where *ochlos onamatōn* means literally "a crowd of names," translated by the NIV as "group." In Revelation 3:4 and 11:13, the NIV translates *onomata* ("names") as "people."

Narrow

In contrast to the wide gate and road, which lead to destruction, Jesus spoke of the "narrow" gate and road that lead to life; narrow because it is God's sole way for entrance into heaven, through faith in Christ, as opposed to the many ways contrived by people through works and self-righteousness (see Matthew 7:13-14; Luke 13:24).

Definitions

1: *stenos* (adjective, Strong's #4728)

Related to the words *stenazō* ("to groan") and *stenagmos* ("groaning"), *stenos* is used figuratively in Matthew 7:13,14 of the gate that provides the entrance to eternal life. It is "narrow" because taking it would be counter to natural inclinations, and "the way" is similarly characterized; so also in Luke 13:24.

2: *thlibō* (verb, Strong's #2346)

Meaning "to press," the verb *thlibō* is translated as "narrow" in Matthew 7:14 (literally, "narrowed"). The image is of being hemmed in, like in a mountain gorge. It is narrow because it is hard to pass through, whereas sin naturally leads one to want to go the easier way, which leads to destruction. For the related noun *thlipsis*, see *Tribulation*.

Quote

"To confess and testify to the truth as it is in Jesus, and at the same time to love the enemies of that truth, his enemies and ours, and to love them with the infinite love of Jesus Christ, is indeed a narrow way."

—Dietrich Bonhoeffer, *The Cost of Discipleship*, translated by R.H. Fuller, with some revision by Irmgard Booth (New York: Touchstone Rockefeller Center, 1995), 190.

Nation

In the New Testament, the same word translated "Gentile" (non-Jew) is the word also translated "nation." The Gentiles were "the nations," all the nations other than the Jewish people. But the Jews as the people of Israel nevertheless also constituted a "nation." In 1 Peter 2:9, Peter took the phrase "holy nation," used before for Israel as the chosen people (compare Deuteronomy 7:6), and applied it to believers in Jesus, not as a replacement of Israel, but in reference to Christians as the whole people of God.

Definition

ethnos (neuter noun, Strong's #1484)

Originally "a multitude," *ethnos* denotes

a. any nation or people (as in Matthew 24:7; Acts 10:35), including the Jewish people (as in Matthew 21:43; Luke 7:5; Acts 10:22), or

b. "the nations" as distinct from Israel when in the plural (as in Matthew 4:15; Romans 11:11; Galatians 2:8).

Quote

"When Jesus, with a solid Jewish pedigree, was recognized as the Messiah and his crucifixion and resurrection became definitive for salvation, it was hard for the Jews, who were the first Christians, to accept Gentiles into the family of faith. They eventually did accept them, but it was not easy going for the first Christian Gentiles."

> —Eugene Peterson, *Practice Resurrection: A Conversation on Growing up in Christ* (Grand Rapids, MI: Eerdmans, 2010), 120.

Nature

"Nature" in the New Testament is about the natural powers of a person or thing, what constitutes them, their birth or origin, or the natural order. For example, Paul talked about people committing acts that are "contrary to nature," in the sense of violating the natural way of things (Romans 1:26).

Definition

phusis (feminine noun, Strong's #5449)

From *phuō* ("to bring forth, produce"), this noun signifies

a. the nature, natural powers, or constitution of a person or thing (as in Ephesians 2:3; James 3:7; 2 Peter 1:4),

b. origin or birth (Romans 2:27), or

c. the natural or regular order of things (Romans 1:26; 2:14; 1 Corinthians 11:14; Galatians 4:8).

Neighbor

A "neighbor" (*plēsion*) in the New Testament is "one who is near," so a person's neighbor could be anyone. Jesus referred to the Old Testament directive to "love your neighbor as yourself" (Leviticus 19:18) as the second greatest commandment (see Mark 12:31).

Definition

plēsion (adverb treated as a noun, Strong's #4139)

This adverb, when treated as a noun, literally means "one who is near." It has a wider range of meaning than the English word "neighbor." There were no isolated farmhouses scattered over the agricultural areas of Palestine. The population gathered in villages and walked from place to place when they worked. So domestic life was touched at every point by a wide circle of "neighbors." Some examples of the aspects of being a neighbor were

a. the helpfulness of neighborliness (Luke 10:36; compare Proverbs 27:10),

b. the intimacy of a neighbor (Luke 15:6,9; Hebrews 8:11), and

c. its sincerity and sanctity (as in Romans 13:10; 15:2; compare Exodus 22:7,10; Proverbs 3:29).

The New Testament also quotes and expands on the command in Leviticus 19:18 to love one's neighbor as oneself (for example, Matthew 5:43; 19:19; 22:39; Mark 12:31,33; Luke 10:27; Galatians 5:14; James 2:8).

Insight

The Hebrew word for "neighbor" in Leviticus 19:18 is *rea'*, meaning "friend" or "companion."

New

The words for "new" in the New Testament (*kainos* and *neos*) refer to things that are unused and of a different nature than what came before (*kainos*), or new in terms of time—more recent (*neos*). For example, the "new" wine in texts like Matthew 9:17 is *neos*, of recent production. *Kainos* is used to refer to things like a "new covenant" (Matthew 26:28) or a "new creation" (2 Corinthians 5:17), with a "new" form or quality, different from what came before.

Definition

kainos (adjective, Strong's #2537)

This word denotes "new," that is, that which is unused, not necessarily things that are "new" in time but things that have a new form or quality to them, being of a different nature than what came before. New things that the gospel brings for present obedience and realization include

a. a new covenant (Matthew 26:28),

b. a new commandment (John 13:34), and

c. a new creation (Galatians 6:15; 2 Corinthians 5:17), among other things.

The new things to be received and enjoyed in the afterlife include

a. a new name for the believer (Revelation 2:17),

b. a new name by which God will be known (Revelation 3:12),

c. a new song (Revelation 5:9),

d. a new heaven and a new earth (Revelation 21:1),

e. the new Jerusalem (Revelation 3:12; 21:2), and

f. Jesus making all things new (Revelation 21:5).

Obey, Obedience

In Scripture, obedience is largely connected to listening. When God gives an instruction, we can obey by "hearing under," which is the literal meaning behind both the noun (*hupakoē*) and the verb (*hupokouō*). Through the obedience of Jesus, "many will be made righteous" (Romans 5:19).

Definitions

1: *hupakoē* (feminine noun, Strong's #5218)

The word for "obedience," the noun *hupakoē* (*hupo*, "under," *akouō*, "to hear"), is used of

a. obedience in general (Romans 6:16),

b. the fulfillment of apostolic counsels (2 Corinthians 7:15; 10:6; Philemon 1:21),

c. the fulfillment of God's claims or commands (Romans 1:5; 16:26),

d. obedience to Christ (2 Corinthians 10:5), and

e. Christ's obedience (Romans 5:19; Hebrews 5:8).

2: *hupakouō* (verb, Strong's #5219)

This verb means "to listen, attend" (as in Acts 12:13) and so "to submit, to obey." It is used of "obedience" to

a. God (Hebrews 5:9; 11:8),

b. Christ, by natural elements and impure spirits (Matthew 8:27; Mark 1:27; 4:41; Luke 8:25),

c. disciples of Christ (Luke 17:6),

d. the faith (Acts 6:7),

e. the gospel (Romans 10:16; 2 Thessalonians 1:8),

f. Christian doctrine (Romans 6:17),

g. apostolic commands (Philippians 2:12),

h. Abraham by Sarah (1 Peter 3:6),

i. parents by children (Ephesians 6:1; Colossians 3:20),

j. masters by servants (Ephesians 6:5; Colossians 3:22),

k. sin (Romans 6:12), and

l. righteousness (Romans 6:18).

Insight

The adjective *hupēkoos* (related to both words above) appears with reference to Jesus being obedient even to death on a cross in Philippians 2:8.

Old

The words for "old" in the New Testament (*archaios* and *palaios*) mean "original, ancient" (*archaios*), and "of what is of long duration, old in years" (*palaios*). The devil is called *archaios*, for example, in Revelation 12:9, and the believer's old self is *palaios* (advanced in years) because it is being superseded by the new self (Romans 6:6).

1: *archaios* (Strong's #744)

Meaning "original, ancient" (from *archē*, "beginning"), *archaios* is used of

    a. persons belonging to a former age (Matthew 5:21,33),

    b. time long gone by (Acts 15:21),

    c. days gone by in a person's experience (Acts 15:7),

    d. an early disciple (Acts 21:16),

    e. things that are old in relation to the new (2 Corinthians 5:17),

    f. the world (2 Peter 2:5), and

    g. the devil (Revelation 12:9; 20:2).

2: *palaios* (adjective, Strong's #3820)

Meaning "of what is of long duration, old in years," *palaios* is used of garments (Matthew 9:16; Mark 2:21; Luke 5:36), wine and wineskins (Matthew 9:17; Mark 2:22; Luke 5:37,39), and treasures of divine truth (Matthew 13:52). It references what belongs to the past, such as the believer's "old self," superseded by what is new (Romans 6:6; Ephesians 4:22; Colossians 3:9), and the "old covenant" of the Law (2 Corinthians 3:14). It also is used of leaven, a metaphor for moral evil (1 Corinthians 5:7,8), and an old commandment (1 John 2:7).

Orphan

"Orphan" or "fatherless person" appears twice in the New Testament (John 14:18; James 1:27).

orphanos (adjective, translated as a noun, Strong's #3737)

Orphanos is an adjective in the New Testament referring to fatherless or orphaned persons. Jesus promised his disciples he would not leave them "as orphans" (John 14:18), and James described "pure and faultless" religion as looking after orphans and widows in their distress (James 1:27).

Overcome (see Conquer)

P

Parable

A "parable" in the New Testament is a "placing beside," as if comparing things. The parables of Jesus are stories about things his hearers would understand, used to teach spiritual truths. One famous parable is that of the Good Samaritan, an illustration of who counts as a neighbor (Luke 10:25-37). Another concerns a self-righteous Pharisee and a repentant tax collector (Luke 18:9-14).

Definition

parabolē (feminine noun, Strong's #3850)

This word literally denotes "a placing beside," or "a placing of one thing beside another," with a view to comparison (though some consider that the idea of comparison is not necessarily contained in the word). In the New Testament, *parabolē* is found almost entirely in the Gospels, with its only other occurrence in Hebrews (9:9; 11:19). It is generally used of an utterance or narrative drawn from nature or human circumstances, the object of which is to teach a spiritual lesson (for example, see the ones in Matthew 13). Occasionally, it is used of a short saying or proverb (as in Matthew 15:15; Mark 3:23; 7:17; Luke 4:23; 5:36; 6:39). It is the lesson that is valuable; the hearers must catch the analogy to be instructed (this is also true of a proverb). Such a narrative or saying, speaking of earthly things for a spiritual meaning, is distinct from a fable, which attributes to things what does not belong to them in nature.

Jesus's parables most frequently convey truths connected with the subject of the kingdom of God. He withheld the meaning from his hearers (as he did from the multitudes in Matthew 13:34) as a divine judgment on the unworthy.

Insights

- Two dangers are to be avoided in seeking to interpret the "parables" in Scripture: that of ignoring the important features, and that of trying to make all the details mean something.

- The word *parabolē* is a common translation in the Septuagint used for the Hebrew word *mashal* (also translated as "proverb" in many contexts). The NIV translates *mashal* as "parable" in Ezekiel 24:3, and the Septuagint uses *parabolē*.

Quote

"Parables are...fictional narratives created by Jesus out of the cultural milieu of his day."

—Sam Tsang, *Right Parables, Wrong Perspectives* (Eugene, OR: Wipf & Stock Publishers, 2015), xi.

Passover

The "Passover" was a celebration in which the Jewish people would commemorate their exodus out of captivity in Egypt. During that celebration they would eat unleavened bread and sacrifice a spotless lamb, or similar unblemished animal, in commemoration of the night when the angel of death passed over their houses, which each had the blood of a spotless lamb on the doorposts (compare Exodus 12 with Deuteronomy 16:1-12). The Passover is important in the New Testament because Jesus's crucifixion took place during the Passover, and the Last Supper was a Passover meal. Also, Christ is literally called "our Passover" in 1 Corinthians 5:7, translated by the NIV as "our Passover lamb."

Definition

pascha (neuter noun, Strong's #3957)

Pascha is the Greek spelling of the Aramaic word for the "Passover," from the Hebrew *pasach*, "to pass over, to spare." It was a feast instituted by God in commemoration of the deliverance of Israel from Egypt, and anticipatory of the expiatory sacrifice of Christ. The word denotes the Passover feast (as in Matthew 26:2; John 2:13,23; 6:4; 11:55; 12:1; 13:1; 18:39; 19:14; Acts 12:4; Hebrews 11:28). It also refers to the Passover meal (Matthew 26:18; Mark 14:16; Luke 22:8,13), and the Passover lamb (as in Mark 14:12; compare Exodus 12:21; see also Luke 22:7). Finally, it is used about Christ himself (1 Corinthians 5:7).

Patience

"Patience" usually refers either to endurance (*hupomonē*) or longsuffering (*makrothumia*) in the New Testament. It is an attribute of God, as well as one he expects of humans toward one another. Patience also is one of the fruit of the Spirit that Paul listed in Galatians 5:22-23.

Definitions

1: *hupomonē* (feminine noun, Strong's #5281)

Literally "an abiding under" (*hupo*, "under," *menō*, "to abide"), *hupomonē* is almost invariably translated as "patience." Patience that grows in trial may become endurance (James 1:3). Many trials further the gospel (2 Corinthians 6:4; 12:12; 2 Timothy 3:10). Some trials may be viewed as chastisement from God (Hebrews 12:7). This kind of patience, endurance, is said to perfect Christian character (James 1:4).

2: *makrothumia* (feminine noun, Strong's #3115)

Translated as "forbearance, patience, longsuffering" (*makros*, "long," *thumos*, "temper"), *makrothumia* is the character quality that, for example, would allow someone to not get angry quickly (Romans 2:4; 9:22; 2 Corinthians 6:6; Galatians 5:22; Ephesians 4:2; Colossians 1:11; 3:12; 1 Timothy 1:16; 2 Timothy 3:10; 4:2; 1 Peter 3:20; 2 Peter 3:15; Hebrews 6:12; James 5:10).

Quotes

"There is no disguising the fact that this means goodness, patience, self-denial, humility, and the continual intervention of a far higher sort of love than Affection, in itself, can ever be. That is the whole point. If we try to live by Affection alone, Affection will 'go bad on us.'"

> —C.S. Lewis, *The Four Loves* (New York: Harcourt, Brace, 1988), 55.

"God is…patient. He puts up with our interruptions; he backtracks and fills us in on the old stories; he repeats the vital information."

> —Eugene Peterson, *Run with the Horses: The Quest for Life at Its Best* (Downers Grove, IL: InterVarsity Press, 2009), 40.

Peace

"Peace" (*eirēnē*) in the New Testament has to do with harmonious relationships. It corresponds with the Hebrew word *shalōm* ("peace, wholeness").

Definition

eirēnē (feminine noun, Strong's #1515)

This word, meaning "peace," corresponding with the Hebrew *shalōm* ("peace, wholeness"), occurs in every book of the New Testament except 1 John. It describes

a. harmonious relationships between people (Matthew 10:34; Romans 14:19),

b. harmony between nations (Luke 14:32; Acts 12:20; Revelation 6:4),

c. friendliness (Acts 15:33; 1 Corinthians 16:11; Hebrews 11:31),

d. freedom from being hurt or bothered (Luke 11:21; 19:42; Acts 9:31),

e. order at the state level (Acts 24:2), and in churches (1 Corinthians 14:33),

f. the harmonized relationships between God and humans, accomplished through the gospel (Acts 10:36; Ephesians 2:17), and

g. the sense of contentment (Matthew 10:13; Mark 5:34; Luke 1:79; 2:29; John 14:27; Romans 1:7; 3:17; 8:6).

Quotes

"God will have his Eden. He is creating a garden in which Adams and Eves will share in his likeness and love, at peace with each other, animals, and nature."

>—Max Lucado, *You'll Get Through This: Hope and Help for Your Turbulent Times* (Philadelphia, PA: Running Press, 2015), 17.

"Just as the resurrection of Jesus opened up the unexpected world of God's new creation, so the Spirit comes to us from that new world, the world waiting to be born, the world in which, according to the old prophets, peace and justice will flourish and the wolf and the lamb will lie down side by side."

>—N.T. Wright, *Simply Christian: Why Christianity Makes Sense* (New York: HarperCollins Publishers, 2006), 124.

Perfect

The idea of being "perfect" (*teleios*) in the New Testament is not about absolute perfection, but more like "completeness" or "maturity." So being "perfect" as your heavenly Father is perfect (Matthew 5:48) is to be complete in your maturity.

Definition

teleios (adjective, Strong's #5046)

Referring to being "perfect" in the sense of completion or maturity, *teleios* shows up in Matthew 5:48 with respect to being complete (in the sense of being mature, with good character) just as God is, reminiscent of being holy as God is holy (Leviticus 19:2). It is used in Romans 12:2 to refer to God's "perfect" (that is, complete) will. In 1 Corinthians 2:6, it refers to those who are perfect in the sense of being "mature." These are the usual senses of the term.

Perseverance (see Patience)

Persecute

To "persecute" someone in the New Testament often means to harass them, though sometimes the verb *diōkō* can mean to cause hindrance, suffering, or harm to them because of their identity or beliefs. Among the people Jesus pronounced blessed in his beatitudes were those persecuted because of righteousness or because of him (Matthew 5:10-11).

Definition

diōkō (verb, Strong's #1377)

This verb has the meanings

a. "to put to flight, drive away" and

b. "to pursue," which is where the meaning "to persecute" comes
   from (see Matthew 5:10-12,44; 10:23; 23:34; Luke 11:49; Acts
   9:4,5; Galatians 1:13,23; Philippians 3:6).

Pharisee

The "Pharisees" were a sect in Judaism that believed in the resurrection of the
dead and in angels and spirits (Acts 23:8). They were well trained in matters of the Law and the Prophets, and some of them held seats on the Sanhedrin (see *Sanhedrin*). Jesus frequently held them to a very high standard
(as in Matthew 23), as they purported to be experts in the Law and teachers of Israel.

Definition

Pharisaios (masculine noun, Strong's #5330)

The term *Pharisaios*, from an Aramiac word meaning "to separate," was
applied to a sect with a different manner of life from that of the general
public. The "Pharisees" and Sadducees appeared as distinct parties in the latter half of the second century BC, though they represented tendencies that
could be found much earlier in Jewish history, tendencies which became
pronounced after the return from Babylon (537 BC). The immediate pre-
decessors of the two parties were, respectively, the Hasideans and the Hellenizers. The latter, precursors of the Sadducees, aimed at removing Judaism
from its narrowness and sharing in the advantages of Greek life and culture.
The Hasideans (from a transcription of the Hebrew *chasidim*, "pious ones")
were a society of men zealous for religion, who acted under the guidance of
the scribes, in opposition to the secular Hellenizing party. Among the Jews,

the Hellenizers were a political faction, while the Hasideans, whose fundamental principle was complete separation from non-Jewish elements, were the strictly legal party, and were ultimately more popular and influential. For many of them, their zeal for the Law led them to almost deify it, and their attitude became merely external, formal, and mechanical. They laid stress upon the formal correctness of an action, and not upon its righteousness. So much of the opposition of the Pharisees to Jesus was inevitable. His manner of life and teaching was essentially a condemnation of theirs, which is why he denounced them (for example, Matthew 6:2,5,16; 15:7,12-14).

Insight

The Pharisees were not all bad. Hypocrisy was not a requirement for becoming a Pharisee. They had hope in the resurrection of the dead (Acts 23:8), unlike the Sadducees, even though many Pharisees and Sadducees alike did not believe in Jesus's resurrection. Nicodemus was a Pharisee, but after coming to Jesus at night to find out more about him (see John 3), he once stood up for Jesus (John 7:50-51) and helped Joseph of Arimathea, probably also a Pharisee, bury Jesus's body (John 19:39). There was also Rabbi Gamaliel, a respected Pharisee who stood up for the apostles when many members of the Sanhedrin wanted to put them to death (Acts 5:34-39). Paul, trained by Gamaliel (Acts 22:3), was also a Pharisee and remained one long after he believed in Jesus, appealing to the Pharisees on the Sanhedrin regarding his hope in the resurrection of the dead (Acts 23:6). In Philippians he regarded his prestigious education and status as a Pharisee to be loss in comparison to knowing Christ (Philippians 3:5,7).

Pitch a Tent (see Tent, Pitch a Tent)

Poor

"Poor" in the New Testament refers to those who had very little money or resources, if any at all. They are frequently the subjects of commands to assist them. People can also be "poor" metaphorically, as in the "poor in spirit" (Matthew 5:3).

Definition

ptōchos (adjective, Strong's #4434)

This word, broadly meaning "poor," occurs in the New Testament

a. literally (such as in Matthew 11:5; 26:9,11; Luke 21:3; John 12:5,6,8; 13:29; James 2:2,3,6), being the constant subjects in the New Testament of commands to assist them (Matthew 19:21; Mark 10:21; Luke 14:13,21; 18:22; Romans 15:26; Galatians 2:10), and

b. metaphorically, in a positive sense (Matthew 5:3; Luke 6:20), and a negative sense (Revelation 3:17).

Pour

The word for "pouring" has several uses in the New Testament, including to refer to a pouring out of the Holy Spirit (as in Acts 2), or of divine wrath (as in Revelation 16), or the shedding of the blood of Jesus.

Definition

ekcheō (verb, Strong's #1632)

Meaning "to pour out" (*ek*, "out"), is used of

a. Christ's action with the changers' money (John 2:15),

b. the Holy Spirit (Acts 2:17,18,33; Titus 3:6),

c. the emptying of the contents of the divine wrath (Revelation 16:1, 4,8,10,12,17),

d. the shedding of the blood of saints by the enemies of God (Revelation 16:6), and

e. the shedding of the blood of Christ, using the alternate form *ekchunnō* (Luke 22:20).

Power

"Power" in the New Testament is about might and authority. *Dunamis* is used more for the idea of "might" (and is sometimes translated "miracle"— see *Miracle*). *Exousia* has more to do with the "authority" aspect of power (see *Authority*).

Definitions

1: *dunamis* (feminine noun, Strong's #1411)

This word, one use of which can generally refer to "power," occurs in the New Testament with reference to

a. God (Matthew 22.19; Mark 14:62),

b. angels (Ephesians 1:21),

c. Christ as a manifestation of God's power (1 Corinthians 1:24),

d. the gospel as a manifestion of God's power (Romans 1:16), and

e. mighty works, or miracles (for example, Mark 6:5).

2: *exousia* (feminine noun, Strong's #1849)

This word denotes "freedom of action, right to act, authority." As used of God, it is absolute, unrestricted (as in Luke 12:5). In Acts 1:7, the unrestricted right to bring an end to history is indicated. Angelic beings are sometimes called *exousias*, "authorities" (Ephesians 3:10; 6:12; Colossians 2:15).

Prayer

Generally, "prayer" is simply talking to God. But in the New Testament, "prayer" can range from thanksgiving to humbly asking God for something. Two of the most common words for prayer in the New Testament are the verb *proseuchomai* and the noun *proseuchē*.

Definitions

1: *proseuchomai* (verb, Strong's #4336)

Meaning "to pray," *proseuchomai* is the most frequent word for prayer in the New Testament. It denotes prayer to God, especially in the Synoptic Gospels and Acts (see also Romans 8:26; Ephesians 6:18; Philippians 1:9; 1 Timothy 2:8; Hebrews 13:18; Jude 1:20).

2: *proseuchē* (feminine noun, Strong's #4335)

Related to *proseuchomai*, the noun *proseuchē* denotes

a. prayer to God, the most frequent noun in this respect (for example, Matthew 21:22; Luke 6:12; Ephesians 6:18; Philippians 4:6), and

b. a "place of prayer," in this case, outside the city wall by a river (Acts 16:13,16).

Quotes

"God foreordains the means as well as the end, and our prayer is foreordained as the means whereby he brings his sovereign will to pass."

> —J.I. Packer, *Concise Theology: A Guide to Historic Christian Beliefs* (Carol Stream, IL: Tyndale House Publishers, 1993), 189.

"We don't have to leave our marriages to chance. We can fight for them in prayer and not give up, because as long as we are praying, there is hope."

> —Stormie Omartian, *The Power of a Praying Wife* (Eugene, OR: Harvest House Publishers, 2014), 19-20.

Preach, Preaching

In the New Testament, "preaching" or "proclamation" usually has to do with preaching the gospel. Jesus said, "this gospel of the kingdom will be preached in the whole world as a testimony to all nations, and then the end will come" (Matthew 24:14).

Definitions

1: *euaggelizō* (verb, Strong's #2097)
Related to the noun *euangelion* (see *Gospel*), the verb *euangelizō* ("to evangelize, to preach the good news") is almost always used of the "good news" or "gospel" concerning the Son of God (as in Luke 1:19; 1 Thessalonians 1:8; see also Acts 13:32; Romans 10:15; Hebrews 4:2).

2: *kērussō* (verb, Strong's #2784)
Related to the noun *kērugma* (neuter noun, Strong's #2782), the verb *kērussō* means

a. "to proclaim" (for example, Matthew 3:1; Mark 1:45; Luke 4:19; 12:3; Acts 10:37; Romans 2:21; Revelation 5:2), and

b. "to preach the gospel" (for example, Matthew 24:14; Mark 13:10; Romans 10:14; 1 Corinthians 15:11,12; 1 Timothy 3:16).

Priest

A "priest" (*hiereus*) is someone who is able to offer sacrifices. A "high priest" (*archiereus*), particularly one so designated by the Levitical order, could represent the whole Israelite people (Leviticus 4:13-20). Duties of the high priest are detailed in Hebrews (5:1-4; 8:3; 9:7,25). According to Hebrews, Jesus is said to be a perpetual high priest in the order of Melchizedek, superior to the temporal high priests in the order of Levi (see *Melchizedek*). High priests mentioned in the New Testament include Annas and Caiaphas (see Luke 3:2).

Definitions

1: *hiereus* (masculine noun, Strong's #2409)

Meaning "one who offers sacrifice and has the charge of such things," *hiereus* is used of

a. a priest of the pagan god Zeus (Acts 14:13),

b. Jewish priests (as in Matthew 8:4; 12:4,5; Luke 1:5; John 1:19; Hebrews 8:4), and

c. believers (Revelation 1:6; 5:10; 20:6).

The Aaronic priesthood had its purpose until the time of Jesus, who is the new perpetual high priest.

2: *archiereus* (masculine noun, Strong's #749)

A word meaning "high priest," one of the Levitical order, *archiereus* can also mean "chief priest," as in a priest who would represent the whole people of Israel (Leviticus 4:13-20). Examples of high priests in the New Testament include Annas and Caiaphas (Luke 3:2). Duties of a high priest are detailed in Hebrews (5:1-4; 8:3; 9:7,25). They were responsible for offering sacrifices once a year, to make atonement both for their own sins and for the sins of the people.

Jesus, however, says the author of Hebrews, is the new high priest (Hebrews 4:15; 5:5,10; 6:20; 7:26; 8:1,3), the one who takes away sin once and for all. He was able to do this because he was without sin and offered up his body. His priesthood is not in the order of Levi (like human high priests) but in the order of Melchizedek (Hebrews 5:10).

Prophet

In the New Testament the "prophets" are often referred to as those who were killed because the people of Israel didn't want to hear their message, which was from God and directed at the people. Jesus referred to himself as a prophet (Matthew 13:57; Mark 6:4). Many times Jesus or a New Testament author referred to the prophetic books of the Old Testament (such as Isaiah) to make a point about a prophecy being fulfilled.

Definition

prophētēs (masculine noun, Strong's #4396)

A *prophētēs* is "one who speaks out or openly," one upon whom the Spirit of God rested (Numbers 11:29). In the case of the Old Testament prophets, their messages were very largely the proclamation of the divine purposes of judgment, salvation, and glory to be accomplished in the future.

In the New Testament, the word is used of

a. the Old Testament prophets (as in Matthew 5:12; Luke 4:27; Romans 11:3),

b. the prophets in general (such as Matthew 10:41; 21:46; Mark 6:4),

c. John the Baptist (Matthew 21:26; Luke 1:76),

d. prophets in the churches (as in Acts 13:1; 15:32; 21:10; Ephesians 2:20; 3:5; 4:11),

e. Christ as a prophet that was promised (examples include John 1:21; 6:14; 7:40),

f. two witnesses to be raised up for special purposes (Revelation 11:10,18),

g. the Cretan poet Epimenides (Titus 1:12), and

h. the writings of the prophets (as in Luke 24:27).

Propitiation (see Atonement)

Psalm

In the original Hebrew text of Psalms, the book was entitled "Praises," and rabbis often called it "The Book of Praises." The noun *psalm* comes from a Greek verb that refers to "the plucking of strings," which implies an association with music—which is why some have called the Psalms "Israel's hymnbook."

Definition

psalmos (masculine noun, Strong's #5568)

Primarily referring to "a sacred song, sung to musical accompaniment, a psalm," *psalmos* occurs in the New Testament with reference to

a. the Old Testament book of Psalms (Luke 20:42; 24:44; Acts 1:20),

b. a particular psalm (Acts 13:33), and

c. psalms in general (1 Corinthians 14:26; Ephesians 5:19; Colossians 3:16).

Queen

The word for "queen" appears a few times in the New Testament, referring to the queen of Sheba, the queen of the Ethiopians, and (in Revelation) Babylon the Great, the symbol for a corrupt empire.

Definition

basilissa (feminine noun, Strong's #938)

The noun for "queen," *basilissa*, occurs four times in the New Testament. Twice it occurs as the "Queen of the South" (Matthew 12:42; Luke 11:31), a reference to the queen of Sheba (1 Kings 10:1), once of the queen of Ethiopia (Acts 8:27), and once in reference to Babylon the Great, the symbol of a corrupt empire (Revelation 18:7; compare Isaiah 47:7,8).

Rabbi

A "rabbi" in New Testament times was a Jewish teacher. It is the word used by the teacher's followers as a term of respect. Literally, *rabbi* means "my master."

Definition

rabbi (masculine noun, Strong's #4461)

Meaning "my master," *rabbi* comes from the Hebrew word *rav* (meaning "master"). When a suffix is added, it becomes *rabbi* ("my master"). In the New Testament the word is used as a courteous title of address. People frequently addressed Jesus as "Rabbi" (Matthew 26:25,49; Mark 9:5; 11:21; 14:45; John 1:38,49; 3:2; 4:31; 6:25; 9:2; 11:8). There is also a synonymous word, *rabbouni* ("Rabboni"), explained by John with the Greek word *didaskale*, a form of address in Greek meaning "Teacher" (see John 20:16; see also Mark 10:51, where the NIV translates *rabbouni* as "Rabbi").

Ransom (see Redemption)

Reconcile, Reconciliation

A prominent verb for "reconciling" in the New Testament, *katallassō* means "changing, exchanging" and therefore "to change from enmity to friendship." This word and those related to it (such as the noun *katallagē*) are used primarily in reference to God restoring his relationship to humans.

Definitions

1: *katallassō* (verb, Strong's #2644)

This verb properly denotes "to change, exchange" (especially with respect to money), so in the New Testament it means "to change from enmity to friendship, to reconcile." With regard to the relationship between God and humanity, the use of this and related words shows that God is the primary force for reconciliation, exercising his grace toward sinful humanity on the basis of the death of Christ (2 Corinthians 5:19). Romans 5:10 expresses this in another way: "If, while we were still God's enemies, we were reconciled to him through the death of his Son, how much more, having been reconciled, shall we be saved through his life!"

2: *katallagē* (feminine noun, Strong's #2643)

Related to *katallassō* (see above), the noun *katallagē* means primarily "an exchange," but in the New Testament translates to "reconciliation," a change on the part of one party (humans, with respect to their former estranged relationship to God), caused by an action on the part of another (God, with respect to sending his Son as an atoning sacrifice for sin). The word occurs four times in the New Testament. The first time it occurs it refers to the reconciliation experienced by believers who accept God's atoning sacrifice (Romans 5:11). The second time, Paul noted that those of his Jewish kin who rejected Jesus at the cross ended up causing this reconciliation to be available to the world, and he longed for his fellow Jews to accept this reconciliation for themselves as well (Romans 11:15). The last two times it occurs are in 2 Corinthians, where Paul wrote of a "ministry of reconciliation" believers have received (2 Corinthians 5:18,19)—that is, because believers have been reconciled to God, they have a "ministry" (or "service" or "duty"—see *Servant, Service*) toward calling others to repentance and therefore reconciliation.

Quotes

"The cross exposes the futility of our self-righteousness; it reminds us that we are sinners, incapable of bringing about our own reconciliation with God. Before the cross we can only stand with bowed heads and a broken spirit."

—Erwin W. Lutzer, *Cries from the Cross* (Chicago: Moody Publishers, 2015), 16.

"God is the consummate forgiver. And we depend every day on His ongoing forgiveness for our sins. The least we can do is emulate His forgiveness in our dealings with one another."

—John MacArthur, *The Freedom and Power of Forgiveness* (Wheaton, IL: Crossway Books, 2019), 10.

Redeem, Redemption

"Redemption" in the New Testament has the connotation of being purchased or released, as in a ransom situation. Words for this include *exagorazō*, a strengthened form of *agorazō* ("to buy"), with the sense of purchasing a slave with a view to the slave's freedom. The verb *lutroō* and its corresponding noun *lutrōsis* ("redemption"), have to do with "a releasing on payment of a ransom." The word *apolutrōsis* means "deliverance," or, more specifically, releasing upon satisfactory payment. These terms are used of God "redeeming" humans, purchasing them by paying their ransom.

Definitions

1: *exagorazō* (verb, Strong's #1805)

As a strengthened form of *agorazō* ("to buy"), the verb *exagorazō* denotes "to buy out," especially in the sense of purchasing a slave with a view to the slave's freedom. It is used metaphorically with reference to

a. the deliverance by Christ of Christian Jews from the Law's curse (Galatians 3:13; 4:5), and

b. meaning "to buy up for oneself" (see Ephesians 5:16; see also Colossians 4:5).

2: *lutroō* (verb, Strong's #3084)

This verb means "to release on receipt of ransom," and can occur

a. in the natural sense of delivering, as in setting Israel free from Roman oppression (Luke 24:21), and

b. in a spiritual sense, relating to the work of Christ in redeeming people from lawlessness (Titus 2:14), and in the sense of redeeming people from an "empty way of life" (1 Peter 1:18).

3: *lutrōsis* (feminine noun, Strong's #3085)

This noun means "a redemption," similar in meaning to the verb *lutroō* (see above). In the New Testament it occurs three times and is used

a. in the general sense of deliverance, such as that of the nation of Israel (Luke 1:68; 2:38), and

b. regarding the redemptive work of Christ (Hebrews 9:12), which brings about deliverance from the guilt and power of sin.

4: *apolutrōsis* (feminine noun, Strong's #629)

A strengthened form of *lutrōsis* (see above), *apolutrōsis* means "a releasing on payment of ransom."

It occurs with reference to

a. deliverance from physical torture (Hebrews 11:35),

b. the deliverance of the people of God at the coming of Christ, with his glorified saints "in a cloud with power and great glory" (Luke 21:27-28),

c. redemption as the result of atonement and forgiveness of sins (Romans 3:24; Ephesians 1:7; Colossians 1:14; Hebrews 9:15), and

d. the deliverance of the believer from the presence and power of sin, and of the body of the believer to corruption, at the second coming (Romans 8:23; 1 Corinthians 1:30; Ephesians 1:14; 4:30).

Quotes

"God called Israel, so that through Israel he might redeem the world; but Israel itself needs redeeming as well. Hence God comes to Israel riding on a donkey, in fulfillment of Zechariah's prophecy of the coming peaceful kingdom, announcing judgment on the system and the city that have turned their vocation in upon themselves and going off to take the weight of the world's evil and hostility onto himself, so that by dying under them he might exhaust their power."

—N.T. Wright, *Simply Jesus* (New York: HarperCollins Publishers, 2011), 38-39.

"How rich is God?...Everything that exists belongs to him. And when he gave the infinitely precious blood of Jesus to redeem us from death, he truly gave according to his infinite riches."

—Michael Youssef, *Leading the Way Through Ephesians* (Eugene, OR: Harvest House Publishers, 2012), 21.

Rejoice (see Joy)

Repent, Repentance

Repentance is a "perceiving afterwards," a changing of the mind. It involves a turning from sin and moving toward faith and good deeds. Jesus began preaching repentance in Matthew 4:17.

Definitions

1: *metanoeō* (verb, Strong's #3340)

This verb literally refers to a "perceiving afterwards" (*meta*, "after," implying change, and *noeō*, "to perceive"—compare *nous*, "mind, seat of moral reflection"). Therefore, it means "to change one's mind or purpose," always in the New Testament of a change for the better, and always with repentance from sin. The word occurs in the Synoptic Gospels (in Luke, nine times), five times in Acts, and twelve times in Revelation. One famous instance is in Matthew 4:17, when Jesus first called people to repentance, in that Gospel.

2: *metanoia* (feminine noun, Strong's #3341)

This noun generally has the same meaning as its related verb (see above). In the New Testament, it usually means "to turn from sin," a change of mind that involves both a turning from sin and a turning to God. In the New Testament, it is

a. the requirement by God on the part of humans (as in Matthew 3:8; Luke 3:8; Acts 20:21; 26:20), and

b. the mercy of God in giving repentance or leading people to it (as in Acts 5:31; 11:18; Romans 2:4; 2 Timothy 2:25).

Quotes

"To confess our sins is to say the same thing as God says about them. Confessing our sins therefore means acknowledging that God's perspective of our transgressions is correct."

> —John MacArthur, *The Freedom and Power of Forgiveness*
> (Wheaton, IL: Crossway Books, 2009), 71.

"Sin always leads to pollution, disintegration, and perversion, and what is worse, it hinders our fellowship with God...In short, the remedy is confession (1 John 1:9) and learning to walk in the Spirit...thankfully, Jesus bore the penalty of our sins and His blood cleanses our conscience and gives us hope and purpose, and we're spared the eternal consequences."

> —Erwin W. Lutzer, "Sin Confessed and Unconfessed,"
> Moody Church Media, https://www.moodymedia.org/
> articles/sin-confessed-and-unconfessed/.

Resurrection

"Resurrection" (*anastasis*) in the New Testament is a "raising up" or "rising," literally a "standing up." Jesus's resurrection is central to the New Testament; without it, our faith is in vain (1 Corinthians 15:14). The New Testament also refers to a general "resurrection" of the dead at the end of days (as in Acts 23:6), with theological roots in Daniel 12:2.

Definition

anastasis (feminine noun, Strong's #386)

The noun *anastasis* means "a raising up" or "rising" (*ana*, "up," and *histēmi*, "to stand"—so literally, "a standing up"). This word can refer to

    a. Jesus's resurrection (Acts 1:22; 2:31; 4:33; Romans 1:4; 6:5; Philippians 3:10; 1 Peter 1:3; 3:21),

b. the resurrection of those who are Christ's at his second coming (1 Corinthians 15:21,42),

c. the resurrection of the rest of the dead after the millennium (John 5:29; compare Revelation 20:5),

d. those raised in more immediate connection with Christ's resurrection (Acts 26:23; Romans 1:4),

e. resurrection spoken of in general terms (Matthew 22:23; Mark 12:18; Luke 20:27; Acts 4:2; Hebrews 6:2), and

f. those who were raised in Old Testament times, to die again (Hebrews 11:35).

Quotes

"Just as the resurrection of Jesus opened up the unexpected world of God's new creation, so the Spirit comes to us from that new world, the world waiting to be born, the world in which, according to the old prophets, peace and justice will flourish and the wolf and the lamb will lie down side by side."

—N.T. Wright, *Simply Christian: Why Christianity Makes Sense* (New York: HarperCollins Publishers, 2006), 124.

"The site of Jesus's tomb was known to both Christian and Jew alike, so it could have been checked by skeptics. In fact, nobody, not even the Roman authorities or Jewish leaders, ever claimed that the tomb still contained Jesus's body. Instead they were forced to invent the absurd story that the disciples, despite having no motive or opportunity, had stolen the body—a theory that not even the most skeptical critic believes today."

—Lee Strobel, *The Case for Christ: A Journalist's Personal Investigation of the Evidence for Jesus* (Grand Rapids, MI: Zondervan, 1998), 263.

Reward

The word for "reward" in the New Testament primarily refers to wages, and then also to the granting of other good or valuable things. Jesus said that those who are persecuted because of him will receive a great reward in heaven (Matthew 5:12).

Definition

misthos (masculine noun, Strong's #3408)

This word primarily denotes "wages, hire," and then generally "reward," that which is

a. received in this life (Matthew 5:46; 6:2,5,16; Romans 4:4; 1 Corinthians 9:17,18), or of evil "rewards" (Acts 1:18), and

b. wages to be received after death (Matthew 5:12; 10:41,42; Mark 9:41; Luke 6:23,35; 1 Corinthians 3:8,14; 2 John 1:8; Revelation 11:18; 22:12).

Rich

The New Testament uses several words related to wealth or riches. One of them, the adjective *plousios*, often used as a noun, is used many times to speak of spiritual riches. One can be "rich" literally or metaphorically; for example, God is said to be "rich" in mercy (Ephesians 2:4). Wealth is also said to be transitory; it will one day be gone (see James 1:10-11).

Definition

plousios (adjective, Strong's #4145)

This word, meaning "rich," is used in the New Testament

a. literally, as an adjective (Matthew 27:57; Luke 12:16; 14:12;

16:1,19) or as a noun, as in a rich man or rich men (such as Matthew 19:23,24; Mark 10:25; 12:41; Luke 16:21,22; 18:25; James 1:10,11; Revelation 6:15; 13:16), and

b. metaphorically, of God's richness in his mercy (Ephesians 2:4) or of Christ (2 Corinthians 8:9), or of believers (James 2:5; Revelation 2:9; 3:17).

Righteousness

"Righteousness" (*dikaiosunē*) is a multifaceted concept in the New Testament. The Greek word can simply refer to the "righteousness" expected of humans (Matthew 5:6; Romans 6:13). It can also refer to justice (Romans 3:26), or to the "righteousness" God offers believers, in the sense of justification (Romans 5:17).

Definition

dikaiosunē (feminine noun, Strong's #1343)

Meaning "the character or quality of being right or just," *dikaiosunē* expresses an attribute of God (as in Romans 3:5), the context of which shows that *dikaiosunē theou* ("the righteousness of God") means essentially the same thing as God's faithfulness—in other words, that which is consistent with God's own nature and promises. Romans 3:25,26 speaks of his righteousness as exhibited in the death of Christ.

Dikaiosunē also denotes right action (as in Matthew 5:6,10,20; John 16:8,10; James 1:20; 3:18; 2 Peter 1:1). Paul used the word this way (Romans 6; Ephesians 6:14), but usually he used it as related to justification, teaching that the person who trusts in Christ "might become the righteousness of God," or justified by God.

Rule

There are many words that can be translated as "rule" in the New Testament. One of them is *poimainō* (meaning "to act as a shepherd"—see *Shepherd*).

Definition

poimainō (verb, Strong's #4165)

Primarily meaning "to act as a shepherd, tend or feed flocks," *poimainō* is translated with the meaning "to rule" three times of its eleven occurrences (Revelation 2:26; 12:5; 19:15).

Sacrifice

"Sacrifices" were important in the Old Testament as offerings either to false deities or to God himself. The atonement offering, thank offering, and other offerings expressed devotion and obedience to the Lord. In the New Testament, the idea is important regarding Jesus's death on the cross as a "sacrifice" for sin. There were other uses of the word also, such as when Paul told believers to offer their bodies as living "sacrifices," holy and pleasing to God (Romans 12:1-2). As for "atoning sacrifice," that is the NIV's way of rendering the word *hilastērion*, meaning "atonement" (see *Atonement*).

Definitions

1: *thusia* (feminine noun, Strong's #2378)

This word primarily denotes an "act of offering," and then "that which is offered." It is used of

a. idolatrous sacrifice (Acts 7:41),

b. animal or other sacrifices, as offered under the Law (Matthew 9:13; 12:7; Mark 12:33; Luke 2:24; 13:1; Acts 7:42; 1 Corinthians 10:18; Hebrews 5:1; 7:27; 8:3; 9:9; 10:1,5,8,11),

   c. Christ, in his sacrifice on the cross (Ephesians 5:2; Hebrews 9:23,26; 10:26), and

   d. various metaphorical uses (Romans 12:1; Philippians 2:17; 4:18; Hebrews 13:15,16; 1 Peter 2:5).

2: *thuō* (verb, Strong's #2380)

This verb is used of "sacrificing by slaying a victim," and it is used with respect to

   a. the sacrifice of Christ (1 Corinthians 5:7),

   b. the Passover sacrifice (Mark 14:12; Luke 22:7), and

   c. idolatrous sacrifices (Acts 14:13,18).

3: *prosphora* (feminine noun, Strong's #4376)

Literally, "a bringing to," *prosphora* denotes a sacrificial "offering" in the New Testament. It is used of

   a. Christ's sacrifice (Ephesians 5:2; Hebrews 10:10,14,18),

   b. offerings under or according to the law (Acts 21:26; Hebrews 10:5,8),

   c. gifts in kind conveyed to needy Jews (Acts 24:17), and

   d. the presentation of believers themselves, saved from among the Gentiles to God (Romans 15:16).

4: *prospherō* (verb, Strong's #4374)

Primarily, this word means "to bring to" or "to offer." It refers to

   a. the sacrifice of Christ himself (Hebrews 8:3) and with respect to his status as high priest (Hebrews 9:14,25,28; 10:12),

   b. offerings under or according to the Law (Matthew 8:4; Mark 1:44; Acts 7:42; 21:26),

   c. offerings prior to the Law (Hebrews 11:4,17),

   d. gifts offered to Christ (Matthew 2:11),

e. prayers offered by Christ (Hebrews 5:7),

f. vinegar offered to him on the cross (Luke 23:36),

g. the slaughter of the disciples by persecutors, who think they are "offering" service to God (John 16:2), and

h. money "offered" by Simon the sorcerer (Acts 8:18).

Quotes

"One life is forfeit; another life is sacrificed instead."

—John Stott, *The Cross of Christ* (Downers Grove, IL: Inter-Varsity Press, 2006), 138, speaking of the atonement.

"Jesus loved us sacrificially, which is why he was willing to come to earth, live with us, and give himself up as our perfect sacrifice. The incarnation—God taking the form of a human—also enabled Jesus to experience what we have experienced and be there for us with an affirming love. Christ demonstrated real love for us, and he wants to love others that way through us. When we accept God's sacrificial and affirming love and in turn love others with this same sacrificial and affirming love, we are living out the truth of Christ's real love."

—Josh McDowell and Sean McDowell, *Sacrifice—Experience a Deeper Way to Love* (Eugene, OR: Harvest House Publishers, 2012), 56.

"When I read in the Bible that these sins separated me from God, who is holy and morally pure, this resonated as being true. Certainly God, whose existence I had denied for years, seemed extremely distant, and it became obvious to me that I needed the cross of Jesus to bridge that gulf."

—Lee Strobel, *The Case for Christ: A Journalist's Personal Investigation of the Evidence for Jesus* (Grand Rapids, MI: Zondervan, 1998), 268.

Sadducee

The "Sadducees" were a Jewish sect more secular than the Pharisees—they didn't believe in the supernatural, including the resurrection of the dead (which, for the Pharisees, was probably based on Daniel 12:2), and only believed in the first five books of the Bible. They also rejected the oral law that was upheld by the Pharisees.

Definition

Saddoukaios (masculine noun, Strong's #4523)

Related to the Hebrew word *tzᵉdakah*, "righteousness," *Saddoukaios* referred to the Jewish party of the "Sadducees," which was far more secular in character than the Pharisees (see *Pharisees*). They denied the resurrection of the dead and did not believe in angels or spirits, which Paul knew and was able to take advantage of when he declared himself a Pharisee on trial for his belief in the resurrection of the dead (Matthew 22:23; Mark 12:18; Luke 20:27; Acts 23:6-8; compare Daniel 12:2). Because of this denial of the resurrection of the dead, and because they only believed in the first five books of the Bible (the Mosaic Law), the Sadducees at one point posed a riddle to Jesus involving a legal matter, which, from their perspective, created a logical problem for the idea of the resurrection (Matthew 22:23-33; Mark 12:18-27; Luke 20:27-40). Jesus was not intimidated by their debate tactic and pointed out that God is not a God of the dead but of the living (Matthew 22:32; Mark 12:27; Luke 20:38), a direct response to their lack of belief in the resurrection at the end of the world. In Jesus's time the Sadducees held a monopoly on functions related to the priesthood and the temple. In his commentary, Grant R. Osborne points out, "The chief priests were mostly Sadducees, while the teachers of the law were mostly Pharisees."[7]

Salvation (see Save, Salvation)

Samaritan

Many Jews of Jesus's day looked down on the people group known as the "Samaritans" (from Samaria) because they had different religious beliefs, disagreed about where to worship, and were often considered untrustworthy. Nevertheless, Jesus associated with a Samaritan woman despite the cultural taboo (John 4:9), and featured a Samaritan as the hero of his parable about loving one's neighbor (Luke 10:25-37).

Definition

Samaritēs (masculine noun, Strong's #4541)

The Jews of Jesus's day often considered the "Samaritans" to be like halfbreeds, believing their religious practices were corrupted by non-Jewish sources. Wherever they came from, it is clear the Samaritans had their own understanding of where to worship the God of Israel.[8] Despite racial and religious hostility between Jews and Samaritans, Jesus, a Jewish man, associated with a Samaritan woman (John 4:9). On the Samaritan belief in a different place of worship than that of the Jews, Jesus said that one day those who worship the Father would worship him in "the Spirit and in truth" (John 4:20-24). Many Jews of Jesus's day would never have expected a Samaritan to be made the hero of a parable, but Jesus did exactly that in his famous story about loving one's neighbor as oneself, regardless of who it is that does the helping or who it is that needs the help (Luke 10:25-37). Luke mentioned that the one leper who came back to thank Jesus for healing happened to be a Samaritan (Luke 17:16). Perhaps because of Jesus's conversation with the Samaritan woman, her realization that he was a prophet, her testimony to the other Samaritans, and the reception Jesus received among them (John 4:39-40), some Jews revealed their prejudices and accused Jesus of being a Samaritan, as well as demon-possessed (John 8:48).

Quotes

"The Samaritan [in the parable of Luke 10:25-37] had the capacity for universal altruism. He had a piercing insight into that which is beyond the external accidents of race, religion, and nationality. One of the great tragedies of man's long trek along the highway of history has been the limiting of neighborly concern to tribe, race, class, or nation."

—Martin Luther King Jr., "On Being a Good Neighbor," page 3, The King Center, accessed July 3, 2017, http://www.thekingcenter.org/archive/document/being-good-neighbor-0.

"Jesus addressed both the attitude and the inquiry of the law expert using the parable [in Luke 10:25-37]. Right from the start of this account, the law expert thought that he was qualified to judge Jesus, but in asking the law expert to identify with the victim, Jesus showed the law expert to be helpless, much like the victim of the robbery. His neighbor might even appear to be the least likely candidate, his imaginary enemy the Samaritan, but his arrogance would keep him from seeing the possibility."

—Sam Tsang, *Right Parables, Wrong Perspectives* (Eugene, OR: Wipf & Stock, 2015), 34.

Sanhedrin

The "Sanhedrin" was a governing body in Judea during the time of Jesus, composed of Jewish religious leaders, many of them Pharisees and Sadducees. Acts 5:21 defined it as "the full assembly of the elders of Israel." It was the Sanhedrin that condemned Jesus and handed him over to the Romans. Members of the Sanhedrin were also often at variance with the apostles. But some members of this governing body, including a few of the Pharisees, dissented from the Sanhedrin's plans against Jesus and, later, their plans against the apostles (see *Pharisee*). The word for "Sanhedrin," however, could also refer to any deliberating session of persons.

Definition

sunedrion (neuter noun, Strong's #4892)

The literal meaning of *sunedrion* is "a sitting together" (*sun*, "together," *hedra*, "a seat"); its biblical uses refer to

a. any assembly or session of persons deliberating or adjusting, as in the Septuagint's translation of Psalm 26:4; Proverbs 22:10; Jeremiah 15:17. In the New Testament, examples include Matthew 10:17; Mark 13:9. But in particular, *sunedrion* refers to

b. the "Sanhedrin" itself, the great council at Jerusalem, which consisted of possibly 71 members, prominent members of the families of the high priest, elders, and scribes. Jewish sources trace the origin of this to Numbers 11:16. The more important causes came up before this council. The Roman rulers of Judea allowed them to try such cases, and even to pronounce sentence of death, with the condition that such a sentence would be valid only if confirmed by the Roman procurator. In Matthew 5:22, Jesus said that anyone who says a mean word to a brother or sister "is answerable to the court," the *sunedrion*, possibly meaning the actual "Sanhedrin." It is also the Sanhedrin that was "looking for false evidence against Jesus so that they could put him to death" (Matthew 26:59). And "the apostles were brought in and made to appear before the Sanhedrin to be questioned by the high priest" because they were preaching in Jesus's name, against the orders of this body (Acts 5:27). Paul also was brought before the Sanhedrin (Acts 22:30–23:10). Not all members of the Sanhedrin were out to condemn Jesus's followers, however—Gamaliel, a respected member, warned the others to be careful as to what they did to the apostles, lest they find themselves fighting against God (Acts 5:33-39).

"It's a bit ironic that the burial of Jesus should be conducted, not by those who had boasted they would never leave, but by two members of the Sanhedrin—two representatives of the religious group that killed the Messiah."

—Max Lucado, *God Came Near: No Wonder They Call Him the Savior* (Sisters, OR: Multnomah Publishers, 1986), 92.

"That the Jewish authorities would condemn Jesus of blasphemy...flows not from his claim to be Messiah but from his loftier claim to be Daniel's exalted Son of Man coming on the clouds of heaven."

—Craig L. Blomberg, *The Historical Reliability of the New Testament: Countering the Challenges to Evangelical Christian Beliefs* (Nashville, TN: B&H Academic, 2016), 144-145.

Satan (see Devil)

Save, Salvation

"Salvation" in the New Testament primarily refers to God's rescue of human beings through Christ's atoning death on the cross. That Christ has been raised also gives hope for the rest of his followers that they too will be raised on the last day—otherwise, their faith is in vain (see 1 Corinthians 15:17). It is only through Jesus that we can be saved (Acts 4:12), and this comes by faith, by declaring Jesus is Lord, and believing that God raised him from the dead (Romans 10:9-10).

1: *sōzō* (verb, Strong's #4982)

Meaning "to save," the verb *sōzō*, like its related noun *sōtēria* (see below), can be used with reference to

a. material and temporal deliverance from danger, suffering, or even sickness, in which cases it can mean "save," "heal," "deliver," or "rescue" (Matthew 8:25; 9:22; Mark 5:34; 13:20; Luke 8:48; 23:35; James 5:15; etc.),

b. the spiritual and eternal salvation granted immediately by God to those who believe in Jesus (as in Acts 2:47; Romans 8:24; Ephesians 2:5,8; etc.),

c. the present experience of God's power to deliver believers from the bondage of sin (Matthew 1:21; Romans 5:10; 1 Corinthians 15:2; Hebrews 7:25; James 1:21),

d. future deliverance of believers at the second coming of Christ (for example, Romans 5:9),

e. the deliverance of "all Israel" (Romans 11:26), and

f. other instances pertaining to God's saving of persons, including the giving of blessings to those who are saved (as in Luke 19:10; John 10:9; 1 Corinthians 10:33; 1 Timothy 1:15).

2: *sōtēria* (feminine noun, Strong's #4991)

This word denotes "deliverance, preservation, salvation." It is used in the New Testament with reference to

a. material and temporal deliverance from danger (Luke 1:69,71; Acts 27:34; 7:25; Philippians 1:19; Hebrews 11:7),

b. spiritual and eternal deliverance granted immediately to those who accept his conditions of repentance and faith in the Lord Jesus, in whom alone it is to be obtained (Acts 4:12), and upon confessing him as Lord (Romans 10:9-10; see also Romans 1:16; Ephesians 1:13),

c. the present experience of God's power to deliver from bondage to sin (Philippians 2:12),

d. future deliverance at the second coming of Christ (Romans 13:11; 1 Thessalonians 5:8,9), and

e. other instances involving salvation given from God to humans, such as all the blessings given to humans by him (2 Corinthians 6:2; Hebrews 5:9; 1 Peter 1:9,10; Jude 1:3).

Insight

The Septuagint also uses this word to translate the Hebrew word *shalōm* ("peace"), as in Genesis 26:31 (see *Peace*).

Quotes

"Why was it that God 'did not spare his own Son, but gave him up for all' (Rom 8:32)? Because of his grace. It was his own free decision to save which brought the atonement."

> —J.I. Packer, *Knowing God* (Downers Grove, IL: InterVarsity Press, 1993), 133-134.

"When the devil throws our sins up to us and declares that we deserve death and hell, we ought to speak thus: 'I admit that I deserve death and hell. What of it? Does this mean I shall be sentenced to eternal damnation? By no means. For I know One who suffered and made satisfaction in my behalf. His name is Jesus Christ, the Son of God. Where he is, there I shall be also!'"

> —Martin Luther *Letters of Spiritual Counsel*, trans. and ed. Theodore G. Tappert (Vancouver, BC: Regent College, 2003), 86-87.

"For those who have received the most precious gift of Christ's redeeming blood...you have reason to look forward to the glories of Heaven, for you will be perfected, you will be joyful, you will once again be active, and right *now* you can be certain that you are *nearing home*."

> —Billy Graham, *Nearing Home: Life, Faith, and Finishing Well* (Nashville, TN: Thomas Nelson, 2011), 180.

Scribe

The Jewish "scribes" in the time of Jesus were often connected with the Pharisees (Luke 5:21, "teachers of the law" in NIV) and chief priests (Luke 9:22). The scribes would teach the Law, develop it, and use it in connection with the Sanhedrin and various local courts. They spent much time studying the Old Testament Scriptures. But they, like the Pharisees, were often hypocrites and self-righteous, and therefore received many stern rebukes from Jesus (see Matthew 23).

Definition

grammateus (masculine noun, Strong's #1122)

From *gramma* ("letter of the alphabet, writing"), this term means "a scribe, a man of letters, a teacher of the law." The "scribes" or "teachers of the law" are mentioned frequently in the Synoptic Gospels, particularly in connection with the Pharisees (Matthew 23; Luke 5:21) and sometimes the chief priests (Matthew 2:4; Mark 8:31; 10:33; 11:18,27; Luke 9:22). John's Gospel mentions them only once (John 8:3). They are mentioned three times in Acts (4:5; 6:12; 23:9) and elsewhere only in 1 Corinthians 1:20. They were considered qualified to teach in the synagogues (Mark 1:22).

Life under the scribes could be a burden. Like the Pharisees, the "scribes" or "teachers of the law," as Jesus said, "tie up heavy, cumbersome loads and put them on other people's shoulders, but they themselves are not willing to lift a finger to move them" (Matthew 23:4). In this regard, instead of helping with true moral and spiritual life (as they were supposed to do), the scribes often prevented true access to God (Luke 11:52).

Insight

Jesus was harder on the scribes than he was on the Pharisees and Sadducees, because of their pastoral responsibilities in being experts in, and teachers of, the Scriptures.

Scripture

To the people in the New Testament and its authors, the "Scriptures" consisted of the Old Testament, as it was only the Old Testament that was complete at that time. The New Testament was still being written. The "Scriptures" were frequently quoted as having been fulfilled in Jesus, and Paul used them to argue for his point about God crediting righteousness to people through faith (see, for example, Galatians 3:6, where Paul quoted Genesis 15:6).

Definition

graphē (feminine noun, Strong's #1124)

This word primarily means "a drawing, painting," and then "a writing." It refers to

a. the Old Testament Scriptures as a whole (as in Matthew 21:42; 22:29; John 5:39; Acts 17:11; 18:24; Romans 1:2), or to a single Old Testament reference (as in Mark 12:10; Romans 4:3; Galatians 3:8,22), and

b. the Old Testament Scriptures and any existing New Testament text at the time (see below) as "God-breathed" or "inspired" Scripture (2 Timothy 3:16). Of course, Christians today can interpret 2 Timothy 3:16 as pertaining to the New Testament as well as the Old (as could any Christians who lived after the New Testament canon was completed).

Insight

First Timothy 5:18 seems to quote Luke 10:7. That might show that at least that part of what we now know as the New Testament was considered "Scripture" by another New Testament author.

"Because the Bible is *God's Word*, it has *eternal relevance*; it speaks to all humankind, in every age and in every culture."

> —Gordon D. Fee and Douglas Stuart, *How to Read the Bible for All Its Worth* (Grand Rapids, MI: Zondervan, 2003), 21.

"But in Scripture itself God's purpose is not just to save human beings, but to renew the whole world."

> —N.T. Wright, *Scripture and the Authority of God* (New York: HarperCollins Publishers, 2011), 27.

"Eventually I dared to venture into those 'other parts' of the Bible. The strange and confusing parts. Whenever I read a chapter that didn't make sense, which was often, I'd write it out. With each word, with each line, I said it out loud. And I asked the Holy Spirit to teach me the truth of God's Word."

> —Denise J. Hughes, *Word Writers®—Ephesians: Experience the Bible...Writing Word by Word* (Eugene, OR: Harvest House Publishers, 2016), 9.

Seed

The New Testament refers to "seed" in the natural or botanical sense, but also in terms of the offspring of humans, even distant descendants. Paul in Galatians 3:16 interpreted the singular use of "seed" in Genesis 17:19 (translated "descendants" by the NIV) as referring to one "seed" or descendent in particular, namely, Christ (see Galatians 3:19).

sperma (neuter noun, Strong's #4690)

Related to *speirō* ("to sow, plant a seed"), the noun *sperma* has the following usages:

a. agricultural and botanical (for example, Matthew 13:24,27,32; 1 Corinthians 15:38; 2 Corinthians 9:10),

b. physiological (Hebrews 11:11),

c. metaphorical in the sense of natural offspring (Matthew 22:24,25; Romans 1:3; Paul's reference to Christ as the "seed" of Abraham in Galatians 3:16,19; Hebrews 2:16; Revelation 12:17), and

d. metaphorical in the sense of spiritual offspring (Romans 4:16,18; 9:8; Galatians 3:29).

Quote

"Faith is like a seed, planted in the earth, which grows into a plant. This familiar image, found in many of the parables of the kingdom, points to the dynamic nature of the Christian life."

—Alister McGrath, *Knowing Christ* (New York: Doubleday, 2002), 195.

Self-control

Self-control (*enkrateia*), literally meaning "strength inside" (*en*, "in," *krateia*, "strength") is about the ability to control oneself, one's own person. Paul listed it as one of the fruit of the Spirit in Galatians 5:22-23.

Definition

egkrateia (feminine noun, Strong's #1466)

Literally meaning "strength inside," *egkrateia* ("self-control") is about the ability to control ourselves despite what we may want to do or feel. The term occurs only four times in the New Testament. Paul talked about this in front of Felix in Acts 24:25. He also mentioned it in his list of the fruit of the Spirit in Galatians 5:22-23. It occurs twice in 2 Peter 1:6.

Quote

"Refuse to 'live by the sword.' When threatened with the loss of someone or something that we value, we can become enraged at the perpetrator and resort to acts of aggression. If we don't develop a more effective way of dealing with such threats, we will become victims of our own aggression."

—Deborah Smith Pegues, *30 Days to Taming Your Anger:
How to Find Peace When Irritated, Frustrated, or Infuriated*
(Eugene, OR: Harvest House Publishers, 2013), 47.

Servant, Service

"Service" (or "ministry") is a very important concept in the New Testament. Jesus said in Mark 10:43 that whoever wants to become great among his disciples must be a "servant." Jesus also said that whoever wants to be greatest or first must be a "slave" (*doulos*—see Matthew 20:27; see also *Slave*). The word translated "servant" (*diakonos*) is also the word for "deacon" (1 Timothy 3:8,12) and "minister" (1 Timothy 4:6). Paul spoke of the *diakonia* ("service" or "ministry") of reconciliation given to believers in 2 Corinthians 5:18.

Definitions

1: *diakonia* (feminine noun, Strong's #1248)
Referring to "the office and work of a *diakonos* or 'minister,'" this word denotes "service," "ministry," and refers to

a. household duties (Luke 10:40), and

b. religious and spiritual work, such as

   i. apostolic ministry (Acts 1:25; 6:4; 12:25; 21:19; Romans 11:13),

   ii. the ministry of believers in general (Acts 6:1; Romans 12:7; 1 Corinthians 12:5),

   iii. the ministry of the Holy Spirit in the gospel (2 Corinthians 3:8), and

   iv. the ministries of righteousness (2 Corinthians 3:9) and reconciliation (2 Corinthians 5:18).

2: *diakonos* (masculine noun, Strong's #1249)

This word primarily denotes a "servant," whether as one doing work in servitude or as an attendant rendering free service. The word is probably connected with the verb *diōkō*, "to hasten after, pursue" (but not in *diōkō*'s other sense of "to persecute"). It occurs in the New Testament with reference to

a. household servants (John 2:5,9),

b. the civil ruler (Romans 13:4),

c. Christ (Romans 15:8; Galatians 2:17 NASB),

d. the followers of Christ in relation to their Lord (John 12:26; Ephesians 6:21; Colossians 1:7; 4:7), and to each other (Matthew 23:11; Mark 9:35; 10:43), and

e. to the servants of Christ in preaching, teaching, and other functions in churches (Romans 16:1; 1 Corinthians 3:5; 2 Corinthians 3:6; 6:4; 11:23; Ephesians 3:7; Philippians 1:1; etc.).

f. Once *diakonos* is used where angels seem to be intended (Matthew 22:13).

The main difference between *diakonos* and *doulos* ("a bondservant, slave") is that a *diakonos* is a servant primarily in relationship to their work, while a *doulos* is primarily defined in relation to their master.

A *diakonos* can also be understood as a "minister" or "deacon" (for example, 2 Corinthians 3:6; 6:4; 11:15; Ephesians 6:21; 1 Thessalonians 3:2; 1 Timothy 3:8,12; 4:6).

Quote

"Reliable servants. They're the binding of the Bible. Their acts are rarely recited and their names are rarely mentioned. Yet were it not for their loyal devotion to God, many great events would never have occurred."

—Max Lucado, *God Came Near: No Wonder They Call Him the Savior* (Sisters, OR: Multnomah Publishers, 1986), 112.

Sexual Immorality

The general word for "sexual immorality," *porneia*, is fairly comprehensive in covering sinful sexual acts. It is used literally with reference to immoral sexual acts (such as in 1 Corinthians 6:13,18), and metaphorically for idolatry, in Revelation.

Definition

porneia (feminine noun, Strong's #4202)

This word is used

a. of immoral sexual intercourse (John 8:41; Acts 15:20,29; 21:25; 1 Corinthians 5:1; 6:13,18; 7:2; 2 Corinthians 12:21; Galatians 5:19; Ephesians 5:3; Colossians 3:5; 1 Thessalonians 4:3; Revelation 2:21; 9:21). In Matthew 5:27 and 19:9, it stands for or includes adultery, though it is distinguished from adultery in Matthew 15:19 (see also Mark 7:21). It is also used

b. metaphorically, in referring to pagan idolatry (Revelation 14:8; 17:2,4; 18:3; 19:2). This may also be the sense in Revelation 2:21, as it may be about syncretism in Christian faith.

Quotes

"The trouble is that the modern world, like much of the ancient one, has come to regard what is sometimes called an active sex life as not only the norm but something nobody in his or her right mind does without. The only question is, what particular forms of sexual activity do you find exciting, fulfilling, or life-enhancing? The early and normative Christian tradition...stands out at this point against the normal approach of paganism ancient and modern and utters a vehement no."

—N.T. Wright, *Simply Christian: Why Christianity Makes Sense* (New York: HarperCollins, 2006), 231.

"In a group of men and women who are struggling with sexual addiction you would not find them sharing how much they really enjoyed sex (unlike overeaters). But everyone there would assume sexuality is pleasurable—and a good and great thing to have if managed properly. The problem is the misuse of a good thing."

—David Eckman, *Sex, Food, and God: Breaking Free from Temptations, Compulsions, and Addictions* (Eugene, OR: Harvest House Publishers, 2006), 18.

Sheep

Isaiah 53:6 says, "We all like sheep have gone astray; each of us has turned to our own way, and the LORD has laid on him the iniquity of us all." In the New Testament as well, the imagery of "sheep" is used to describe wayward persons who need to be herded by Jesus, the "good shepherd" who "lays down his life for the sheep" (John 10:11—see *Shepherd*).

Definition

probaton (neuter noun, Strong's #4263)

Among the Greeks this word was used of small cattle, sheep, and goats. In the New Testament, it refers to "sheep" only. It is used

a. naturally (as in Matthew 12:11,12),

b. metaphorically,

    i. of those who belong to the Lord,

    ii. of the lost sheep of the house of Israel (Matthew 10:6),

    iii. of those under the care of Jesus, the good shepherd (John 10:1-27; see also Matthew 26:31; Hebrews 13:20),

    iv. of those who in the future judgment will be shown to have been kind to his brothers and sisters (Matthew 25:33), or

    v. with reference to the clothing of false shepherds (Matthew 7:15), and

c. comparatively, as in relation to

    i. Christ (Acts 8:32),

    ii. the disciples (Matthew 10:16),

    iii. true followers of Christ in general (Romans 8:36),

    iv. the former wayward condition of those who had come under his care (1 Peter 2:25), or

    v. the multitudes who sought the help of Christ in the days of his flesh (Matthew 9:36; Mark 6:34).

The word can also be used to denote "a little sheep," as it occurs in the plural in John 21:16,17.

Quotes

"Most of the images of Jesus's teaching drew upon the common experience of Jews living in the first century: shepherd and sheep, sower and seed, wine and wineskins, master and servants."

—Chuck Swindoll, *Jesus: The Greatest Life of All* (Nashville, TN: Thomas Nelson, 2008), 144.

"Sheep rarely last long without a shepherd. They easily fall prey to wolves. They wander and become hopelessly lost, and they cannot see twenty feet beyond their noses. Isn't this a picture of mankind—a straying flock that possesses similar characteristics? Sheep need a deliverer. Jesus is our eternal Deliverer."

—Billy Graham, *Where I Am: Heaven, Eternity, and Our Life Beyond* (Nashville, TN: Thomas Nelson, 2015), 13.

Shepherd

A "shepherd" tends a flock of sheep. Jesus referred to himself as the "good shepherd" who looks after his sheep (John 10:1-27). Jesus is also referred to as a "shepherd" to whom lost sheep return. When reinstating Peter, Jesus asked him to feed (that is, "shepherd" or care for) his sheep (John 21:15-17), thus asking Peter to be a pastor to Jesus's followers.

Definitions

1: *poimēn* (masculine noun, Strong's #4166)

The noun *poimēn* ("shepherd") is used

   a. in its natural sense, referring to one whose job it is to tend sheep (Matthew 9:36; 25:32; Mark 6:34; Luke 2:8,15,18,20; John 10:2,12),

   b. metaphorically, of Christ (Matthew 26:31; Mark 14:27; John 10:11,14,16; Hebrews 13:20; 1 Peter 2:25), and

   c. metaphorically, of those who act as pastors in churches (Ephesians 4:11).

2: *poimainō* (verb, Strong's #4165)

This verb means "to act as a shepherd" (from *poimēn*, "a shepherd"—see above), and is used

a. literally (as in Luke 17:7; 1 Corinthians 9:7), and

b. metaphorically, of Christ (Matthew 2:6), of those who are to act as spiritual shepherds under him (John 21:16; 1 Peter 5:2; Acts 20:28), and of those who wrongly act as predatory shepherds who "feed only themselves" (Jude 1:12).

3: *boskō* (verb, Strong's #1006)

This verb means "to feed" (primarily with reference to a herdsman feeding his herd). Its uses are

a. literal (Matthew 8:30,33; Mark 5:11,14; Luke 8:34; 15:15), and

b. metaphorical, of a spiritual ministry (John 21:15,17).

Quote

"Who is the active one? Who is in charge? The shepherd. The shepherd selects the trail and prepares the pasture. The sheep's job—our job—is to watch the shepherd. With our eyes on our Shepherd, we'll be able to get some sleep."

—Max Lucado, *Safe in the Shepherd's Arms: Hope and Encouragement from Psalm 23* (Nashville, TN: J. Countryman, 2002), 28.

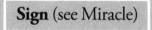

Sign (see Miracle)

Sin

"Sin" is "missing the mark" of being in right relationship with God. We have all sinned and fallen short of God's glory (Romans 3:23). It is what separates people from God. Jesus dealt with sin on the cross so that those who believe in him can have eternal life.

Definitions

1: *hamartia* (feminine noun, Strong's #266)

This noun depicts, literally, "a missing of the mark," but this etymological meaning is largely lost sight of in the New Testament. *Harmartia* is the most comprehensive term for moral error or failure. It is used of "sin" as

  a. a principle or source of action, or an inward element producing acts (Romans 3:9; 5:12,13,20; 6:1,2; 7:7,8; see also 7:9,11,13),

  b. a governing principle or power (Romans 6:6; 5:21; 6:12,14,17; 7:11,14,17,20,23,25; 8:2; 1 Corinthians 15:56; Hebrews 3:13; 11:25; 12:4; James 1:15),

  c. a generic term, distinct from specific terms such as *hamartēma* yet sometimes inclusive of concrete wrongdoing, such as in John 8:21,34,46; 9:41; 15:22,24; 19:11 (in Romans 8:3, "God [sent] His own Son in the likeness of sinful flesh"; that final phrase is literally, "flesh of sin"; where "flesh" stands for the body, the instrument of indwelling "sin"), and

  d. a sinful deed, an act of "sin" (Matthew 12:31; Acts 7:60; James 1:15; 2:9; 4:17; 5:15,20; 1 John 5:16).

2: *hamartēma* (neuter noun, Strong's #265)

This word, akin to *hamartia*, denotes "an act of disobedience to Divine law." It is translated as plural in Mark 3:28; Romans 3:25; and 2 Peter 1:9; and as singular in Mark 3:29 (some manuscripts have *krisis*, "condemnation"); see also 1 Corinthians 6:18.

3: *anamartētos* (adjective, Strong's #361)

This means "without sin" and is found in John 8:7. In the Septuagint, see Deuteronomy 29:19.

4: *hamartanō* (verb, Strong's #264)

Literally, "to miss the mark," it is used in the New Testament of "sinning"

  a. against God

       i. by angels (2 Peter 2:4),

ii. by man (Matthew 27:4; Luke 15:18,21; see also Ephesians 4:26; 1 Timothy 5:20; Titus 3:11; Hebrews 3:17; 10:26; 1 John 1:10; 2:1; 3:6,8,9),

b. against Christ (1 Corinthians 8:12),

c. against man:

i. a brother (Matthew 18:15,21; Luke 17:3,4; 1 Corinthians 8:12),

ii. against the father by the Prodigal Son (Luke 15:18,21),

d. against Jewish law, the temple, and Caesar (Acts 25:8),

e. against one's own body, by fornication (1 Corinthians 6:18), and

f. against earthly masters by servants (1 Peter 2:20).

5: *proamartanō* (verb, Strong's #4258)

This verb means "to sin previously" (*pro*, "before"), and occurs in 2 Corinthians 12:21; 13:2.

Quotes

"Instead of following Christ, let the Christian enjoy the consolations of his grace! That is what we mean by cheap grace, the grace which amounts to the justification of sin without the justification of the repentant sinner who departs from sin and from whom sin departs. Cheap grace is not the kind of forgiveness of sin which frees us from the toils of sin."

> —Dietrich Bonhoeffer, *The Cost of Discipleship* (New York: SCM Press, 1995), 44.

"When the devil throws our sins up to us and declares that we deserve death and hell, we ought to speak thus: 'I admit that I deserve death and hell. What of it? Does this mean I shall be sentenced to eternal damnation? By no means. For I know One who suffered and made satisfaction in my behalf. His name is Jesus Christ, the Son of God. Where he is, there I shall be also!'"

> —Martin Luther, *Letters of Spiritual Counsel*, trans. and ed. Theodore G. Tappert (Vancouver, BC: Regent College, 2003), 86-87.

Sister (see Brother)

Slave

A "slave" (*doulos*) in the New Testament is a bondservant, someone in subjection to another, often in a master/slave relationship. Paul called himself a *doulos* of Jesus Christ (Romans 1:1), as did James (James 1:1). In both of those instances, the NIV uses the translation "servant." Paul also commanded "slaves" to obey their masters, and for masters to treat their slaves well (Ephesians 6:5-9).

Definition

doulos (adjective used as a noun, Strong's #1401)

An adjective meaning "in bondage," *doulos* is frequently used as a noun in the New Testament ("one in bondage") and is the most common word translated as "servant." It is used with reference to

a. natural conditions (as in Matthew 8:9; Ephesians 6:5; Colossians 4:1), and

b. in a metaphorical sense—spiritual, moral, and ethical conditions (John 8:34; Acts 16:17; Romans 1:1; 6:17,20; Titus 1:1; James 1:1).

Quote

"Time and time again throughout the pages of Scripture, believers are referred to as *slaves of God* and *slaves of Christ*. In fact, where the outside world called them 'Christians,' the earliest believers repeatedly referred to themselves in the New Testament as the Lord's slaves."

—John MacArthur, *Slave: The Hidden Truth About Your Identity in Christ* (Nashville, TN: Thomas Nelson, 2010), 12.

Son

The word for "son" in the New Testament (*huios*) primarily denotes a male offspring. It is used of Jesus in titles such as "Son of Man" (a reference to the divine figure in Daniel 7:13-14), or "Son of God," indicating his unique relationship to God, or even "Son of David," indicating his messianic credential as a descendant of King David. The word usually translated "son" is used far more frequently than "daughter" (see *Daughter*), and frequently refers to offspring without reference to gender.

Definition

huios (masculine noun, Strong's #5207)

This word primarily signifies the relation of offspring to parent (see John 9:18-20; Galatians 4:30). It is often used metaphorically of prominent moral characteristics. It is used in the New Testament with reference to

a. male offspring (Galatians 4:30),

b. legitimate, as opposed to illegitimate offspring (Hebrews 12:8),

c. descendants, without reference to sex (Romans 9:27 NASB),

d. friends attending a wedding (Matthew 9:15 NASB—see the note),

e. those who enjoy certain privileges (Acts 3:25),

f. those who act in a certain way, whether evil (Matthew 23:31) or good (Galatians 3:7),

g. those who manifest a certain character, whether evil (Acts 13:10; Ephesians 2:2 NASB) or good (Luke 6:35; Acts 4:36; Romans 8:14),

h. the destiny that corresponds with the character, whether evil (Matthew 23:15) or good (Luke 6:35), and

i. the dignity of the relationship with God into which people are brought by the Holy Spirit when they believe in Jesus (Romans 8:19; Galatians 3:26).

Insight

The related word *huiothesia* (in the New Testament, used only by Paul) is translated by the NIV as "adoption to sonship." It occurs in Galatians 4:5 and has to do with the place and condition of a son given to one to whom it does not naturally belong. Significantly, it occurs after Galatians 3:28, where Paul said, "There is neither Jew nor Gentile, neither slave nor free, nor is there male and female, for you are all one in Christ Jesus." In other words, social status no longer matters in Christ Jesus. In Galatians 4:5, then, it is significant that Jew and Greek, slave and free, and male and female, regardless of their status in the culture—all of them are adopted as God's children.[9]

Son of God (see Son)

Son of Man (see Son)

Spirit

The word for "spirit" (*pneuma*) can also mean "breath" or "wind" like its Hebrew counterpart *ruach*. The "Holy Spirt" in the New Testament refers to the third Person of the Trinity. He is the one promised by Jesus in John 14:26 to teach the disciples "all things" and remind them of what Jesus said. *Pneuma* can also refer to the "spirit" of a person, that is, the immaterial aspect of humans.

Definition

pneuma (neuter noun, Strong's #4151)

The noun *pneuma* can refer to "wind," "breath," and "spirit," like its Hebrew counterpart *ruach*. It has many uses in the New Testament, but it tends to refer to

a. wind (translated by the NIV as "spirits" in Hebrews 1:7, but compare with Amos 4:13),

b. breath (2 Thessalonians 2:8),

c. the immaterial, invisible part of people (Luke 8:55; Acts 7:59; 1 Corinthians 5:5; James 2:26),

d. unclean spirits (Matthew 8:16; Luke 4:33; etc.), and

e. the Spirit or—with the adjective *hagios*, "holy," in its neuter form—the Holy Spirit, the third Person of the Trinity (John 14:26; Acts 2:4; Galatians 5:16-18,22-23).

Quotes

"The Spirit focuses not on His own things, but the things of Christ."

—Joni Eareckson Tada, *A Place of Healing: Wrestling with the Mysteries of Suffering, Pain, and God's Sovereignty* (Colorado Springs, CO: David C. Cook, 2010), 124.

"I believe we can move beyond these sterile disputes [between Catholics and Protestants about communion] by putting our discussion of worship within our larger picture of heaven and earth, of God's future and our present, and of the way in which those two pairs come together in Jesus and the Spirit."

—N.T. Wright, *Simply Christ: Why Christianity Makes Sense* (New York: HarperCollins, 2006), 156.

"Jesus appears to have been identified as the one upon whom the Spirit of God rested. The anointing of Jesus with the Spirit at the time of his baptism is of particular importance in this respect."

—Alister McGrath, *Christian Theology: An Introduction, Sixth Edition* (West Sussex: John Wiley & Sons Ltd., 2017), 232.

Steal

The eighth commandment prohibits "stealing" (Exodus 20:15). As a result, this concept is mentioned throughout the New Testament. The verb *kleptō* ("to steal"), for example, occurs in Romans 2:21, where Paul says, "You who preach against stealing, do you steal?"

Definition

kleptō (verb, Strong's #2813)

Related to *kleptēs* ("thief"—see *Thief*), the noun *kleptō* means "to steal" and occurs 13 times in the New Testament (Matthew 6:19,20; 19:18; 27:64; 28:13; Mark 10:19; Luke 18:20; John 10:10; twice in Romans 2:21; 13:9; twice in Ephesians 4:28).

Strong

One can translate many words in the New Testament as "strong"; among them are *dunatos* and *ischuros*. *Dunatos* (related to *dunamis*—see the entries *Power* and *Miracle*) can mean "possible," but it can also mean "strong" or "powerful." Paul said that though he was weak, Christ was *dunatos*—"strong" (2 Corinthians 12:9-10). In Revelation 18:8, God is said to be *ischuros* (the NIV uses "mighty," but it can also be translated as "strong").

Definitions

1: *dunatos* (adjective, Strong's #1415)

This word, meaning "possible" in some contexts but "powerful, mighty, strong" in many others, is translated as "strong" in Romans 15:1, contrasted with those who are "weak" in the faith (see *Weak*). Paul also contrasted his own weakness with the fact that Christ is "strong" in 2 Corinthians 12:9-10.

In 2 Corinthians 13:9, Paul was glad to see the believers in Corinth were "strong," referring to their spiritual condition.

2: *ischuros* (adjective, Strong's #2478)

The word *ischuros* means "strong, mighty," and it is used of persons and things such as

a. God (Revelation 18:8),

b. angels (Revelation 5:2; 10:1; 18:21),

c. "the strong man" (Matthew 12:29), and

d. the church at Corinth (1 Corinthians 4:10), among other uses.

Quotes

"We shouldn't spend time thinking about ourselves and how weak we are. Instead we should think about God and how strong He is. Just as the sensors built into the power suit respond by voice recognition and infuse the suit with power, we are told to respond to God's voice and He will be our strength."

> —Billy Graham, *Nearing Home: Life, Faith, and Finishing Well* (Nashville, TN: Thomas Nelson, 2011), 73.

"Yes, I pray that my pain might be removed, that it might cease; but more so, I pray for the strength to bear it, the grace to benefit from it, and the devotion to offer it up to God as a sacrifice of praise."

> —Joni Eareckson Tada, *A Place of Healing: Wrestling with the Mysteries of Suffering, Pain, and God's Sovereignty* (Colorado Springs, CO: David C. Cook, 2010), 35.

"After that tremendous struggle [of Jesus in Gethsemane] the strength of love mastered the weakness of manhood; He put that cup to His lips and never shrank, but He drank right on until not a dreg was left; and now the cup of wrath is empty, no trace of the terrible wine of the wrath of God can be found within it."

> —Charles Haddon Spurgeon, "The Crown of Thorns," in *Spurgeon's Sermons on the Cross of Christ* (Grand Rapids, MI: Kregel, 1993), 16.

Stumbling Block

More than one word exists in the New Testament related to "stumbling" or "a stumbling block" (as in, that which causes offense). One of them, *skandalon*, is the word from which we get our English word "scandal," but its use in the New Testament can refer to a trap, snare, or stumbling block. It is always used metaphorically, especially of things that may cause offense or arouse prejudice, such as the cross. Sometimes it refers to actions that are unhelpful or cause difficulty (as in Romans 14:13), while other times it refers to righteousness that comes by faith, an offense to some who rely on the law (Romans 9:33).

Definition

skandalon (neuter noun, Strong's #4625)

Originally the name of a part of a trap to which the bait is attached, *skandalon* can mean "stumbling block," and it can refer to

a. Christ (Romans 9:33; 1 Peter 2:8; 1 Corinthians 1:23) and his cross (Galatians 5:11),

b. that which is evil (Matthew 13:41; the NIV translates the phrase *panta ta skandala* here as "everything that causes sin"),

c. an aspect of Christian liberty that may cause those weak in the faith to stumble (Romans 14:13), and

d. the offense that a loving believer should not harm their brother or sister with (1 John 2:10).

Quote

"[The incarnation] is the real stumbling block in Christianity. It is here that Jews, Muslims, Unitarians, Jehovah's Witnesses, and many of those who feel the difficulties concerning the virgin birth, the miracles, the atonement, and the resurrection have come to grief."

—J.I. Packer, *Knowing God* (Downers Grove, IL: InterVarsity Press, 1993), 53.

Submit

Paul asked wives to "submit" to their husbands "as the church submits to Christ" (Ephesians 5:24), while at the same time asking husbands to love their wives "as Christ loved the church and gave himself up for her" (verse 25—see *Love*). He asked believers in general to "submit to one another" (verse 21).

Definition

hupotassō (verb, Strong's #5293)

Meaning "to subject, to subordinate," the verb *hupotassō* can be used

a. to mean "to put in subjection, to subject" (for example, Romans 8:20; 1 Corinthians 15:28), and

b. in the reflexive or passive form of the word, "to submit oneself, to be in submission to" (such as Luke 2:51; Romans 8:7; Ephesians 5:21,24; James 4:7).

Quotes

"When we select certain scriptures to support the case of women's subjugation...we are in danger of taking selected verses to define dogma while disregarding the overall principles of God's Word and the overwhelming evidence that women have equal rights in his original plan. When we look at the creation account it is clear that God created humankind equally competent, creative, and responsible because both male and female bear the imprint of God himself. It would take the subsequent fall from grace of both genders to set the stage for the centuries of fear, misunderstanding, and competition that divide their roles. They were created for mutuality and oneness, not subjugation and separateness."

—Alice Scott-Ferguson, *Reconcilable Differences: Two Women Debate God's Roles for Women* (Colorado Springs, CO: Cook Communications Ministries, 2006), 141.

"One of the most beautiful metaphors for the blending of masculine and feminine roles is seen in the ice-dancing couple. Perfectly in sync with one another, he leads and she follows. Mutual trust and communication are essential. He is strong enough to lift her up and exalt her, but she must stay balanced and land on her own two feet gracefully. She leans on him when necessary, but he stays acutely sensitive to her every movement. In complete harmony they glide through their dance, creating something far grander and far more glorious than either of them could create alone."

—Nancy Parker Brummett, *Reconcilable Differences: Two Women Debate God's Roles for Women* (Colorado Springs, CO: Cook Communications Ministries, 2006), 54.

Suffer

"Suffering" in the New Testament is especially important with respect to what happened to Jesus on the cross, and to what his followers face for following him. Jesus predicted he would suffer, for example, in Matthew 16:21. Believers are said to be blessed if they suffer because of righteousness (1 Peter 3:14).

Definition

paschō (verb, Strong's #3958)

Meaning "to suffer," this verb is used of

a. the suffering endured by Christ (for example, Matthew 16:21; 17:12; 1 Peter 2:21,23; 3:18), and

b. the suffering of followers of Christ in general (for example, Acts 9:16; 2 Corinthians 1:6; Galatians 3:4; 1 Thessalonians 2:14; 2 Thessalonians 1:5; 1 Peter 3:14,17; 4:1; 5:10; Revelation 2:10), or because of wrong behavior (1 Peter 4:15).

Quotes

"Jesus, the one who since Satan's fall had despised pain and suffering as one of the awful results of man's sin, handicapped Himself on earth when His back ached and His muscles cramped and when He sweat real sweat and cried real tears and bled real blood."

> —Joni Eareckson Tada, *A Place of Healing: Wrestling with the Mysteries of Suffering, Pain, and God's Sovereignty* (Colorado Springs, CO: David C. Cook, 2010), 239.

"Even if we could live a life with no conflict, suffering, or mistakes, it would be a shallow existence."

> —Brennan Manning, *The Ragamuffin Gospel: Good News for the Bedraggled, Beat-Up, and Burnt Out* (Colorado Springs, CO: Multnomah Books, 2005), 175.

"Jesus behaves from the start *both* with the sovereign authority of one who knows himself charged with the responsibility to inaugurate God's kingdom *and* with the recognition that this task will only be completed through his suffering and death."

> —N.T. Wright, *Simply Jesus* (New York: HarperCollins Publishers, 2011), 172.

Sufficient

That which is "sufficient" or "enough" is expressed in the New Testament with the word *hikanos* (in certain contexts also meaning "able," "many," "large," "long," or "worthy"). The only time *hikanos* is translated as "sufficient" by the NIV in the New Testament is in 2 Corinthians 2:6, where Paul said the punishment from the community was "sufficient" for (presumably) the man who had taken his father's wife (mentioned in 1 Corinthians 5:1), as he had evidently repented. In 2 Corinthians 12:9, Paul used the verb *arkeō* to indicate that he was told God's grace was "sufficient" for him. There are other words also in the New Testament to express what is "enough" or "sufficient."

Definitions

1: *hikanos* (adjective, Strong's #2425)

This verb, often meaning "worthy" (for example, Matthew 3:11), "large" (Matthew 28:12), or "long" (as with a duration of time—see Luke 20:9), can also be translated as "sufficient" (2 Corinthians 2:6) or "enough" (for example, Luke 22:38).

2: *arkeō* (verb, Strong's #714)

This word can mean "to suffice, be enough," and it occurs in John 6:7 (ESV) when Philip said that two hundred denarii "would not be enough" to buy the bread needed to feed the people who came to listen to Jesus. This verb also appears when Philip asked Jesus to show him and the other disciples the Father; that that would be enough (John 14:8). Paul used this verb in 2 Corinthians 12:9 to express that God's grace was "sufficient" for him.

Quotes

"A Christian ruled by grace knows that God is quite capable of speaking loudly enough to be heard!"

> —Steve McVey, *Grace Rules* (Eugene, OR: Harvest House Publishers, 1998), 124.

"As God didn't allow the Israelites to store up manna, he doesn't let us store up grace. He always gives us enough, but we can't deposit it for the future. We have to get it fresh, every day."

> —Randy Alcorn, *Grace: A Bigger View of God's Love* (Eugene, OR: Harvest House Publishers, 2016), 17.

Supplication (see Prayer)

Sword

A "sword" in the Bible can be literal or metaphorical. Paul described the "sword of the Spirit" as "the word of God" in Ephesians 6:17.

Definitions

1: *machaira* (feminine noun, Strong's #3162)

A *machaira* is "a short sword or dagger" (Matthew 26:47,51,52; Luke 21:24; 22:38). The word is used to describe the "word of God" in Hebrews 4:12 (as a two-edged "sword," discerning inner thoughts), and the "sword" of the Spirit in Ephesians 6:17. Sometimes it refers to ordinary violence (as in Matthew 10:34) or the instrument of a magistrate or judge (Romans 13:4).

2: *rhomphaia* (feminine noun, Strong's #4501)

This word is of somewhat doubtful origin and would refer to "a Thracian weapon of large size." Whether it is a sword or spear is not certain, but it is usually longer than a *machaira* (see above). It occurs literally in Revelation 6:8 and metaphorically as an instrument of anguish (Luke 2:35), and of judgment (Revelation 1:16; 2:12,16; 19:15,21), there probably figurative of the Lord's declarations of wrath.

"Jesus could have chosen to argue with the devil, but he did not. Instead, he used his powerful offensive weapon, the sword of the Spirit. He had hidden God's Word in his heart, so he was ready and mightily equipped when the moment of battle came. His sword was well balanced and finely sharpened. He was ready for spiritual warfare."

—Rick Stedman, *Praying the Armor of God: Trusting God to Protect You and the People You Love* (Eugene, OR: Harvest House Publishers, 2015), 54-55.

Synagogue

The "synagogue" was a gathering place where Jews would congregate. Jesus often preached in synagogues, as did Paul. It was in a Jewish synagogue, for example, where Jesus read from Isaiah 61, in Luke 4:16-21.

Definition

sunagōgē (feminine noun, Strong's #4864)

Literally "a bringing together" (*sun*, "together," *agō*, "to bring"), *sunagōgē* denotes

    a. "a gathering of things, a collection of persons, an assembly of a Jewish religious gathering" (as in Acts 9:2). James referred to a synagogue of Jewish believers in James 2:2 (the NIV translates *sunagōgē* there as "meeting"). A "synagogue of Satan" is mentioned in Revelation 2:9 and 3:9, referring to people who claimed to be Jews but were not. The word *sunagōgē* can also refer to

    b. the building in which the gathering is held (Matthew 6:2; Mark 1:21).

Insight

The Jewish "synagogue" probably originated at the time of the Babylonian exile. Having no temple, the Jews assembled on the Sabbath to hear the Law read; the practice continued in various buildings after the return.

Tabernacle (see Tent, Pitch a Tent)

Tartarus (see Hell)

Teach, Teacher, Teaching

"Teaching," or giving instruction, was a common practice of Jesus (Matthew 5:2; 7:29). Jesus's disciples often addressed him as "Teacher" (among other titles—see *Rabbi* and *Master*).

Definitions

1: *didaskō* (verb, Strong's #1321)
This verb is used

    a. absolutely, in the sense of "to give instruction" (as in Matthew 4:23; 9:35; Romans 12:7; 1 Corinthians 4:17; 1 Timothy 2:12; 4:11), and

b. with a direct object, such as with persons (Matthew 5:2); see also Matthew 7:29; 15:9; 22:16.

2: *didaskalos* (masculine noun, Strong's #1320)

This is rendered "teacher" or "teachers." Jesus's disciples called him "Teacher" (for example, in Matthew 8:19), as did others, throughout the Gospels (see Matthew 17:24). James warned the recipients of his letter that not many should become "teachers" (James 3:1).

Quotes

"[Jesus] was an immensely popular teacher despite His unassuming nature and ordinary looks. The places He taught could scarcely hold the tightly packed multitudes that mobbed Him everywhere He went."

—Chuck Swindoll, *Jesus: The Greatest Life of All* (Nashville, TN: Thomas Nelson, 2008), 3.

"Our responsibility as believers in Christ is to proclaim the wisdom of His Word. God has taught every generation, through blight or blessing, to look to Him as the source of all things."

—Billy Graham, *Nearing Home: Life, Faith, and Finishing Well* (Nashville, TN: Thomas Nelson, 2011), 36.

Temple

A "temple" was a sacred building connected with God or with pagan deities, depending on the religious faith involved. The Jewish temple had associations with the divine presence, especially the "Holy of Holies" or "Most Holy Place," where the ark of the covenant was kept and where the high priest would offer sacrifices to God. Jesus described his own body as a temple in John 2:19-22. Paul said that the believer's body is a "temple of the Holy Spirit," and that the sexually immoral person sins against their own body (1 Corinthians 6:18-19 ESV).

Definitions

1: *hieron* (neuter noun, Strong's #2411)

Hieron is used as a noun; it is also the neuter of the adjective *hieros*, meaning "sacred." It denotes "a sacred place, a temple," such as that of Artemis (Diana) in Acts 19:27. It can also refer to the temple in Jerusalem (Mark 11:11), meaning the entire building with its precincts or some part thereof, as distinct from the *naos* (see below), the "inner sanctuary." Apart from the Gospels and Acts, it is mentioned only in 1 Corinthians 9:13. Christ taught in one of the courts of the temple, to which all the people had access. *Hieron* (unlike *naos*) is never used figuratively. The Jewish temple mentioned in the Gospels and Acts was begun by Herod in 20 BC, and ultimately destroyed by the Romans in AD 70.

2: *naos* (masculine noun, Strong's #3485)

As "a shrine or sanctuary," *naos* was used

a. among the pagans to denote the shrine containing an idol (Acts 17:24; 19:24),

b. among the Jews in reference to "the inner sanctuary" of the Jewish temple, into which only the priests could lawfully enter (see Luke 1:9,21,22). Jesus, from the tribe of Judah and therefore not a priest while on the earth (Hebrews 7:13,14; 8:4), did not enter the *naos* at all—nor did he have to, as his death was by itself a sacrifice for sin once and for all. The word is also used

c. by Christ metaphorically, of his own physical body (John 2:19,21), and

d. metaphorically in apostolic teaching (such as Paul's reference to the body of the believer as a temple in 1 Corinthians 6:19), among other such uses.

Quotes

"Before Jewish access to the Temple Mount area was gained as a result of the Six-Day War in June 1967, our knowledge of the Herodian Second Temple was limited to a small section of a retaining wall (known as the 'Wailing' or Western Wall) revered as the 'only remnant' of the Temple that survived the Roman destruction in A.D. 70."

> —Randall Price, *The Stones Cry Out* (Eugene, OR: Harvest House Publishers, 1997), 190.

"When you become a transformed follower of Jesus you do not receive a personal, private relationship between just 'Jesus and you.' Each of us is made part of a community of Jesus-followers—the family, Christ's body, a holy temple where the Spirit of God lives, the bride of Christ, and the agency through which Christ is reaching out to the lost world."

> —Josh McDowell and Sean McDowell, *The Unshakable Truth: How You Can Experience the 12 Essentials of a Relevant Faith* (Eugene, OR: Harvest House Publishers, 2010), 381.

Tempt, Test

"Temptation" in the New Testament involves being enticed to sin. For example, Jesus was tempted to sin in Matthew 4:1-11, but the devil failed in his attempt. One might also call it "testing," since the same word lies beneath both "tempt" and "test." Sometimes the context makes the difference clear, as in Revelation 2:10, where Jesus said he would "test" some of the believers in the church of Smyrna by allowing them to suffer imprisonment.

Definition

peirazō (verb, Strong's #3985)

This verb means either (1) the negative action of "to tempt," or (2) the more positive action of "to test, prove."

For the first meaning, "to tempt," see the use of the verb in Matthew 4:1-11, where Jesus was tempted by the devil in the wilderness ("tempter" in verse 3 translates the substantive participial form of the verb, meaning "the one who tempts").

For the second meaning, "to test," some examples include when the Pharisees tried to "test" Jesus as to his ability to interpret Scripture (by asking him if it was "lawful for a man to divorce his wife for any and every reason," Matthew 19:3), as well as when Jesus in Revelation 2:10 said he would "test" some of the believers of the church in Smyrna by allowing them to be cast into prison by the devil.

Quotes

"Desiring their freedom, [God] therefore refuses to carry [humans], by their mere affections and habits, to any of the goals which He sets before them: He leaves them to 'do it on their own.' And there lies our opportunity. But also, remember, there lies our danger. If once they get through this initial dryness successfully, they become much less dependent on emotion and therefore much harder to tempt."

> —the character of Screwtape writing to Wormwood: C.S. Lewis, *The Screwtape Letters* (New York: HarperCollins Publishers, 1996), 7-8.

"This living a lifestyle of intentional gratitude became an unintentional test in the trustworthiness of God—and in counting blessings I stumbled upon the way out of fear."

> —Ann Voskamp, *One Thousand Gifts: A Dare to Live Fully Right Where You Are* (Grand Rapids, MI: Zondervan, 2010), 151.

Tent, Pitch a Tent

In the New Testament, the Greek word *skēnē* is largely a reference to the Old Testament "tabernacle," the "tent" in the wilderness that was the precursor to the temple for the Israelites. It was where the ark of the covenant was kept in the "Holy of Holies" or "Most Holy Place," where the high priest would enter annually to offer a sacrifice of atonement for himself and the whole community. The related word *skēnoō* means "to pitch one's tent" and is famously used in John 1:14: "The Word [that is, Jesus] became flesh and made his dwelling among us." The NIV translates the form of the word *skēnoō* there as "made his dwelling," but literally, it says that he "tabernacled," "tented," or "pitched his tent" among us.

Definitions

1: *skēnē* (feminine noun, Strong's #4633)

Skēnē refers to "a tent, booth, tabernacle," and it is used of

a. tents as dwellings (Matthew 17:4; Mark 9:5; Luke 9:33; Hebrews 11:9),

b. the Mosaic tabernacle (Acts 7:44; Hebrews 8:5; 9:8,21), or the outer part of it (Hebrews 9:2,6), or the inner part of it (Hebrews 9:3),

c. the heavenly prototype (Hebrews 8:2; 9:11; Revelation 13:6; 15:5; 21:3),

d. the eternal abodes of the saints (Luke 16:9),

e. the temple in Jerusalem, as continuing the service of the tabernacle (Hebrews 13:10),

f. the house of David (metaphorically, of his people—Acts 15:16), and

g. the portable shrine of the god Molek (Acts 7:43).

2: *skēnoō* (verb, Strong's #4637)

Meaning "to pitch a tent" or "to tabernacle" (related to the noun *skēnē* above), the verb *skēnoō* occurs in John 1:14 of when Jesus came among us as God in the flesh. Thus he "made his dwelling" in the world or "pitched his tent," that is, dwelling in the tabernacle of his human body. In total *skēnoō* occurs five times in the New Testament (including John 1:14; Revelation 7:15; 12:12).

Quotes

"The city [of Bethlehem] hums. The merchants are unaware that God has visited their planet. The innkeeper would never believe that he had just sent God into the cold."

—Max Lucado, *God Came Near: No Wonder They Call Him the Savior* (Sisters, OR: Multnomah Publishers, 1986), 21.

"How are we to think of the Incarnation? The New Testament does not encourage us to puzzle our heads over the physical and psychological problems that it raises, but to worship God for the love that was shown in it."

—J.I. Packer, *Knowing God* (Downers Grove, IL: InterVarsity Press, 1993), 58.

Test (see Tempt, Test)

Testimony

A "testimony" in the New Testament is an attestation or "witness" (as with giving evidence) to the important details surrounding the life, death, and resurrection of Christ. John was "the disciple whom Jesus loved" (see John 21:20), and one of the sons of Zebedee (Matthew 10:2). The people who identified him as "the disciple who testifies to these things" (and who may have helped him compose his Gospel) also said that they knew his "testimony" (*marturia*) was true (John 21:24).

Definitions

1: *marturia* (feminine noun, Strong's #3141)

This word, meaning "witness, evidence, testimony," is personally acquired information about Jesus Christ, as in John 21:24 (where it has the sense of "record" but is rendered "testimony" in the NIV), and in Acts 22:18, where after his baptism Paul was warned by the Lord, "Quick!...Leave Jerusalem immediately, because the people here will not accept your testimony about me."

2: *marturion* (neuter noun, Strong's #3142)

This word also means "a testimony, a witness." In 2 Thessalonians 1:10, "our testimony to you" refers to the fact that the missionaries, aside from proclaiming the truths of the gospel, had given witness to the power of those truths. In 1 Timothy 2:6, "the testimony given at the proper time" (ESV) refers to the time divinely appointed for it, namely the present age, from Pentecost (Acts 2) until the church is complete.

Quotes

"There is no better way to show an example of what it means to be a Christian than your own testimony. A testimony is a simple sharing of what Christ has done in your life. It can be a powerful tool if developed properly."

> —Josh McDowell and Sean McDowell, *The Unshakable Truth: How You Can Experience the 12 Essentials of a Relevant Faith* (Eugene, OR: Harvest House Publishers, 2010), 234.

"In this world and throughout the ages, every Christian is a testimony to the loving grace of the Father."

> —Steve McVey, *Grace Walk* (Eugene, OR: Harvest House Publishers, 1995), 160.

Thank

Giving "thanks" or expressing gratitude in Scripture is frequently expressed to God himself. Jesus gave thanks to the Father at various times before sharing food (including at the Last Supper). Paul also gave thanks to God many times, often for the Christians to whom he was writing. In fact, we get the word "Eucharist" (a term for the observance of communion) from the verb meaning "to thank," *eucharisteō*, which is what Jesus did at the first communion with his disciples, at the Last Supper (Matthew 26:27; Mark 14:23; Luke 22:17,19; 1 Corinthians 11:24). Besides *eucharisteō*, the New Testament has other verbs meaning "to thank" and nouns translated as "thankfulness."

Definition

eucharisteō (verb, Strong's #2168)

Meaning "to thank," this verb occurs

a. with reference to actions taken by Christ (Matthew 15:36; 26:27; Mark 8:6; 14:23; Luke 22:17,19; John 6:11,23; 11:41; 1 Corinthians 11:24),

b. in the beginning of many of Paul's letters (including Romans, 1 Corinthians, Ephesians, Philippians, Colossians, 1 and 2 Thessalonians, and Philemon), and

c. regarding others who are giving thanks (Romans 14:6; 1 Corinthians 14:17; Revelation 11:17), among other uses.

Quotes

"We are never thankful for what we think we deserve. We are always deeply thankful for great kindness we know we *don't* deserve."

—Randy Alcorn, *Grace: A Bigger View of God's Love* (Eugene, OR: Harvest House Publishers, 2016), 83.

"We must be thankful to all the people who have helped us, we must honour them and love them. But never, never pin your whole faith on any human being; not if he is the best and wisest in the whole world."

> —C.S. Lewis, *Mere Christianity* (New York: HarperCollins Publishers, 1980), 191.

Thief

A thief is one who steals (see *Steal*; see also *Bandit*). The day of judgment ("the day of the Lord") will come like a "thief in the night," according to 1 Thessalonians 5:2. Jesus metaphorically called the teachers who came before him "thieves" in John 10:8.

Definition

kleptēs (masculine noun, Strong's #2812)
The word *kleptēs* ("thief") is used

a. literally (Matthew 6:19,20; 24:43; Luke 12:33; John 10:1,10; 12:6; 1 Corinthians 6:10; 1 Peter 4:15),

b. metaphorically of false teachers (John 10:8), and

c. figuratively, such as with its use related to the day of judgment (for example, 1 Thessalonians 5:2).

Thorn

"Thorn" (*akantha*) is an important image in the New Testament. Jesus made use of the image of thorns (*akanthas*, the plural form in Greek) in part of a parable about where seeds are sown (Matthew 13:7). Paul spoke about a "thorn" (*skolops*) in his flesh in 2 Corinthians 12:7.

1: *akantha* (feminine noun, Strong's #173)

Meaning "a brier, a thorn," *akantha* is always used in the plural in the New Testament (Matthew 7:16; Luke 6:44; twice in Matthew 13:7, 22, with parallels in Mark and Luke). It is also used of the crown of thorns placed on Christ's head in mock imitation of the garlands worn by emperors (Matthew 27:29; John 19:2). They are an effect of the divine curse on the ground (Genesis 3:18; contrast Isaiah 55:13). The word *akantha* also occurs in Hebrews 6:8.

2: *skolops* (masculine noun, Strong's #4647)

Originally denoting "anything pointed," like a "stake," *skolops* means "thorn" and occurs in the New Testament only once, in 2 Corinthians 12:7, describing Paul's "thorn" in the flesh. What is stressed is not so much the size of the (probably) metaphorical thorn but the acuteness of the suffering, and the spiritual lesson learned.

Time

A "time," "appointed time," or "season" in the New Testament is for the most part either "a space of time" (*chronos*), "a season" (*kairos*), or "any time or span of time" (*hōra*, usually meaning "hour").

1: *chronos* (masculine noun, Strong's #5550)

This denotes "a space of time," whether short (as in Matthew 2:7) or long (as in Luke 8:27; 20:9). It could also refer to a succession of shorter "times" (for example, Acts 20:18) or longer ones (for example, Romans 16:25).

2: *kairos* (masculine noun, Strong's #2540)

When used of time in the New Testament, this word means "a fixed or definite period, a season," sometimes an opportune or "right time" (as in Romans 5:6). The NIV translates the plural of this word as "dates" in 1 Thessalonians 5:1.

3: *hōra* (feminine noun, Strong's #5610)

This can mean "any time or period fixed by nature," though it is translated as "hour" in most contexts of the New Testament. But it means "moment" in Matthew 8:13, for example, and "time" (as in "a particular point of time") in Mark 13:11.

Quotes

"Each of us has a family tree reaching back into the mists of time. Down the ages, like runners in a great relay race of history, others have passed this Good News from one generation to another."

>—Alister McGrath, *Mere Apologetics: How to Help Seekers and Skeptics Find Faith* (Grand Rapids, MI: Baker Books, 2012), 13.

"Pagan oppression was the sign of the present evil age; the age to come would bring freedom and peace, when YHWH [that is, Yahweh] vindicated his people after their long period of suffering."

>—N.T. Wright, *Jesus and the Victory of God* (Minneapolis, MN: Fortress Press, 1996), 577.

Tongue

A word for both "language" and "tongue" in the New Testament is *glōssa*. It is used in James to talk about the "tongue's" destructive potential with respect to the speech it can produce (James 3:5,6,8). In 1 Corinthians 12:10, Paul also spoke of a gift of tongues that some are said to have.

Definition

glōssa (feminine noun, Strong's #1100)

The *glōssa* ("tongue") is described in James as capable of great destruction, in the sense of what speech can do (James 3:5,6,8). Sometimes it means a "tongue" in the sense of a "language" (for example, Revelation 5:9; 7:9; 10:11; 11:9; 13:7; 14:6; 17:15). In Acts 2:4-13, an occurrence of "tongues" took place that most of the hearers recognized as a supernatural phenomenon.

Quotes

"Can you recall a time when you made detracting remarks about someone? What was your motive in doing so? Why did you feel the need to diminish that person's character in the eyes of another? Were you speaking out of the pain of being hurt by her? Did you envy her accomplishments? If so, have you not learned how to let your envy motivate you to achieve your own goals rather than cause you to defame another? It is likely you grudgingly admire and desire something the other person possesses."

—Deborah Smith Pegues, *30 Days to Taming Your Tongue*
(Eugene, OR: Harvest House Publishers, 2005), 43.

"In America, we cherish freedom of speech. But with freedom comes responsibility. Responsible citizens in a democracy, and Christians in any form of society, must learn what is helpful and even necessary to say, even when unpleasant—such as in challenging injustice against others—and what remains only destructive...And almost all people suffer from the tendency to pass on interesting rumors to others without scrupulously checking their accuracy, especially in the Internet age, which produces a torrent of misinformation, half-truths, and personal opinions all subtly mixed together with genuine facts for just about any Google search that one executes!"

—Craig L. Blomberg and Mariam J. Kamell, *Zondervan Exegetical Commentary on the New Testament: James*, ed. Clinton E. Arnold (Grand Rapids, MI: Zondervan, 2008), 165.

Torah (see Law)

Tree

"Tree" in the New Testament can refer to an important tree, as in the "tree" of life (see Revelation 2:7), or can refer to the cross (for example, 1 Peter 2:24 ESV—see *Cross*).

Definitions

1: *xulon* (neuter noun, Strong's #3586)

A *xulon* is "wood, a piece of wood, anything made of wood," often referring to a "tree" (see Luke 23:31). It refers to the cross, for example, in 1 Peter 2:24 ESV, and to the "tree" of life in Revelation 2:7 and 22:2.

2: *dendron* (neuter noun, Strong's #1186)

This word means "a living, growing tree," known, for example, by the fruit it produces (for example, Matthew 12:33; Luke 6:44). It is also used in Jude 1:12 metaphorically of evil teachers.

Insight

In Luke 13:19, a mustard seed is said to grow into a *dendron*, a tree—illustrating how the kingdom of God can begin small but become great.

Trespass (see Sin)

Tribe

A "tribe" is "a company of people united by kinship or location." The word occurs frequently in Revelation. One important biblical use of the word is in reference to the twelve tribes of Israel (for example, Revelation 7:4-8).

Definition

phulē (feminine noun, Strong's #5443)

This word refers to "a company of people united by kinship or habitation, a clan, tribe." It is used of

a. the peoples of the earth (Matthew 24:30; see Revelation 1:7; 5:9; 7:9; 11:9; 13:7; 14:6), and

b. the tribes of Israel (Matthew 19:28; Luke 2:36; 22:30; Acts 13:21; Romans 11:1; Philippians 3:5; Hebrews 7:13,14; James 1:1; Revelation 5:5; 7:4-8).

Tribulation

The word for "tribulation," *thlipsis*, is related to a verb that denotes a pressing or squeezing. In the New Testament it refers to affliction in general, but the most famous use of the term is in reference to "the great tribulation" of Revelation 7:14, a terrible ordeal to be endured, with a tremendous amount of suffering.

Definition

thlipsis (feminine noun, Strong's #2347)

This word, meaning literally "a pressing" or "a squeezing," is translated as "tribulation" in Revelation 7:14 where it refers to "the great tribulation," a time of severe trouble. Elsewhere it might be translated "trouble" (for example, Matthew 13:21) or "distress" (as in Matthew 24:21).

Quotes

"I'd like...to just remind you when you find yourself wrestling with hard times, financial shortfalls, or maybe severe pain, that your [larger Christian spiritual] family suffers those things too—and seeks provision from the Lord."

> —Joni Eareckson Tada, *A Place of Healing: Wrestling with the Mysteries of Suffering, Pain, and God* (Colorado Springs, CO: David C. Cook, 2010), 175.

"General tribulation is to be distinguished from the end-times tribulation period. All Christians may expect a certain amount of general tribulation in their lives."

> —Ron Rhodes, *The End Times in Chronological Order: A Complete Overview to Understanding Bible Prophecy* (Eugene, OR: Harvest House Publishers, 2012), 119.

True, Truly, Truth

"Truth," that which is genuine or corresponds to reality, is most associated in the Bible with God himself. Jesus, being God's Son and God Incarnate, is the way, the "truth," and the life (John 14:6). He is the "truth" because he points toward actual reality, contrasted with all the counterfeits offered in this world.

Definitions

1: *alēthēs* (adjective, Strong's #227)

That which is *alēthēs* is "unconcealed, manifest, real, true to fact," and the word occurs in the New Testament with reference to

   a. persons who are truthful (Matthew 22:16; Mark 12:14; John 3:33; 7:18; 8:26; Romans 3:4; 2 Corinthians 6:8), and

b. things that are "true," "valid," or "real," conforming to reality (John 4:18; 5:31,32; 6:55; 8:13,14,17; 10:41; 19:35; 21:24; Acts 12:9; Philippians 4:8; Titus 1:13; 1 Peter 5:12; 2 Peter 2:22; 1 John 2:8,27).

2: *alēthinos* (adjective, Strong's #228)

The adjective *alēthinos* is an alternate form of the word *alēthēs* (see above). One difference is that *alēthinos*, in addition to meaning "true" or "real," can also mean "ideal" or "genuine." This adjective occurs with reference to

a. God (John 7:28),

b. Christ (1 John 2:8),

c. God's words (John 4:37; Revelation 19:9), and

d. his worshipers (John 4:23), and their hearts (Hebrews 10:22, translated "sincere" in the NIV), among other uses.

3: *alēthōs* (adverb, Strong's #230)

Meaning "surely" or "truly," *alēthōs* is related to the adjectives listed above and appears, for example, in Matthew 14:33 and Acts 12:11. It occurs a total of 18 times in the New Testament.

4: *alētheia* (feminine noun, Strong's #225)

The noun *alētheia*, meaning "truth" (and related to the three words listed above), is used in the New Testament

a. objectively, signifying the reality behind the appearance of a thing (for example, Romans 9:1; 2 Corinthians 11:10), particularly of Christian doctrine, as in John 14:6 (referring to Jesus being the "truth"), and Galatians 2:5 (referring to the "truth" of the gospel), and

b. subjectively, with truthfulness or truth expressed in sincerity and integrity of character (for example, John 8:44; 3 John 1:3).

Insight

Sometimes Jesus prefaced something he was about to say with the following phrase: "Truly I say to you..." (for example, Luke 18:17). In the Synoptic Gospels there is only one "truly," but in John when Jesus spoke in this way the word for "truly" is repeated (for example, John 1:51, translated as "very truly" in the NIV). The word for "truly" in that phrase, isn't *alēthōs* (see above). Instead, it's *amēn*, a Hebrew term carried over into Greek that also means "truly." This is the word we say at the end of prayers, confirming the truth of what we just said.

Quotes

"If you look for truth, you may find comfort in the end. If you look for comfort you will not find either comfort or truth."

> —C.S. Lewis, *Mere Christianity* (New York: HarperCollins
> Publishers, 1980), 55.

"Christian consciousness begins in the painful realization that what we had assumed was the truth was in fact a lie. Prayer is immediate: 'Deliver me from the liars, God! They smile so sweetly but lie through their teeth.' Rescue me from the lies of advertisers who claim to know what I need and what I desire...from the person who tells me of life and omits Christ, who is wise in the ways of the world and ignores the movements of the Spirit."

> —Eugene Peterson, *A Long Obedience in the Same Direction:
> Discipleship in an Instant Society* (Downers Grove, IL: Inter-
> Varsity Press, 2000), 27.

Type

Literally a "blow" or an "impression or mark from a blow," the word for "type" can refer to the nail "marks" in Jesus's hands (John 20:25), or to a "type" in the sense of an "example" in Scripture for the edification of those who came later (as Paul understood about the stories of the people of Israel in the wilderness—see 1 Corinthians 10:6).

tupos (masculine noun, Strong's #5179)

Primarily meaning "a blow" or "an impression left by a blow" (as in John 20:25), it can also refer to the impression made by a stamp or die, an image, an "idol" (see Acts 7:43), or a form, mold, or pattern (Romans 6:17; Acts 7:44; Hebrews 8:5).

Unclean

Many things and even people were considered "unclean" in the Scriptures. A spirit might be unclean or impure (meaning a demon—see, for example, Mark 6:7). It is used of an "impure" person in Ephesians 5:5.

Definition

akathartos (adjective, Strong's #169)

Meaning "unclean, impure," this word is used of

a. unclean spirits, frequently in the synoptic Gospels (though not in John's Gospel), and also in passages like Acts 5:16 and Revelation 16:13,

b. things that are ceremonially unclean (such as in Acts 10:14,28), and

c. things that are morally unclean (such as in 2 Corinthians 6:17; Ephesians 5:5).

Understanding

"Understanding" in the New Testament is about being able to put facts, thoughts, or ideas together. Many people were amazed at Jesus's ability to understand (Luke 2:47).

Definition

sunesis (feminine noun, Strong's #4907)

Related to the verb *suniēmi*, literally "to put together," the noun *sunesis* denotes

a. understanding, the mind, or intelligence (Mark 12:33),

b. understanding in the sense of reflexive thought (Luke 2:47; 1 Corinthians 1:19; Ephesians 3:4; Colossians 1:9; 2:2; 2 Timothy 2:7).

Unleavened Bread (see Bread)

V

Veil

"Veil" is used for (1) the curtain (*katapetasma*) between the Holy Place and the Holy of Holies in the temple (and earlier in the tabernacle) that symbolized the division between God and most of humankind, which was torn when Jesus died on the cross, (2) the "veil" (*kaluma*) or "covering" Moses put over his face after he was on Mount Sinai, and (3) the "covering around" (*peribolaion*) the head, meaning a woman's long hair, according to the apostle Paul (1 Corinthians 11:15), a word that only occurs elsewhere in the New Testament in Hebrews 1:12 describing a "robe."

Definitions

1: *katapetasma* (neuter noun, Strong's #2665)
Literally "that which is spread out," this word refers to a "curtain," specifically

a. the inner "curtain" of the tabernacle (Hebrews 6:19; 9:3),

b. the corresponding "curtain" which was torn in the temple when Jesus died on the cross (Matthew 27:51; Mark 15:38; Luke 23:45), and

c. metaphorically of the flesh of Christ (Hebrews 10:20).

2: *kalumma* (neuter noun, Strong's #2571)

Literally "a covering," *kalumma* is used in the New Testament

    a. of the veil Moses put over his face after he came down from Mount Sinai, because his face was radiant (2 Corinthians 3:13), and

    b. metaphorically of the spiritually darkened vision suffered by Israel, until they recognize Jesus as the Messiah (2 Corinthians 3:14-15).

3: *peribolaion* (neuter noun, Strong's #4018)

A "covering" (literally a "covering around"), this word was used by Paul of the hair around a woman's head (1 Corinthians 11:15).

Quotes

"A huge woven veil separated the Holy of Holies from the rest of the Temple...By rending the Temple veil [at Jesus's death], God was saying, in effect, 'In the death of My Son, Jesus Christ, there is total access into My holy presence...'"

    —John MacArthur, *The MacArthur New Testament Commentary: Matthew 24–28* (Chicago, IL: Moody Publishers, 1989), 273.

"[With the tearing of the veil] Jesus's death has unmasked the fact that the 'tear'...in the 'old garment' is irreparable [Mark 2:21]; the symbolic order as it is centrally embedded in the sanctuary has been overthrown."

    —Ched Myers, *Binding the Strong Man* (Maryknoll, NY: Orbis Books, 2008), 390.

Virgin

Mary was a "virgin" (*parthenos*) when she conceived Jesus by means of the Holy Spirit (see Luke 1:27; compare Matthew 1:23, quoting from Isaiah 7:14).

Definition

parthenos (feminine noun, Strong's #3933)

The word *parthenos* is used of

a. the virgin Mary (Matthew 1:23, quoting Isaiah 7:14; Luke 1:27),

b. the ten virgins in a parable Jesus told (Matthew 15:1,7,10),

c. the daughters of Philip the evangelist (Acts 21:9),

d. the unmarried women the apostle Paul gave instructions to regarding marriage (1 Corinthians 7:25,28,34,36-38),

e. a local church, figuratively, in its relation to Christ (2 Corinthians 11:2), and

f. pure persons, metaphorically (Revelation 14:4).

Quotes

"By the virgin birth, God kept Jesus from possessing a sin nature from Joseph."
—Ron Rhodes, *What Does the Bible Say About...?* (Eugene, OR: Harvest House Publishers, 1997), 99.

"Jesus, preexistent and coeternal with the Father, left His position of glory, and took on flesh through the virgin birth (John 1:1,14). The incarnation of Christ serves as the gateway for redemption by Christ unifying Himself with the plight of humanity and undeservingly bearing the weight of our sin. The virgin birth, surrounded by debate due to its incomprehensibility, is plainly taught in the Scriptures, but the text in no way implies any Roman Catholic doctrine concerning Mary's perpetual virginity (Matthew 1:17-25). In fact, Scripture records that Mary had other children who were Jesus' half-siblings (Matthew 13:54-56).

"We believe that the virgin birth preserved the sinlessness of Jesus, since the creation of the infant in the womb of Mary was a direct, divine act."

—Erwin W. Lutzer, "The Virgin Birth," Moody Church Media, https://www.moodymedia.org/articles/virgin-birth/.

Water

"Water" is important in the New Testament for baptism. "Water" and blood came out of Jesus's side when he was on the cross (John 19:34, possibly what is referenced in 1 John 5:6). Jesus also told the Samaritan woman that God could offer her "living water" (John 4:10).

Definition

hudōr (neuter noun, Strong's #5204)

The word for "water" in the New Testament, *hudōr*, refers to literal water (John 18:34, the water from Jesus's side; see also 1 John 5:8), water used for symbolic purposes, such as the water John used for baptism of repentance (Matthew 3:11), and symbolic water, such as the "living water" Jesus told the Samaritan woman at the well about (John 4:10).

Quotes

"If you believe, the Father drew you to Him. He brought you to the fountain of living waters to drink fully of the blessed Holy Spirit."

> —Kay Arthur and Pete De Lacy, *The God Who Cares and Knows You* (Eugene, OR: Harvest House Publishers, 2008), 57.

"After a few moments, Jesus stands and removes his outer garments. He wraps a servant's girdle around his waist, takes up the basin, and kneels before one of the disciples. He unlaces the sandal and gently lifts the foot and places it in the basin, covers it with water, and begins to bathe it. One by one, one grimy foot after another, Jesus works his way down the row."

> —Max Lucado, *Just Like Jesus: Learning to Have a Heart Like His* (Nashville, TN: Thomas Nelson, 2003), 17.

Way

Jesus described himself as "the way and the truth and the life," and said it was only through him that anyone could come to the Father (John 14:6). The early Christians also said they followed "the Way" (for example, Acts 24:14). The word for "the way" could mean "the path" or "the road."

Definition

hodos (feminine noun, Strong's #3598)

This word can denote

    a. "a natural path, road, way," and frequently has this meaning in the Synoptic Gospels (for elsewhere, see Acts 8:26; 1 Thessalonians 3:11; James 2:25; Revelation 16:12),

    b. a traveler's way, literally,

    c. a traveler's way, metaphorically—a course of conduct or a way of thinking, as in a way that leads to destruction (Matthew 7:13), contrasted with a way that leads to life (Matthew 7:14), and

d. "the Way," as in the term the early followers of Jesus used for their movement (for example, Acts 24:14), among other meanings.

Weak, Weakness

In the New Testament, human "weakness" is often contrasted with the strength of God, though in one case it is used in an ironic sense—when Paul wrote, "The weakness of God is stronger than human strength" (1 Corinthians 1:25). Paul also called the "strong" to be sensitive toward the "weak," with the "strong" being those who felt freedom from legalistic rules, and the "weak" being those who did things such as observing special days and not eating meat (Romans 14).

Definitions

1: *asthenēs* (adjective, Strong's #772)

This word means "without strength, weak," and it occurs with reference to

a. physical weakness (Matthew 26:41; Mark 14:38; 1 Corinthians 1:27; 4:10; 11:30; 2 Corinthians 10:10; 1 Peter 3:7),

b. "weak and worthless elemental things," in the spiritual sense, that have no power to save (Galatians 4:9),

c. moral or ethical qualms (1 Corinthians 8:7,10; 9:22), and

d. God's actions, according to human estimation, in a rhetorical sense, that is, the so-called "weakness of God" (1 Corinthians 1:25).

2: *adunatos* (adjective, Strong's #102)

This word means "not powerful," and thus "weak." In Romans 15:1, "those without strength" are contrasted with the "strong," those who feel freer in Christ to do certain things (see also Romans 14:1-3).

Quote

"We shouldn't spend time thinking about ourselves and how weak we are. Instead we should think about God and how strong He is...we are told to respond to God's voice and He will be our strength."

—Billy Graham, *Nearing Home: Life, Faith, and Finishing Well* (Nashville, TN: Thomas Nelson, 2011), 73.

A "well," "spring," or "fountain" (*pēgē*) features in the story of Jesus and the Samaritan woman (John 4:4-42). Jesus sat down by Jacob's *pēgē* ("well," John 4:6 NIV). When a Samaritan woman came to draw water from the *pēgē* and encountered Jesus, they began a conversation in which he brought up his ability to give "living water" (John 4:10), which would enable a person to never thirst again, and that would become a *pēgē* of water welling up inside them (John 4:13-14).

Definition

pēgē (feminine noun, Strong's #4077)

"A spring" or "fountain," *pēgē* occurs with reference to

a. "an artificial well," as in one fed by a spring (John 4:6),

b. the indwelling Spirit of God, a spring within that makes a person never thirst again (a metaphor set in contrast to an ordinary well, see John 4:13-14),

c. metaphorical springs (2 Peter 2:17),

d. natural fountains or springs (James 3:11,12; Revelation 8:10; 14:7),

e. eternal life and the future blessings coming from it, also metaphorically speaking (Revelation 7:17; 21:6), and

f. a flow of blood (Mark 5:29).

Wide, Width

Four words translate to "wide" or "width" in the New Testament: (1) *euruchōros* ("spacious"), as in the broad road in Matthew 7:13, parallel with (2) the *platus* ("wide") gate, (3) the verb *platunō* ("to make broad") as used by Paul when he said that he and his companions opened their hearts wide to the Corinthians (2 Corinthians 6:11), and (4) *platos* ("width"), translated by the NIV as "how wide" in Ephesians 3:18.

Definitions

1: *euruchōros* (adjective, Strong's #2149)

From *eurus* ("broad") and *chōros* ("place"), this adjective signifies "wide, broad, spacious" (see Matthew 7:13).

2: *platus* (adjective, Strong's #4116)

This word (denoting that which has a "flat or broad surface") is parallel with *euruchōros* (which described the road in Jesus's illustration—see above), and is used to describe the "wide" gate that leads to destruction (Matthew 7:13).

3: *platunō* (verb, Strong's #4115)

Related to *platus* (see above), the verb *platunō* is used literally of phylacteries (prayer boxes that Pharisees would wear on their foreheads), that were made wide to show how pious one supposedly was (Matthew 23:5), and figuratively, "to be enlarged," as in widening one's heart (2 Corinthians 6:11,13).

4: *platos* (neuter noun, Strong's #4114)

Related to *platus* (see above), this noun denotes "breadth" or "width," "how wide" something is (see Ephesians 3:18; Revelation 20:9; 21:16 ESV).

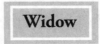

Widow

A "widow" was a woman who no longer had a husband, a difficult status for a woman to have in Bible times given that without a husband's earnings, she was often left with few options for sustenance and survival if other family members did not intervene and care for her.

Definition

A "widow" was a woman without a husband, who therefore could be in a poor financial situation. Jesus said that the scribes ("teachers of the law") loved to show off and get the more important seats in the synagogues while also they unjustly "[devoured] widows' houses" (Mark 12:38-40). Mark 12:41-44 describes an episode where many rich people were putting large amounts of money into the temple treasury, but "a poor widow" put in only "two very small copper coins." Jesus then called his disciples to him and said, "Truly I tell you, this poor widow has put more into the treasury than all the others. They all gave out of their wealth; but she, out of her poverty, put in everything—all she had to live on." Also, James referred to helping orphans and widows in their distress as part of "religion that God our Father accepts as pure and faultless" (James 1:27).

chēra (feminine noun, Strong's #5503)

There are many occurrences of the word *chēra* in the New Testament (such as Mark 12:40,42,43; Luke 2:37; 4:25,26; Luke 7:12; 18:3,5; 20:47; 21:2,3; Acts 6:1; 9:39,41; twice in 1 Timothy 5:3; 1 Timothy 5:4,5,11; twice in 1 Timothy 5:16; James 1:27). It occurs figuratively in Revelation 18:7 of a forsaken city.

Wife (see Woman)

Will

The "will" of God is that which God "desires," "designs," or "wants." Paul told the Roman Christians they should not "conform to the pattern of this world but be transformed" by the renewing of their minds, and thus "be able to test and approve what God's will is—his good, pleasing and perfect will" (Romans 12:2).

Definition

thelēma (neuter noun, Strong's #2307)

This word means

   a. objectively, the will or desires of God (as in Matthew 18:14; Mark 3:35; Romans 2:18; 12:2), and

   b. subjectively, the will of human desires (for example, John 1:13; Ephesians 2:3; 2 Peter 1:21).

Quotes

"It is foolish for any of us to think we can determine our own destiny apart from God! At best, man apart from God is a wilting flower—here today and gone tomorrow."

> —Steve McVey, *Walking in the Will of God: Discovering the Grace and Freedom of His Plan for You* (Eugene, OR: Harvest House Publishers, 2009), 13.

"Your highest calling, the most important part of your destiny, is to reflect God's glory. The primary way to do that is to align yourself underneath His rule and according to His will. Making that a priority for your life choices, thoughts, and goals will bring you closer to your destiny than any seminar, self-help strategy, or good intention ever could."

—Tony Evans, *Discover Your Destiny: Let God Use You Like He Made You* (Eugene, OR: Harvest House Publishers, 2013), 73.

Wine

"Wine" is significant in the New Testament, for example, as the symbol for Christ's blood poured out for many for the forgiveness of sins (Matthew 26:28; see also 1 Corinthians 11:25). Jesus turned water into wine at the wedding at Cana (John 2:1-11). Jesus also said that no one pours new wine into old wineskins, lest they burst (Mark 2:22).

Definition

oinos (masculine noun, Strong's #3631)

This is the general word for "wine." The mention of the bursting of the wineskins (Matthew 9:17; Mark 2:22; Luke 5:37—see also below) implies fermentation. See also Ephesians 5:18. In John 2:1-11, Jesus turned water into wine. The drinking of wine could be a stumbling block to those who chose not to drink (Romans 14:21). Contrast 1 Timothy 5:23, where Paul encouraged Timothy to have a little wine for his stomach because of his frequent illnesses.

Quote

"Most of the images of Jesus's teaching drew upon the common experience of Jews living in the first century: shepherd and sheep, sower and seed, wine and wineskins, master and servants."

—Chuck Swindoll, *Jesus: The Greatest Life of All* (Nashville, TN: Thomas Nelson, 2008), 144.

Wineskin

The word *askos* refers to "a leather bottle, a wineskin," and occurs in Matthew 9:17, Mark 2:22, and Luke 5:37. New wine would tear old wineskins.

Definition

askos (masculine noun, Strong's #779)

The word *askos* refers to "a leather bottle, a wineskin." A whole goatskin, for example, would be used with the openings bound up, and, when filled, tied at the neck. They were tanned with acacia bark and left hairy on the outside. New wines, by fermenting, would tear old skins (compare Joshua 9:13; Job 32:19). Hung in the smoke to dry, the skin-bottles became shriveled.

Quote

"What happens is, the wine ferments and when something ferments, gas is released and it expands. It expands and expands. So it was critical to use new wineskins, new skins because they were subtle, they were soft and they would expand with that fermentation process. As the dregs went to the bottom they would be able to expand. Then the wine would be poured out into another skin and it would still continue some process of fermentation, some process of the dregs falling out. It could go from skin to skin to skin until it was pure and there were no dregs, or sour vinegar, left at the bottom. But particularly the new wine had to be first put in subtle skin to allow for that expansion."

—John MacArthur, "The Uniqueness of the Gospel," Luke 5:33-39, https://www.gty.org/library/sermons-library/42-68/the-uniqueness-of-the-gospel.

Wisdom

Wisdom (*sophia*) can be earthly (see James 3:15), or can be the wisdom of God, contrasted with the world's wisdom (1 Corinthians 1:21,24).

Definition

sophia (feminine noun, Strong's #4678)

"Wisdom" is used with reference to

a. God (Romans 11:33; 1 Corinthians 1:21,24; 2:7; Ephesians 3:10; Revelation 7:12),

b. Christ (Matthew 13:54; Mark 6:2; Luke 2:40,52; 1 Corinthians 1:30; Colossians 2:3; Revelation 5:12),

c. personified wisdom (Matthew 11:19; Luke 7:35; 11:49 NASB), and

d. human wisdom in spiritual matters (Acts 6:3,10; 7:10; 1 Corinthians 2:6; 12:8; Ephesians 1:8,17; Colossians 1:9,28; 3:16; 4:5; James 1:5; 3:13,17; 2 Peter 3:15; Revelation 13:18; 17:9), or in the natural realm (Matthew 12:42; Luke 11:31; Acts 7:22; 1 Corinthians 1:17,19-21,22; 2:1,4-6,13; 3:19; 2 Corinthians 1:12; Colossians 2:23), and in its most debased form (James 3:15).

Quotes

"Paul's concerns at Corinth were complex. The church was in danger of being influenced by early forms of Gnosticism, which held that individuals were saved by a secret, arcane knowledge. Others at Corinth prized intellectual sophistication and were not prepared to tolerate anything that seemed to lack this or any other mark of cultural erudition. Paul rightly rejects any such notions, insisting the Christian gospel must be taken on its own terms, even if it counters prevailing cultural notions of acceptability at Corinth. Yet this is about challenging secular notions of wisdom, not abandoning human notions of rationality!"

> —Alister McGrath, *Mere Apologetics: How to Help Seekers and Skeptics Find Faith* (Grand Rapids, MI: Baker Books, 2012), 90.

"In the *Christian's experience,* Christ is wisdom, as well as power. If you want to be a thoroughly learned man the best place to begin, is to begin at the Bible, to begin at Christ."

> —C.H. Spurgeon, "Christ—the Power and Wisdom of God," May 17, 1857, http://www.romans45.org/spurgeon/sermons/ 0132.htm.

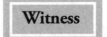

Witness

The New Testament word *martus* means "one who bears witness." It is where we get our English word "martyr," though the English word refers to one who dies for the faith and therefore bears witness to it, while the Greek word *martus* does not necessarily include death. A *martus* might die for their faith (see Acts 22:20, for example, where the NIV uses "martyr"), but it could also mean someone who could testify as to the truth of something (as in 1 Timothy 5:19).

Definition

martus (masculine noun, Strong's #3144)

This noun denotes "one who can or does bear witness, or give a testimony, about what they saw, heard, or know." It is used of

a. God (Romans 1:9; 2 Corinthians 1:23; Philippians 1:8; 1 Thessalonians 2:5,10),

b. Christ (Revelation 1:5; 3:14),

   c. martyrs, those who "witness" for Christ by their death (Acts 22:20; Revelation 2:13; 17:6),

   d. two special persons, prophesied to "witness" in Jerusalem (Revelation 11:3),

   e. one who might "witness" in a forensic sense (Matthew 18:16; 26:65; Mark 14:63; Acts 6:13; 7:58; 2 Corinthians 13:1; 1 Timothy 5:19; Hebrews 10:28), and

   f. one who might "witness" in a historic or spiritual sense (Luke 11:48; 24:48; Acts 1:8,22; 2:32; 3:15; 5:32; 10:39,41; 13:31; 22:15; 26:16; 1 Thessalonians 2:10; 1 Timothy 6:12; 2 Timothy 2:2; Hebrews 12:1; 1 Peter 5:1).

Quotes

"By being witness to our own story, we are indirectly witnessing that the gospel is *real*, not just something that is *true*."

> —Alister McGrath, *Mere Apologetics: How to Help Seekers and Skeptics Find Faith* (Grand Rapids, MI: Baker Books, 2012), 154.

"In this world and throughout the ages, every Christian is a testimony to the loving grace of the Father."

> —Steve McVey, *Grace Walk* (Eugene, OR: Harvest House Publishers, 1995), 160.

Woman

Many of Jesus's early followers were "women." Women were the first to discover the empty tomb and proclaimed it to the male disciples, who did not believe them at first (Luke 24:11). The word for "woman" is also the word for "wife" (*gunē*).

Definition

gunē (feminine noun, Strong's #1135)

A *gunē*, also meaning "wife," is a "woman," and this word can refer to a woman who is either married or unmarried. Jesus used the form of address of the term *gunē* to speak to individual women, not out of derision but out of respect or endearment (Matthew 15:28; John 2:4). In Galatians 4:4, the phrase "born of a woman" is in accordance with the subject—that is, the real humanity of Jesus. Paul's point was not about the virginity of Mary (though there is no reason to doubt that he believed this), but rather about the humanity of Jesus, as all people are indeed "born of a woman."

Work (see Deed)

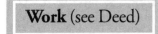

World

"World" in the New Testament can refer to the whole earth, the observable natural order, the present condition of human affairs (*kosmos*), or the known inhabited world (*oikonoumenē*). The ways of the *kosmos* are often contrasted with the ways of God.

Definitions

1: *kosmos* (masculine noun, Strong's #2889)

Primarily "order, arrangement, ornament, adornment" (as in 1 Peter 3:3), *kosmos* is similar to the concept of *aiōn* (meaning "age" or "duration," sometimes meaning "world"). It can refer to

    a. the world, as in the earth or universe (for example, Matthew 13:35; John 21:25; Acts 17:24; Romans 1:20; 1 Timothy 6:7; Hebrews 4:3; 9:26),

b. the earth as contrasted with heaven (1 John 3:17 NASB; perhaps also Romans 4:13),

c. humanity (for example, Matthew 5:14; John 1:9 NASB; 3:16; 1 John 3:17 NASB; frequently in Romans, 1 Corinthians, and 1 John),

d. Gentiles, as distinguished from Jews (for example, Romans 11:12,15),

e. the present condition of human affairs, in alienation from and opposition to God (for example, John 7:7; 8:23; 14:30; 1 Corinthians 2:12; Galatians 4:3; 6:14; Colossians 2:8; James 1:27; 1 John 4:5; 5:19),

f. the sum of temporal possessions (Matthew 16:26; 1 Corinthians 7:31), and

g. the tongue as a "world of evil" (James 3:6), expressive of the variety and magnitude of its effects for evil.

2: *oikoumenē* (feminine noun, Strong's #3625)

Meaning "the inhabited earth," *oikonoumenē* is used of

a. the whole inhabited world (Matthew 24:14; Luke 4:5; 21:26; Romans 10:18; Hebrews 1:6; Revelation 3:10; 16:14),

b. just the inhabitants themselves (Acts 17:31; Revelation 12:9),

c. the Roman Empire (Luke 2:1; Acts 11:28; 24:5),

d. the inhabitants of the Roman Empire (Acts 17:6; 19:27), and

e. the inhabited world in a coming age (Hebrews 2:5).

Quotes

"Rescue me from the person who tells me of life and omits Christ, who is wise in the ways of the world and ignores the movements of the Spirit."

> —Eugene Peterson, *A Long Obedience in the Same Direction: Discipleship in an Instant Society* (Downers Grove, IL: Inter-Varsity Press, 2000), 27.

"Christianity is a fighting religion. It thinks God made the world—that space and time, heat and cold, and all the colours and tastes, and all the animals and vegetables, are things that God 'made up out of His head' as a man makes up a story. But it also thinks that a great many things have gone wrong with the world that God made and that God insists, and insists very loudly, on our putting them right again."

> —C.S. Lewis, *Mere Christianity* (New York: HarperCollins Publishers, 1980), 64.

Worry

Jesus told his followers not to "worry" or "be anxious" about anything (Matthew 6:25,27,28). To illustrate this he said, "Look at the birds of the air; they do not sow or reap or stow away in barns, and yet your heavenly Father feeds them. Are you not much more valuable than they?" (Matthew 6:26). The word is not always used with a negative sense; for example, Paul used it to mean "have concern for" in 1 Corinthians 12:25.

Definition

merimnaō (verb, Strong's #3309)

This verb means "to be anxious about, to have a distracting care" (as in Matthew 6:25,27,28; see also Matthew 10:19; Luke 10:41; Luke 12:11; 1 Corinthians 7:32-34; 1 Corinthians 12:25; Philippians 2:20; Philippians 4:6).

Quotes

"Like any habit, worry can be broken. To do so will take patience, intention, and understanding. We must pay attention to our bodies, examine our thinking, and look closely at our feelings."

> —Linda Mintle, *Letting Go of Worry: God's Plan for Finding Peace and Contentment* (Eugene, OR: Harvest House Publishers, 2011), 18.

"God is not insecure and neither is the child of God who is alive and free in Christ."

> —Neil T. Anderson and Rich Miller, *Freedom from Fear: Overcoming Worry and Anxiety* (Eugene, OR: Harvest House Publishers, 1999), 70.

Worthy (see Sufficient)

Worship

"Worship" in both Old and New Testaments refers to showing reverence for or paying homage to someone. God desires that he alone should be worshiped (Deuteronomy 6:13 NASB; see also Luke 4:8), and because Jesus was God in human form, worship of him is the same as worship of God.

Definition

proskuneō (verb, Strong's #4352)

This verb means "to pay homage, express reverence to" (from *pros*, "to, toward," and *kuneō*, "to kiss"), and is the most frequent word rendered "to worship." It is used of

a. an act of homage or reverence toward God (for example, Matthew 4:10; John 4:21-24; 1 Corinthians 14:25; Revelation 4:10; 11:16),

b. an act of homage or reverence toward Christ (for example, Matthew 2:2,8,11; 8:2; 9:18; 14:33; 15:25; 28:9,17; Hebrews 1:6),

c. prostration before a person (Matthew 18:26),

d. worship of the dragon by people (Revelation 13:4),

e. worship of the beast, the dragon's human instrument (Revelation 13:4,8,12; 14:9,11),

f. worship of the image of the beast (Revelation 13:15; 14:11; 16:2),

g. worship of demons (Revelation 9:20), and

h. worship of idols (Acts 7:43).

Quotes

"True worship contrasts Creator and creature, transcendence and finitude, heavenly glory and earthly idols."

> —Jim Houston, *The Disciple: Following the True Mentor* (Colorado Springs, CO: David C. Cook, 2007), 185.

"While God wants us to worship Him, we cannot worship Him just any way we will. The One who made us to worship Him has decreed how we shall worship Him. He accepts only the worship that He Himself has decreed."

> —A.W. Tozer, *Whatever Happened to Worship?* rev. ed. (Camp Hill, PA: Wing Spread Publishers, 2012), Kindle edition.

Wrath (see Anger)

Writing (see Scripture)

Y, Z

Yeast (see Leaven)

Zeal

The word *zēlos*, aside from meaning "jealousy" (see *Jealousy*), can also mean "zeal." Used this way, it can refer to things such as zeal for God's house (John 2:17) or Paul's zeal when he persecuted the church (Philippians 3:6).

Definition

zēlos (masculine noun, Strong's #2205)

This word denotes "zeal" or "passion" several times in the New Testament (John 2:17; Romans 10:2; 2 Corinthians 7:7; 2 Corinthians 7:11; Philippians 3:6).

Insight

The word *zēlōtēs* ("zealot") is used with reference to "Simon who was called the Zealot" (Luke 6:15), one of Jesus's disciples. This probably meant that this Simon (different from Simon Peter) advocated revolt against Rome or the like.

Quotes

"You may have lost your zeal for life, or what I like to call your mojo, simply because you are not functioning within your destiny."

> —Tony Evans, *Discover Your Destiny: Let God Use You Like He Made You* (Eugene, OR: Harvest House Publishers, 2013), 77.

"[Paul's] zeal was a mark of the Jews of his time, who fought to maintain the purity of the Jewish way of life from pervasive Hellenistic influences."

> —G. Walter Hansen, "Paul's Conversion and His Ethic of Freedom in Galatians," in *The Road from Damascus: The Impact of Paul's Conversion on His Life, Thought, and Ministry*, ed. Richard N. Longenecker (Eugene, OR: Wipf & Stock Publishers, 2002), 216.

Glossary

Aramaic

Aramaic is a language very closely related to Hebrew. After the Babylonian exile the two languages used the same alphabet. Much of the Book of Daniel is written in Aramaic, with the rest in Hebrew. Aramaic would have been the language Jesus and his disciples primarily spoke (in addition to Hebrew, perhaps). There are various Aramaic phrases throughout the Gospels (such as in Mark 5:41).

Definite article

The definite article in Greek or Hebrew (or any language) is the word equivalent to the English word "the."

Greek

The New Testament was written in *koinē* ("common") Greek because this was the main language of the Eastern Mediterranean world in the time of Jesus.

Hebrew

Hebrew is the language in which almost all of the Old Testament was written. At times the Greek of the New Testament shows some Hebraic or Aramaic patterns of speech and concepts.

Papyrus

Papyrus was a material to be written on, made from an Egyptian plant. In New Testament times it was common to make scrolls out of papyrus.

Pentateuch

The Pentateuch (also known as the Torah or the Law) consists of the first five books of the Bible: Genesis, Exodus, Leviticus, Numbers, and Deuteronomy.

Septuagint

The Septuagint is a translation of the Old Testament from its original Hebrew into Greek, done in the third to second centuries BC by Jewish scholars—seventy of them, according to tradition. The New Testament writers often used the Septuagint as their favorite translation.

Synoptic Gospel

The "Synoptic Gospels," or "synoptics," are the writings of Matthew, Mark, and Luke about the life, ministry, death, and resurrection of Jesus. John's Gospel has some similarities with these three, but Matthew, Mark, and Luke are called *synoptic* (an English word of Greek origin meaning "seeing with") because they use most of the same material. John organized his Gospel differently, and shared unique stories about, and discourses from, Jesus.

Translation

A translation takes the meaning of words, phrases, speech, or bodies of text in one language, and represents them using the words of another language. For example, the Greek word *pneuma* ("spirit, wind, breath") is a translation of the Hebrew word *ruach* (also meaning "spirit, wind, breath").

Transliteration

A transliteration takes the sounds of a word or phrase in one language and represents them using the alphabet of a different language. Greek has a different alphabet from Hebrew and Aramaic, so if a New Testament author, writing in Greek, wanted to write a Hebrew or Aramaic word, they would use the letters of the Greek alphabet to approximate the Hebrew word's sounds. In the same way, in this handbook, every Greek word is transliterated from its Greek spelling to an English spelling, representing its sound as closely as possible. For example, the Greek word Χριστός (meaning "Christ," "Messiah," or "Anointed One") is represented (or "transliterated") with the following spelling: *Christos*.

Notes

1. This *Handbook* is based on the work originally done by Walter Bauer in German, translated from German to English by F. Wilbur Gingrich and William F. Arndt, and later edited by Frederick William Danker.

2. Mark L. Strauss, *Zondervan Exegetical Commentary on the New Testament: Mark*, ed. Clinton E. Arnold (Grand Rapids, MI: Zondervan, 2014), 687. See also Ched Myers, *Binding the Strong Man* (Maryknoll, NY: Orbis Books, 2008), 379-380.

3. Daniel Wallace, *Greek Grammar Beyond the Basics* (Grand Rapids, MI: Zondervan, 1996), 269.

4. Ron Rhodes, *Reasoning from the Scriptures with the Jehovah's Witnesses* (Eugene, OR: Harvest House Publishers, 2009), 108-109. See also Robert Bowman, *Jehovah's Witnesses, Jesus Christ, and the Gospel of John* (Grand Rapids, MI: Baker Book House, 1989), 32.

5. Douglas J. Moo, *The NIV Application Commentary: 2 Peter and Jude* (Grand Rapids, MI: Zondervan, 1996), 101.

6. David E. Garland, *Zondervan Exegetical Commentary on the New Testament: Luke*, ed. Clinton E. Arnold (Grand Rapids, MI: Zondervan, 2011), 760.

7. Grant R. Osborne, *Zondervan Exegetical Commentary on the New Testament: Matthew*, ed. Clinton E. Arnold (Grand Rapids, MI: Zondervan, 2010), 88.

8. Ben Witherington III, *John's Wisdom: A Commentary on the Fourth Gospel* (Louisville, KY: Westminster John Knox Press, 1995), 117.

9. The main point of Paul's letter to the Galatians, as Thomas Schreiner noted in his commentary, is that "Gentiles are now adopted into God's family as his children, that they are now the offspring of Abraham because they are incorporated into Christ." See Thomas R. Schreiner, *Zondervan Exegetical Commentary on the New Testament: Galatians*, ed. Clinton E. Arnold (Grand Rapids, MI: Zondervan, 2010), 271.